Digital Signal Processing in Experimental Research

(Volume 3)

How to Optimally Sample and Resample Images: Theory and Methods

Authored by

Leonid Yaroslavsky

School of Electrical Engineering, Tel Aviv University, Tel Aviv
Israel

Digital Signal Processing in Experimental Research

Volume # 3

How to Optimally Sample and Resample Images: Theory and Methods

Author: Leonid Yaroslavsky

ISSN (Online): 1879-4432

ISSN (Print): 2737-4645

ISBN (Online): 978-981-14-7181-0

ISBN (Print): 978-981-14-7179-7

ISBN (Paperback): 978-981-14-7180-3

need for a court order if at any point you breach any terms of this License Agreement. In no event will any delay or failure by Bentham Science Publishers in enforcing your compliance with this License Agreement constitute a waiver of any of its rights.

3. You acknowledge that you have read this License Agreement, and agree to be bound by its terms and conditions. To the extent that any other terms and conditions presented on any website of Bentham Science Publishers conflict with, or are inconsistent with, the terms and conditions set out in this License Agreement, you acknowledge that the terms and conditions set out in this License Agreement shall prevail.

Bentham Science Publishers Pte. Ltd.
80 Robinson Road #02-00
Singapore 068898
Singapore
Email: subscriptions@benthamscience.net

CONTENTS

PREFACE

Digital imaging and image processing are among the major components of modern information technologies. Their very fundamental operation is a conversion of analog signals of image sensors into digital signals, *i.e.*, into arrays of numbers that are stored and processed in the memory of digital cameras and computers, transmitted *via* digital communication channels and used for re-creating images in display devices. This conversion is implemented through image sampling, *i.e.*, by taking, in one or another way, signal samples at certain positions throughout the image area.

Optimal design and implementation of image sampling require answering the question:

- What is the minimum sampling rate, *i.e.*, the minimal amount of numbers sufficient for representing images with a given accuracy?

- How can one sample images with sampling rates close to the theoretical minimum?

- Is it possible to implement image resampling without introducing additional distortions due to the resampling?

The book answers these questions. It provides both the most updated formulations of the sampling theory and practical algorithms of image sampling with sampling rates close to the theoretical minimum, as well as introduces interpolation error-free methods of image resampling. In addition, the book presents a number of examples of applications of the described methods. The book is supplemented by a MATLAB© program package for exercising.

CONSENT FOR PUBLICATION

Not applicable.

CONFLICT OF INTEREST

The author declares no conflict of interest regarding the contents of each of the chapters of this book.

Leonid Yaroslavsky
School of Electrical Engineering
Tel Aviv University
Israel

Part I

IMAGE SAMPLING

CHAPTER 1

Introduction

1.1. WHAT IS MEANT BY OPTIMAL IMAGE SAMPLING AND RESAMPLING?

Image sampling results in arrays of numbers that represent images in digital storage devices, computers, and communication channels, and can be used for image reproduction in display devices. Of course, images reproduced by the display devices are not identical to the original ones because image sampling always causes certain distortions of the images. Image reproduction fidelity improves with the amount of numerical data that are obtained to represent images. On the other side, the cost of image sampling, storage and transmission increases with this amount as well. Therefore, the design and implementation of the image sampling should be aimed at minimization of the volume of discrete representation of an image for the given image reproduction fidelity. This is what is understood by the optimization of image sampling. One of the goals of this book is to show how one can evaluate the minimal sampling rate given the image reproduction fidelity and to introduce an image sampling and reconstruction method that is capable of reaching sampling rates close to this minimum. For the numerical characterization of image reconstruction fidelity, the mean square error (MSE) of image reconstruction from its sampled presentation is used throughout the book, the measure commonly accepted in the signal theory.

Image resampling, which is required in many image processing applications, might also, in principle, result in additional losses of image quality. Optimal resampling procedures are those that cause minimal, if any, distortions of digital signals that represent images. Yet another goal of the book is to present image resampling algorithms, which do not distort digital image signals at all, and to theoretically and experimentally prove their superiority.

1.2. OVERVIEW OF THE BOOK

The book consists of two parts: Part1 (Chapters 2 - 6) that deals with problems of image sampling, and Part2 (Chapters 7-9) that is devoted to the image resampling issues.

Leonid Yaroslavsky

Chapter 2 opens the Part1 and provides a summary of the classic sampling theory beginning from the sampling theorem for 1D signals as it was formulated by the founding fathers of the sampling theory Vladimir Kotelnikov and Claude Shannon on the basis of the concept of band-limited signals. Also, extensions of the sampling theorem to 1D band-pass signals and to 2D band-limited signals, issues of optimization of sampling lattices for image sampling, image sampling by means of sub-band decomposition as a theoretical model for evaluating the minimal admissible sampling rate, and signal distortions caused by their sampling with insufficiently high sampling rates are discussed.

Chapter 3 reformulates the sampling theorem for real, not band-limited signals. The reformulation does not engage the idealized concept of the signal band-limitedness and is based on mathematical models of the signal sampling devices and devices for the reconstruction of analog signals from their samples. The chapter also offers an analysis of sampling distortions of not bandlimited signals.

Chapter 4 introduces the next step in the generalization of the sampling theorem. It treats sampling as a special case of the general signal discretization by their expansion over a set of basis functions of signal transforms and introduces a discrete signal model and a concept of signal spectrum sparsity that generalizes the concept of the signal band-limitedness. It also formulates, in terms of the signal spectrum sparsity, a discrete sampling theorem and discusses in details its applications to the cases of such signal transforms as Discrete Fourier, Discrete Cosine, Walsh and wavelet transforms. Finally, the general sampling theorem is formulated, into which the discrete sampling theorem converts when the number of samples of the discrete signal model tends to infinity.

Chapter 5 is devoted to the compressed sensing approach to signal sampling, which was advanced as a solution of the problem of minimization of signal sampling rates. The chapter discusses the ubiquitous compressibility of images sampled over the standard Cartesian sampling lattices, demonstrates, on a simple model, how it is possible to reconstruct signals sampled with aliasing, which the compressed sensing approach offers, and shows that the compressed sensing approach still requires a considerable sampling redundancy and does not practically allow to reach signal sampling rates close to the theoretical minimum.

In Chapter 6, a practical method of image sampling and reconstruction with sampling rates close to the theoretical minimum is presented along with the results of its extensive experimental verification. At the end of the chapter, examples are provided of applications of the suggested method to solving such underdetermined problems as color image de-mosaicing, image super-resolution from multiple chaotically sampled video frames, image reconstruction from their sparsely sampled or decimated projections, image reconstruction from their sparsely sampled Fourier spectra, and image reconstruction from the modulus of its Fourier spectrum.

Chapters 7-9 constitute Part 2 of the book, which addresses optimal methods of image resampling. In Chapter 7, signal resampling is formulated as a digital filtering problem, the concepts of the frequency responses and point spread functions of digital filters are introduced, a perfect fractional shift filter-interpolator is derived, and the discrete sinc interpolation is introduced as the gold standard of interpolation of sampled signals.

In Chapter 8, two families of fast computational DFT and DCT based algorithms of image resampling with discrete sinc-interpolation are presented: methods based on the perfect fractional shift filter-interpolator and methods based on the concept of the image spectra zero padding.

In Chapter 9, examples are provided of applications of image resampling with discrete sinc interpolation to quasi-continuous spectral and correlation analysis, image rotation, image reconstruction from projections, precise numerical differentiation and integration of sampled signals, and sliding window image resampling with discrete sinc interpolation. Additionally, methods of image rotation and signal differentiation and integration with discrete sinc interpolation are compared with other known methods and a theoretical and experimental evidence is provided that the discrete sinc interpolation secures, in distinction from all other interpolation methods, error free signal interpolation.

Chapters 2, 3, 5, 6, 8 and 9 are supplemented by MATLAB programs for exercising.

CHAPTER 2

Summary of the Classic Sampling Theory

2.1. SAMPLING BAND-LIMITED SIGNALS

2.1.1. Sampling 1D Band-limited Signals: The Classic Sampling Theorem

The classic sampling theory is based on the concept of *band-limited signals, i.e.,* signals whose Fourier spectrum is non-zero only within a limited interval of frequencies. Let $a(x)$ be such a signal defined on the entire axis x and let its Fourier Transform spectrum $\alpha(f)$

$$\alpha(f) = \int_{-\infty}^{\infty} a(x)\exp(i2\pi fx)dx \tag{2.1}$$

be non-zero only within interval $[-F/2 < f < F/2]$:

$$\alpha(f) = \mathrm{rect}(f/F)\alpha(f), \tag{2.2}$$

where

$$\mathrm{rect}(x) = \begin{cases} 1, & -1/2 < x < 1/2 \\ 0, & otherwise \end{cases} \tag{2.3}$$

is a *rectangular window function*. Such signals are called *band-limited signals.* Expand signal spectrum $\alpha(f)$ on the interval $[-F/2, F/2]$ into a Fourier series:

$$\alpha(f) = \mathrm{rect}\left(\frac{f}{F}\right)\sum_{k=-\infty}^{\infty} \alpha_k \exp\left(i\frac{2\pi kf}{F}\right). \tag{2.4}$$

By the definition of the Fourier series, expansion coefficients $\{\alpha_k\}$ are found as

$$\alpha_k = \frac{1}{F}\int_{-F/2}^{F/2} \alpha(f)\exp\left(-i2\pi\frac{kf}{F}\right)df . \tag{2.5}$$

Integral in the right side of this expression represents samples of the inverse Fourier transform of the signal spectrum $\alpha(f)$, *i.e.*, samples $\{a(k/F)\}$ of the signal $a(x)$ taken at points $\{k/F\}$. Therefore, the spectrum $\alpha(f)$ of the band limited signal is determined by the signal samples $\{a(k/F)\}$ as

$$\alpha(f) = \frac{\text{rect}(f/F)}{F} \sum_{k=-\infty}^{\infty} a\left(\frac{k}{F}\right) \exp\left(i\frac{2\pi kf}{F}\right) \tag{2.6}$$

which implies that band-limited signal $a(x)$ can be precisely reconstructed from its samples:

$$a(x) = \int_{-\infty}^{\infty} \alpha(f) \exp(-i2\pi fx) df =$$

$$\frac{1}{F} \sum_{k=-\infty}^{\infty} a(k/F) \int_{-\infty}^{\infty} \text{rect}(f/F) \exp[-i2\pi f(x-k/F)] df =$$

$$\frac{1}{F} \sum_{k=-\infty}^{\infty} a(k/F) \int_{-F/2}^{F/2} \exp[-i2\pi f(x-k/F)] df = \sum_{k=-\infty}^{\infty} a(k/F) \frac{\sin[\pi F(x-k/F)]}{\pi F(x-k/F)} \tag{2.7}$$

taken at the distance $\Delta = 1/F$ one from another. This statement is known as the classic *Kotelnikov-Shannon (K-Sh-) sampling theorem* [2, 3].

The inter-sample distance $\Delta = 1/F$ is called the *sampling interval*. Function

$$\text{sinc}(x) = \frac{\sin x}{x} \tag{2.8}$$

is called the *sinc-function*. Illustrative plots of sinc-functions for two different distances between their zeros are presented in Fig. (**2.1**). They demonstrate that sinc-functions are oscillating functions that have zeros at coordinates multiple to the sampling interval $\Delta = 1/F$ except for the point $x = 0$, where they equal to 1. Their magnitudes gradually decay with x as $1/x$.

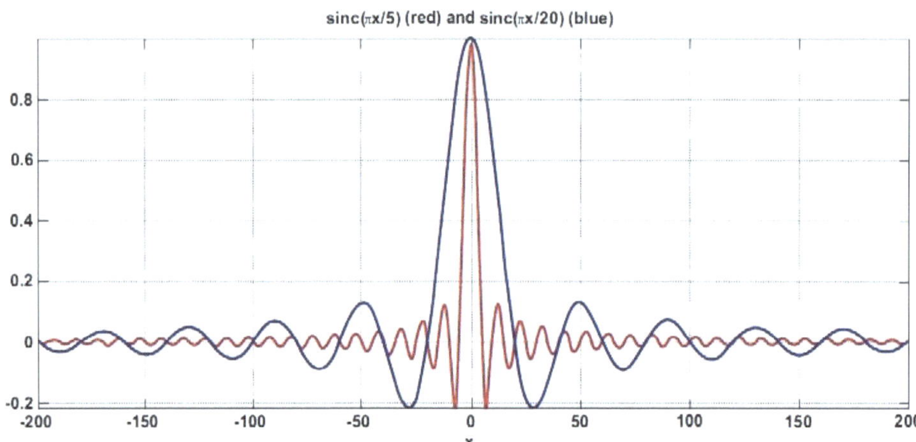

Fig. (2.1). Two examples of sinc-functions.

The sinc-function is a *point spread function* (PSF) of the *ideal low-pass filter* with the frequency response (Fourier transform of the PSF) $\dfrac{1}{F}\mathbf{rect}(f/F)$, which passes through without distortions all signal components with frequencies $|f| \leq F$ and completely stops components with higher frequencies $|f| > F$:

$$\frac{1}{F}\int_{-\infty}^{\infty}\mathbf{rect}(f/F)\exp(-i2\pi fx)df = \frac{1}{F}\int_{-F/2}^{F/2}\exp(-i2\pi fx)df =$$

$$\frac{\exp(i\pi Fx) - \exp(-i\pi Fx)}{i2\pi Fx} = \frac{\sin(\pi Fx)}{\pi Fx} \tag{2.9}$$

Equation (2. **7**) can be rewritten in an alternative form through the sampling interval and sinc-function as

$$a(x) = \sum_{k=-\infty}^{\infty} a(k\Delta)\,\mathbf{sinc}[\pi(x - k\Delta)/\Delta] \tag{2.10}$$

This basic formula for the reconstruction of the band-limited signals implies that band-limited signals are reconstructed from their samples by interpolation of the samples with sinc-function as an interpolation kernel. This interpolation method is called *sinc interpolation.*

Equation (2. **6**) for the spectrum $\alpha(f)$ of the band-limited signal represents this spectrum as a product of the frequency response $\dfrac{1}{F}rect(f/F)$ of the ideal low-pass filter and a function $\tilde{\alpha}(f)$

$$\tilde{\alpha}(f)= \sum_{k=-\infty}^{\infty} a\left(\frac{k}{F}\right)\exp\left(i\frac{2\pi k f}{F}\right),\tag{2. 11}$$

which is the Fourier series expansion of the signal spectrum and, as such, is a periodical function composed of the replicas of signal Fourier spectrum $\alpha(f)$ repeated with a period F :

$$\tilde{\alpha}(f)= \sum_{k=-\infty}^{\infty} a\left(\frac{k}{F}\right)\exp\left(i\frac{2\pi k f}{F}\right)= \sum_{m=-\infty}^{\infty}\alpha(f-mF).\tag{2. 12}$$

This periodical function can be regarded as a Fourier spectrum of a virtual signal $\tilde{a}(x)$ that can be found by the inverse Fourier transform:

$$\tilde{a}(x)= \int_{-\infty}^{\infty}\tilde{\alpha}(f)\exp(-i2\pi f x)df = \sum_{k=-\infty}^{\infty} a\left(\frac{k}{F}\right)\int_{-\infty}^{\infty}\exp\left[-i2\pi f\left(x-\frac{k}{F}\right)\right]df =$$

$$\sum_{-\infty}^{\infty} a\left(\frac{k}{F}\right)\delta\left(x-\frac{k}{F}\right) = \sum_{-\infty}^{\infty}a(k\Delta)\delta(x-k\Delta),\tag{2. 13}$$

where

$$\delta(x)= \int_{-\infty}^{\infty}\exp(\pm i2\pi f x)df\tag{2. 14}$$

is the *Dirac delta-function* that symbolizes the identical transform:

$$a(x)= \int_{-\infty}^{\infty} a(\xi)\delta(x-\xi)d\xi\tag{2. 15}$$

Comparing Eqs. (2.14) and (2. 9) one can see that the delta function is a limit, to which the sinc-function tends when its bandwidth $F \to \infty$:

$$\delta(x) = \lim_{F \to \infty} F \operatorname{sinc}(\pi F x). \tag{2. 16}$$

Eqs. (2.10) through (2.13) simply that

- sampling band-limited signals with sampling interval $\Delta_x = 1/F$ can be treated as generating a virtual signal $\tilde{a}(x)$

$$\tilde{a}(x) = \frac{1}{F} \sum_{k=-\infty}^{\infty} a\left(\frac{k}{F}\right) \delta\left(x - \frac{k}{F}\right), \tag{2. 17}$$

whose spectrum is the periodic replication of the spectrum $\alpha(f)$ of signal $a(x)$ with a replication period $F = 1/\Delta$.

$$\tilde{\alpha}(f) = \sum_{m=-\infty}^{\infty} \alpha(f + Fm) \tag{2. 18}$$

- Signal reconstruction from its samples defined by Eq. (2. 10) can be treated as extraction of the signal spectrum $\alpha(f)$ from the periodically replicated spectrum of the virtual discrete signal by multiplying its periodic spectrum by a rectangular window function $rect(f/F)$,

$$\alpha(f) = rect(f/F)\tilde{\alpha}(f) = rect(f/F) \sum_{m=-\infty}^{\infty} \alpha(f + Fm) \tag{2. 19}$$

i.e., by passing the virtual discrete signal $\tilde{a}(t)$ through the ideal low-pass filter with frequency response $\mathbf{rect}(f/F)$ and point-spread function $\mathbf{sinc}(\pi F x)$, which interpolates signal samples using the sinc-function defined by Eq. (2. 8) as an interpolation kernel. This interpolation method is called *sinc-interpolation*.

The said is illustrated in Fig. (**2.2**).

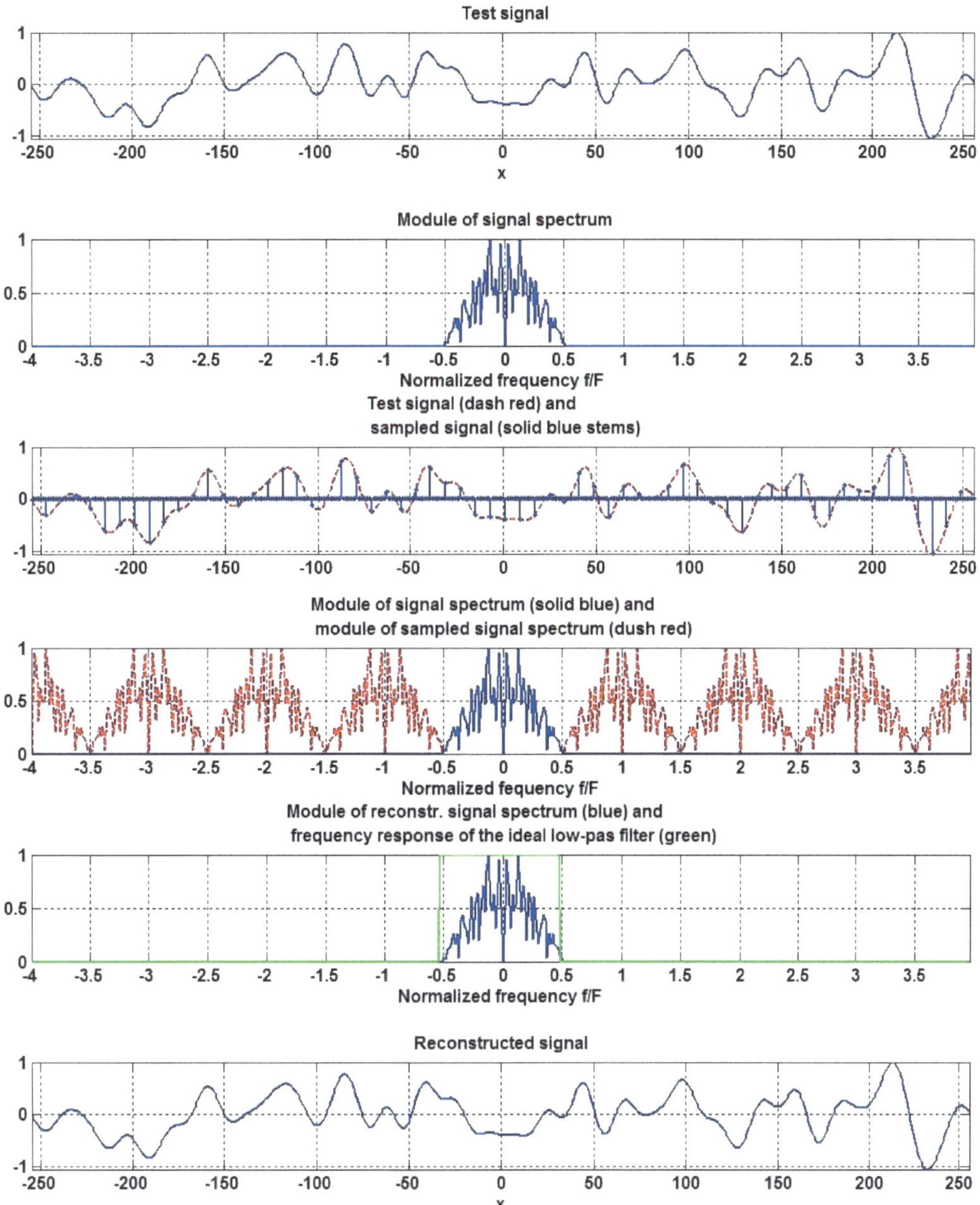

Fig. (2.2). Interpretation of signal sampling as generating a virtual discrete signal with a Fourier spectrum composed from the periodically replicated Fourier spectrum of the signal. From top to bottom: a test signal, module of its Fourier spectrum, the virtual discrete signal composed from samples of the test signal, module of its Fourier spectrum, module of the spectrum of the reconstructed signal, and the reconstructed signal.

The Kotelnikov-Shannon sampling theorem answers the fundamental question, what number of samples of band-limited signals with bandwidth $[-F/2, F/2]$ per unit of the signal length is sufficient for the signal reconstruction from its samples. This number is called the signal *sampling rate*. According to the theorem, it equals F. This rate is called the *Nyquist sampling rate* [3].

The Nyquist sampling rate F is the minimal sampling rate sufficient for reconstruction of band limited signals from their samples. If the signal sampling rate is lower than F, the period of the spectrum periodical replication due to the signal sampling will be lower than the spectrum width and the signal spectrum will overlap with its periodical replicas and can not be extracted from them by the ideal low-pass filter without distortions.

2.1.2   Sampling 1D Band-pass Signals

1D band-limited signals treated in the previous section are called *baseband signals*. Their Fourier spectrum is concentrated within a bounded interval $[-F/2, F/2]$ around zero frequency. This interval is called the *signal baseband*.

1D band-limited signal whose spectrum is concentrated within intervals $[f_0 - F/2, f_0 + F/2]$ and $[-f_0 - F/2, -f_0 + F/2]$ around a non-zero frequency , called the *carrier frequency* are called *pass-band signals*. According to the properties of the Fourier transform, a pass-band signal $a_{PB}(x)$ can be regarded as a result of modulation of a baseband signal $a_{BB}(x)$ by a sinusoidal signal of frequency   :

$$a_{PB}(x) = a_{BB}(x)\sin(2\pi f_0 x) \qquad\qquad (2.20)$$

The classic sampling theorem can be straightforwardly applied to pass-band signals if, before sampling, pass-band signals are converted into corresponding baseband signals by multiplying, or, in the communication engineering jargon, demodu-lating, them by a sinusoidal signal of the carrier frequency   and   the   subsequent low-pass filtering the demodulation result within the baseband $[-F/2, F/2]$. This band-pass-to-baseband signal conversion is illustrated in Fig. (2.3).

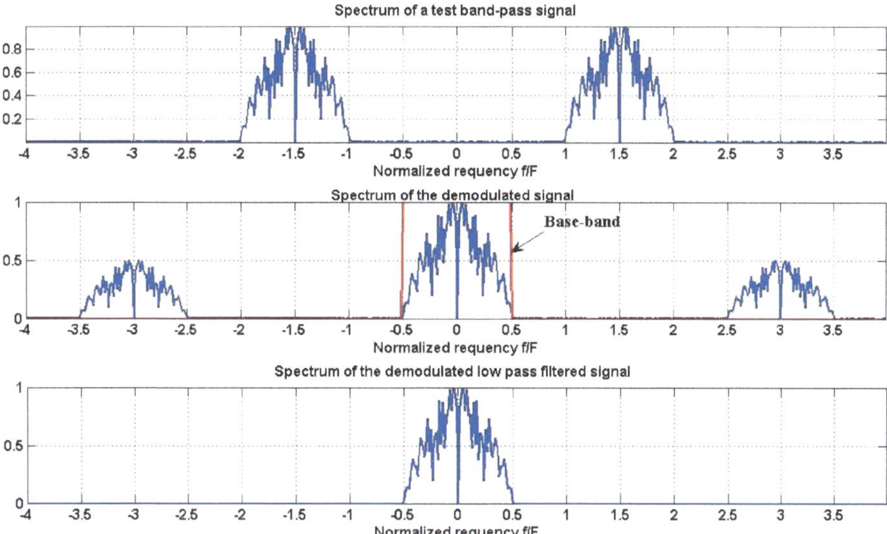

Fig. (2.3). Conversion of a band-pass signal to a baseband signal (from top to bottom): moduli of spectra of a pass-band signal and of its demodulated, and demodulated with subsequent low-pass filtering copies.

Correspondingly, reconstruction of pass-band signals from their sampled representation can be carried out by reconstruction of their baseband copies using sinc interpolation and subsequent modulation of the obtained baseband signal by a sinusoidal signal of the carrier frequency f_0. This implies that the sampling rate for band-pass signals is the same as that for their corresponding baseband signals, *i.e.*, it equals the width F of the baseband signal spectrum.

2.1.3   Separable Sampling 2D Band-limited Signals

Images are two-dimensional (2D) signals. The classic 1D sampling theorem can in a straightforward way be extended to 2D signals if their Fourier spectra are bounded by a rectangle. Let $a(x,y)$ be a signal defined on the entire plane (x,y) and let its Fourier Transform spectrum $\alpha(f_x, f_y)$

$$\alpha(f_x, f_y) = \int\limits_{-\infty}^{\infty} \int\limits_{-\infty}^{\infty} a(x,y)\exp\left[i2\pi(f_x x + f_y y)\right]dxdy \tag{2.21}$$

be non-zero only within an interval $\left[-F_x/2 \le f_x \le F_x/2; -F_y/2 \le f_y \le F_y/2\right]$:

$$\alpha\left(f_x,f_y\right)=\mathbf{rect}\left(f_x/F_x\right)\mathbf{rect}\left(f_y/F_y\right)\alpha\left(f_x,f_y\right)\qquad(2.22)$$

Due to the separability of the spectrum band-limitation (Eq. (2. 22)), one can directly extend Eqs. (2.10), (2.12), and (2.13) to the 2D case and obtain that this signal can be precisely reconstructed from its samples $a\left(k/F_x,l/F_y\right)$ taken at nodes $\left(k/F_x,l/\mathbf{F}_y\right)$ of a regular *rectangular (Cartesian) sampling lattice* (Fig. **2.4**) with sampling intervals $\left(\Delta_x=1/F_x,\Delta_y=1/F_y\right)$ by their 2D separable sinc interpolation:

$$a(x,y)=\sum_{k=-\infty}^{\infty}\sum_{l=-\infty}^{\infty}a\left(k\Delta_x,l\Delta_y\right)\mathbf{sinc}\left[\pi\left(x-k\Delta_x\right)/\Delta_x\right]\mathbf{sinc}\left[\pi\left(x-k\Delta_y\right)/\Delta_y\right],\quad(2.23)$$

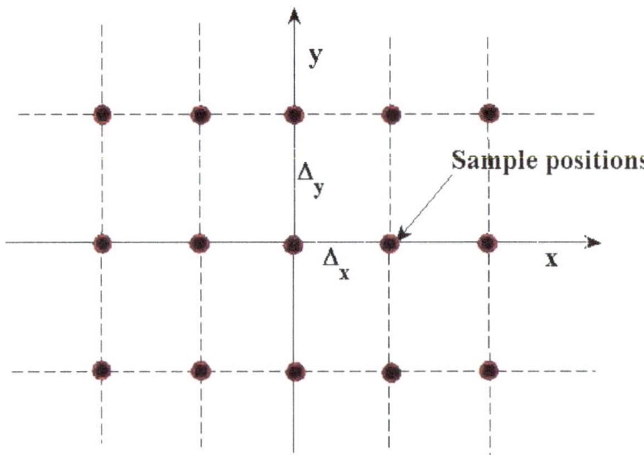

Fig. (2.4). 2D rectangular (Cartesian) sampling lattice.

This statement represents a 2D formulation of the K-Sh sampling theorem. It assumes that signal sampling and reconstruction are carried out in a separable way, say, row-wise and then column-wise.

In full analogy with the above 1D case, one can also conclude that:

- separable sampling 2D band-limited signals with sampling intervals $\left(\Delta_x=1/F_x,\Delta_y=1/F_y\right)$ can be treated as generating a virtual signal $\tilde{a}(x,y)$ whose spectrum is a periodic replication of the spectrum $\alpha\left(f_x,f_y\right)$ of the signal $a(x,y)$

$$\tilde{\alpha}(f_x, f_y) = \sum_{m=-\infty}^{\infty} \sum_{n=-\infty}^{\infty} \alpha(f_x + F_x m, f_y + F_y n) \qquad (2.24)$$

with replication periods in two coordinates $F_x = 1/\Delta_x$ and $F_y = 1/\Delta_y$ (Fig. **2.5**);

- signal reconstruction from its samples defined by Eq. (2.10) can be treated as the extraction of the signal spectrum $\alpha(f_x, f_y)$ from the spectrum of the virtual discrete signal

$$\tilde{a}(x) = \frac{1}{F_x F_y} \sum_{k=-\infty}^{\infty} a(k\Delta_x, l\Delta_y) \delta(x - k\Delta_x) \delta(y - k\Delta_y) \qquad (2.25)$$

by multiplying its periodic spectrum by a rectangular window function $\mathbf{rect}(f_x/F_x)\mathbf{rect}(f_y/F_y)$, i.e., by passing the virtual discrete signal $\tilde{a}(t)$ through the ideal low-pass filter with frequency response $\mathbf{rect}(f_x/F_x)\mathbf{rect}(f_y/F_y)$ and point-spread function $\mathbf{sinc}(\pi x/\Delta_x)\mathbf{sinc}(\pi y/\Delta_y)$, which interpolates signal samples row-wise and column-wise using the sinc-functions as interpolation kernels.

- the minimal number N samples of a band-limited image of the size $S_{xy} = X \times Y$ sufficient for its precise reconstruction equals

$$N = X/\Delta_x \times Y/\Delta_y = S_{x,y} S_{f_x, f_y}, \qquad (2.26)$$

where S_{f_x, f_y} is the area of the rectangle that bounds the image spectrum.

2.2. OPTIMIZATION OF SAMPLING LATTICES FOR IMAGE SAMPLING

Image standard sampling over Cartesian lattices secures the minimal sampling rate only for images with spectra bounded by rectangles. If the image spectrum is bounded by another shape, sampling lattices in other coordinate systems will be optimal in terms of the minimization of the image sampling rate. Two the most immediate examples of the spectral bounding shapes other than the rectangle are image spectrum bounding by a superellipse and by a circle.

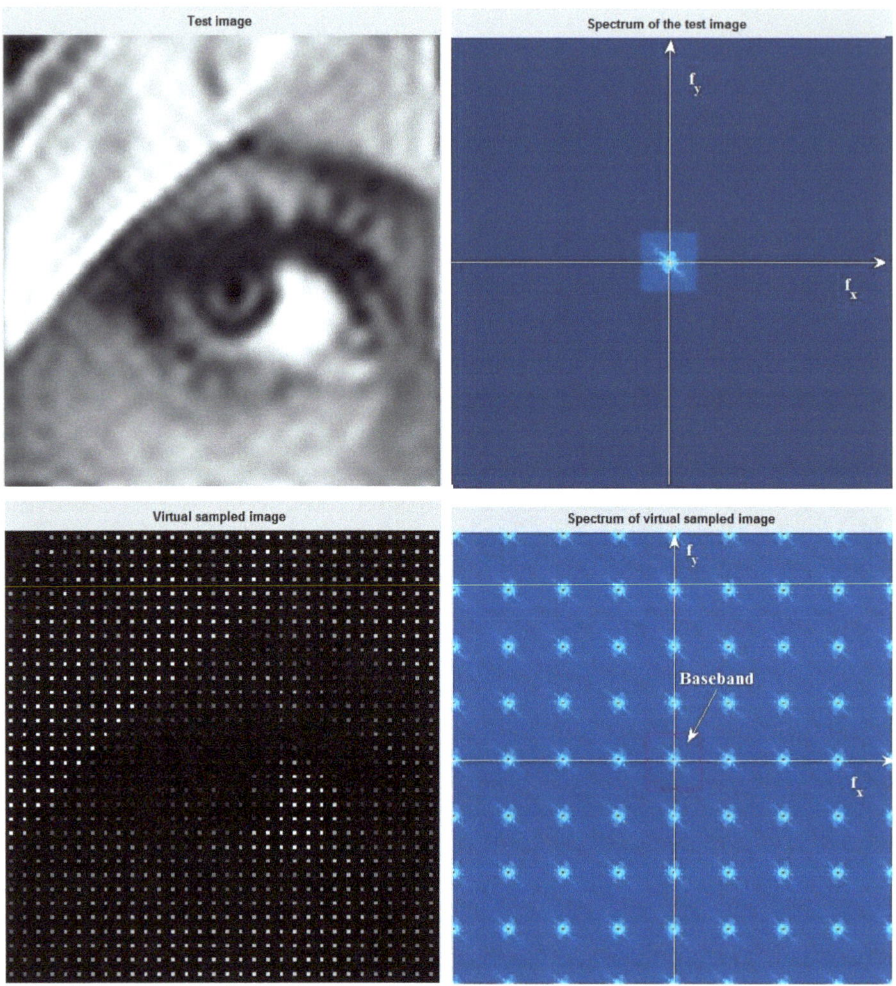

Fig. (2.5). Interpretation of the separable image sampling over a rectangular lattice as the generating a virtual sampled image (bottom left), whose spectrum (bottom right) is a periodically replicated spectrum of the image spectrum.

Image regular sampling in any coordinate system results in the corresponding periodical replication of the image spectrum in a reciprocal coordinate system in the Fourier domain. Therefore the sampling rate will be minimal if spectra periodical replicas are most close to one another, *i.e.*, if they are most densely packed in the spectral domain. For the superellipse as a spectrum bounding shape (Fig. **2.6**), the most dense packing of superellipse spectra is achieved when spectrum replicas are periodically repeated in 45° tilted Cartesian coordinates (Fig.

2.6e). Such an image sampling lattice is called the *rhomboid sampling lattice* (Fig. **2.6f**). This case is conformed to properties of the human vision, which is known to be less sensitive to the diagonal spatial frequencies than to the horizontal and vertical ones. The area of the 45° tilted square (Fig. **2.6d**) that circumscribes the superellipse and is the element of the periodical spectral pattern (Fig. **2.6e**) in the rhomboid sampling lattice, is two times less than the area of the square (Fig. **2.6a**) with vertical and horizontal sides, which is the element of the periodical spectral pattern (Fig. **2.6c**) in the canonic vertical/horizontal Cartesian sampling lattice. Therefore using the rhomboid sampling lattice instead of the canonic one yields a two-fold reduction of the image sampling rate. This method of image sampling and displaying has found an application in the print industry (Fig. **2.7**).

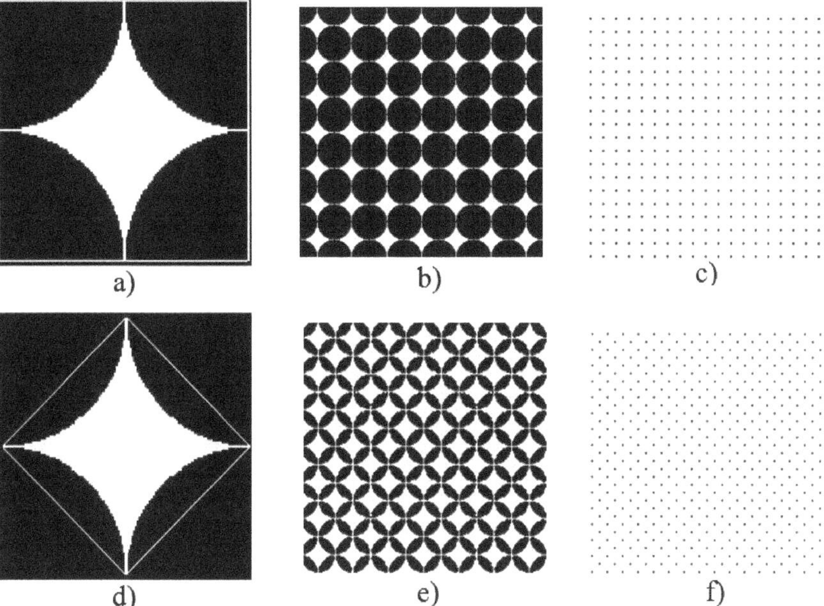

Fig. (2.6). Spectrum bounding shape "superellipse" inscribed in a square with horizontal and vertical sides (**a**) and inscribed in a 45° rotated square (**d**); patterns of superellipses periodically replicated in the vertical and horizontal coordinates (**b**) and in the 45° tilted coordinates (**e**); the Cartesian sampling lattice (**c**) and the rhomboid sampling lattice (**f**).

Fig. (2.7). An example of an image sampled over the rhomboid sampling lattice.

The case of image spectra bounded by a circle (Fig. **2.8**) is conformed to many natural images that have isotropic spectra. Using the *hexagonal sampling lattice* (Fig. **2.8f**) for sampling such images enables achieving the most dense packing of circular periodically replicated copies of image spectra (Fig. **2.8d**) and yields 13.4% saving of the sampling rate with respect to the canonic sampling over the Cartesian sampling lattice. This estimate is found as a relative difference between the area $4R^2$ of the square (Fig. **2.8a**) that circumscribes a circle of radius R and the area $2\sqrt{3}R^2 \approx 3.46R^2$ of the hexagon (Fig. **2.8d**) that circumscribes the same circle and is the element of the hexagonal periodical pattern.

It is no surprise that one can find numerous examples of a hexagonal arrangement of light-sensitive cells in eyes of humans and animals (see, for instance, Fig. **2.9**) because this permits placing the maximal number of cells of a given size on a given area. Hexagonal sampling lattices are also used in the print industry for color printing and in some image displays.

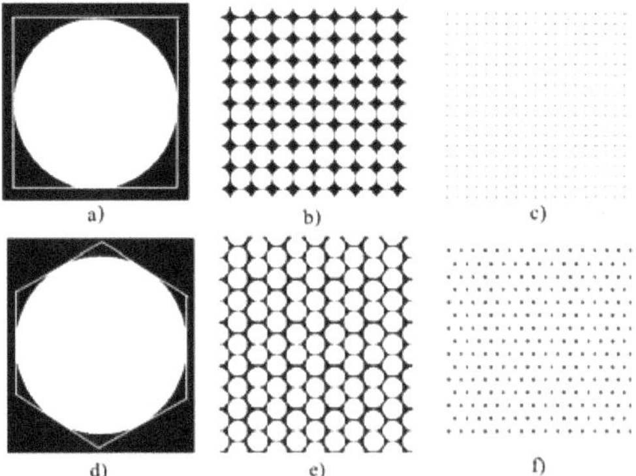

Fig. (2.8). Circular spectrum bounding shape inscribed in a square (**a**) and in a hexagon (**d**), circular spectra periodically replicated in the Cartesian coordinates (**b**) and in the hexagonal coordinates (**e**), and the corresponding Cartesian (**c**) and hexagonal (**f**) sampling lattices.

Fig. (2.9). Hexagonal arrangements of cones in the fovea of the human eye retina (left) and of compound eyes of insects (right).

2.3. IMAGE SAMPLING THROUGH THEIR SUB-BAND DECOMPOSITION AND EVALUATING THE IMAGE MINIMAL SAMPLING RATE

The described examples of canonic rectangular, rhomboid and hexagonal sampling lattices for image sampling demonstrate that, whatever regular periodical sampling lattice is used, the sampling rate always equals the area of the repeated element of the periodical spectral pattern. This allows hypothesizing that, in general, for any shape that bounds the image spectrum the image lowest sampling rate equals the total area of this shape, *i.e.*, the minimal amount N of numbers sufficient for precise reconstruction of images with bounded spectrum equals the product $S_{x,y}S_{f_x,f_y}$ of the image and its spectrum areas

$$N \geq S_{x,y}S_{f_x,f_y},\qquad(2.27)$$

This statement can be proved using the concept of image *sub-band decomposition.* In the sub-band decomposition, image $a(x,y)$ is decomposed into a sum

$$a(x,y) \cong \sum_k a^{(k)}(x,y)\qquad(2.28)$$

of a certain number K of components $\left\{a^{(k)}(x,y)\right\}$ with spectra of rectangular shapes that all together approximate the image spectrum as it is illustrated in Fig. **(2.10)**.

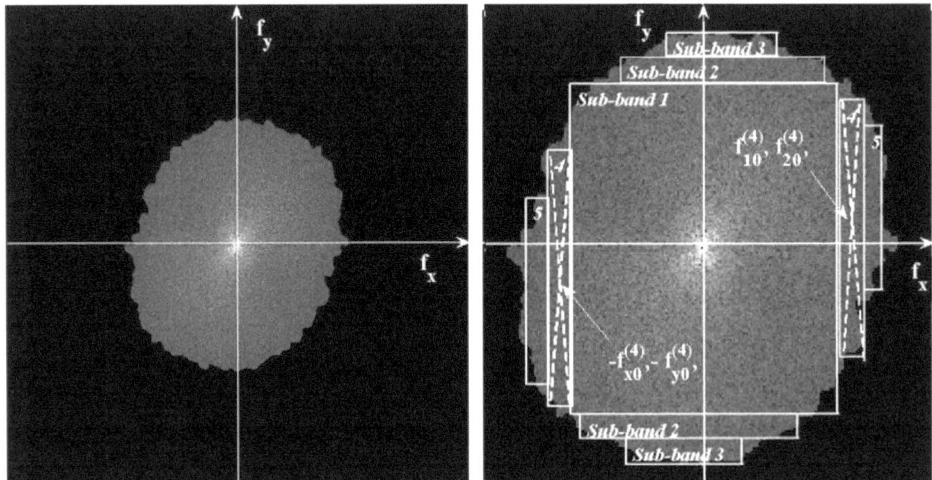

Fig. (2.10). Image spectrum (left) and its sub-band decomposition (right). Carrier frequencies ($f_{x0}^{(4)}, f_{y0}^{(4)}$) for the pass-band components are indicated only for the fourth component in order to not overburden the image.

For each of the components, the rectangular sampling lattice with sampling intervals defined by their dimensions will be optimal according to the sampling theorem for band-limited and band-pass signals. Hence the minimal number N_k of samples required for the precise reconstruction of k-th component with the spectrum of the area $S_{f_x,f_y}^{(k)}$ will equal $S_{x,y} S_{f_x,f_y}^{(k)}$, which, for the entire image, amounts to

$$N_K = \sum_{k=1}^{K} N_k = S_{x,y} \sum_{k=1}^{K} S_{f_x,f_y}^{(k)} \tag{2.29}$$

samples. As soon as a sufficiently large number K of the sub-band components cover the entire area S_{f_x,f_y} of the image spectrum this number tends to

$$\lim_{K \to \infty} N_K = S_{x,y} \lim_{K \to \infty} \sum_{k=1}^{K} S_{f_x,f_y}^{(k)} = S_{x,y} S_{f_x,f_y} \tag{2.30}$$

i.e., to the product $S_{x,y} S_{f_x,f_y}$ of the image area $S_{x,y}$ and the area S_{f_x,f_y} occupied by its bounded spectrum.

2.4. SIGNAL DISTORTIONS CAUSED BY SIGNAL SAMPLING WITH SUB-NYQUIST SAMPLING RATES

For 1D band-limited signals with bandwidth F, the minimal sampling rate sufficient for their precise reconstruction from samples is the Nyquist sampling rate F. It follows from Eq. (2. 19) that if the signal is sampled with a sampling rate $\widetilde{F} < F$, it will be reconstructed distorted due to the penetration into the signal baseband $[-F, F]$ replicas $\alpha(f + F)$ and $\alpha(f + F)$ of the signal spectrum $\alpha(f)$. This is illustrated in Fig. (**2.11**) for the case when the signal sampling rate is 20% lower than the Nyquist rate.

One can numerically evaluate the mean square error of signal reconstruction using the Parseval's relationship for the Fourier Transform:

$$\int_{-\infty}^{\infty} [a(x)]^2\, dx = \int_{-\infty}^{\infty} |\alpha(f)|^2\, df \tag{2.31}$$

According to this relationship, the mean square reconstruction error of a band-limited signal with a baseband F from its samples taken with a rate $\widetilde{F} < F$ equals

$$\int_{-\infty}^{\infty} [a(x) - \tilde{a}(x)]^2\, dx = \int_{\widetilde{F}/2}^{F/2} |\alpha(f + F)|^2\, df + \int_{-F/2}^{-\widetilde{F}/2} |\alpha(-f - F)|^2\, df = 2\int_{\widetilde{F}/2}^{F/2} |\alpha(f + F)|^2\, df \tag{2.32}$$

The most characteristic and clearly visible signal distortions due to the sampling are *strobe effect* and *moiré effect*. The strobe effect is a stroboscopic reduction of frequencies of periodical signal components that exceed the highest frequency $F/2 = 1/2\Delta$ of the signal *sampling baseband* $[-F/2, F/2]$ defined by the sampling interval. The replicated copies of the signal spectra will get inside the baseband and appear with reduced frequencies. Specifically, a periodical component with a frequency $f > F/2$ appears in the reconstructed signal with frequency $(F - f)$ symmetrical to the frequency f relatively to the baseband border frequency $F/2$. Fig. (**2.12**) illustrates this phenomenon for 1-D signals. It presents a result of sampling and reconstruction of a sinusoidal signal $\cos(2\pi f x/512)$ for $f = 48$ and the sampling baseband $F = 64$. One can see in this figure that this signal of frequency 48, which is 3/2 times larger than maximal frequency 32 of the baseband, appears after sampling and reconstruction with frequency 16=64-48 (0.25 in the normalized to the baseband bandwidth frequency scale).

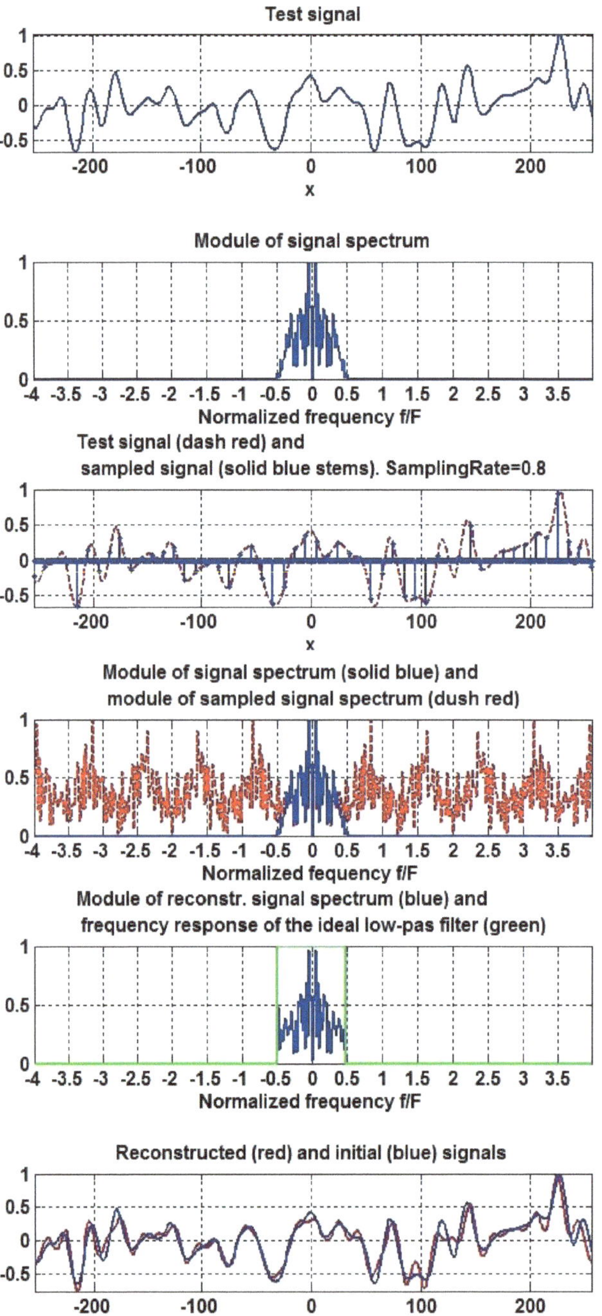

Fig. (2.11). Signal distortions due to signal under-sampling with the rate 0.8 of the Nyquist rate.

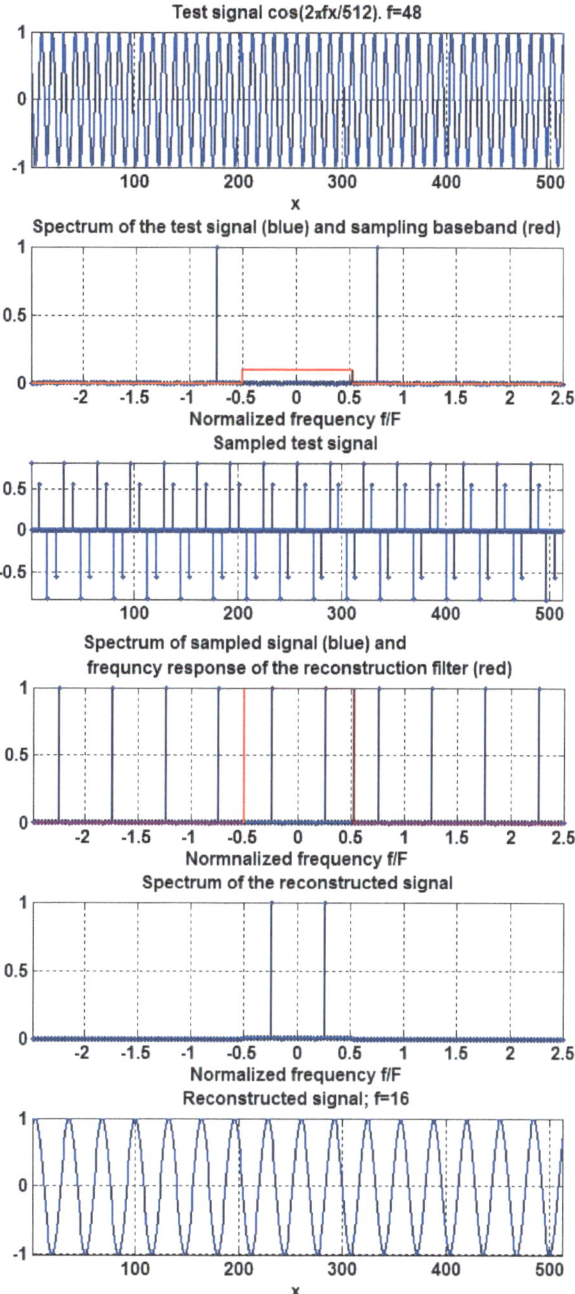

Fig. (2.12). Strobe-effect in sampling a sinusoidal signal with a sampling rate lower than the Nyquist rate (the image was obtained using program Strobe_Moire_Effects_BNTM.m provided in the Exercises).

2D strobe effects are illustrated in Figs. (**2.13** and **2.14**) obtained using programs Aliasing_2D_BNTM.m and Fringe_aliasing_demo_BNTM provided in the Exercises. Fig. (**2.13**) demonstrates the spectra of sampled 2D signals with spatial frequencies within the signal sampling baseband (left) and outside the signal baseband (right). In the latter case, the signal is under-sampled and only the aliasing spectral components get into the sampling baseband.

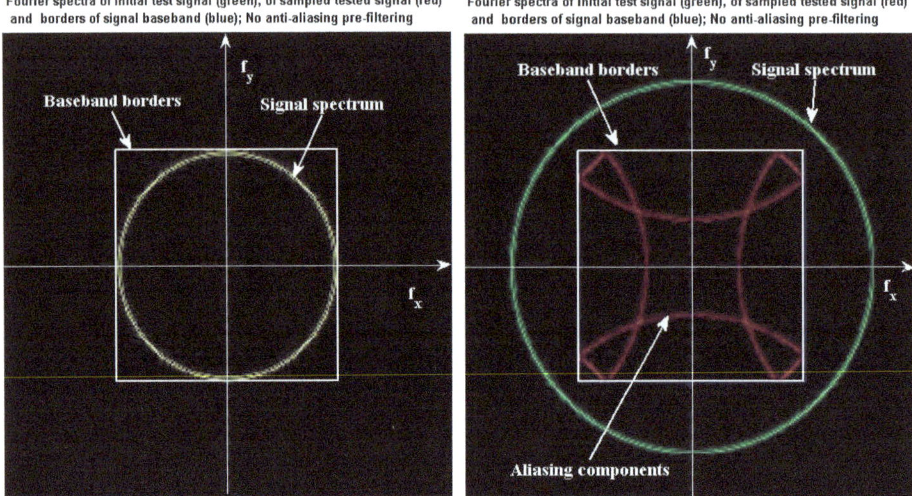

Fig. (2.13). 2D strobe effect illustrated in the spectral domain. Left: a spectrum of a test signal, which contains frequency components with frequencies smaller than the half of the sampling baseband bandwidth. Right: Spectrum of a sampled signal with frequencies larger than the half of the sampling baseband bandwidth and spectrum aliasing components that penetrate the baseband.

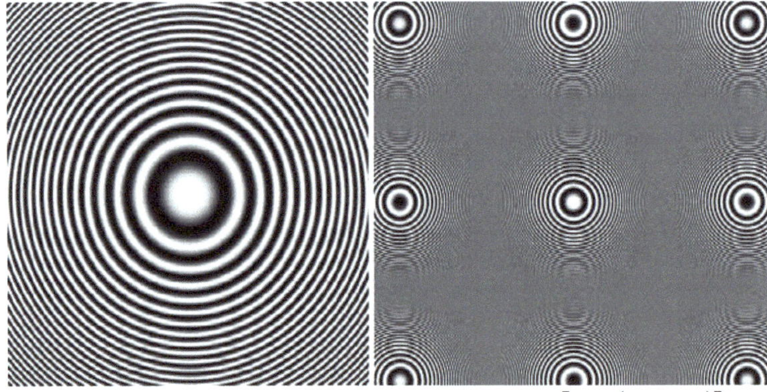

Fig. (2.14). Strobe-effect in sampling a 2D periodical signal $\cos\left[2\pi\kappa\left(x^2 + y^2\right)\right]$ (x, y) are vertical and horizontal coordinates centered at the centers of the images). Left: a signal with local frequencies that do not exceed the highest frequency of the sampling baseband. Right: a signal with a larger value of the parameter κ, which results in the strobe effect due to signal local frequencies that exceed the highest frequency of the sampling baseband.

Fig. (**2.14**) demonstrates the strobe-effect in sampling 2D periodical "chirp" signals $\cos\left[2\pi\kappa\left(x^2 + y^2\right)\right]$ for two values of frequency κ. In the left image, κ is small enough to generate an image, in which local spatial frequencies do not exceed the sampling rate, while in the image to the right, κ is sufficiently large to generate an image with local spatial frequencies larger than the sampling rate, which produces clearly visible strobe effects.

Fig. (**2.15**) demonstrates sampling distortions of periodical components on a real-life image. The upper image in this figure presents a full resolution image; the bottom image is this image down-sampled with aliasing. Fig. (**2.16**) presents the corresponding spectra of these images, where the effects of spectral aliasing can also be easily seen.

Fig. (2.15). An example of sampling distortions of a real-life image. Upper: a full resolution image; bottom: this image downsampled with aliasing.

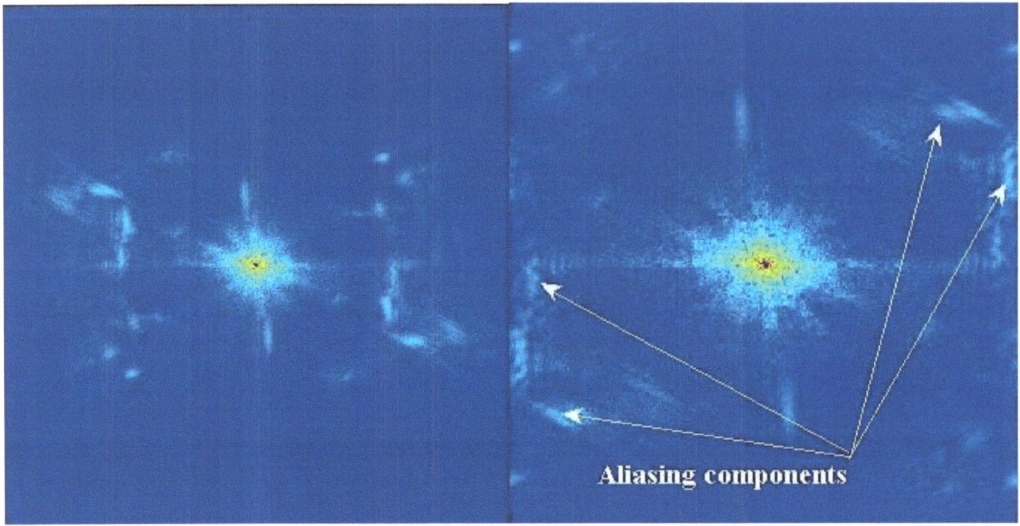

Fig. (2.16). Demonstration of spectra aliasing in the spectral domain. Left: spectrum of a full resolution image of Fig. (**2.15**), upper; right: spectrum of the down-sampled image presented in Fig. (**2.15**), bottom.

While strobe effects appear in form of lowering signal spectral components due to sampling, moiré effects appear in a form of beating between the signal high-frequency components with the ghost high-frequency components from replicas in the spectrum of sampled signals not removed by the reconstruction filter, if its bandwidth is wider than the width of the sampling baseband. These beatings form moiré patterns, hence the name of the effect.

Fig. (**2.17**) generated using the program Strobe_Moire_Effects_BNTM.m illustrates this phenomenon on an example of sampling and reconstruction of a test sinusoidal signal.

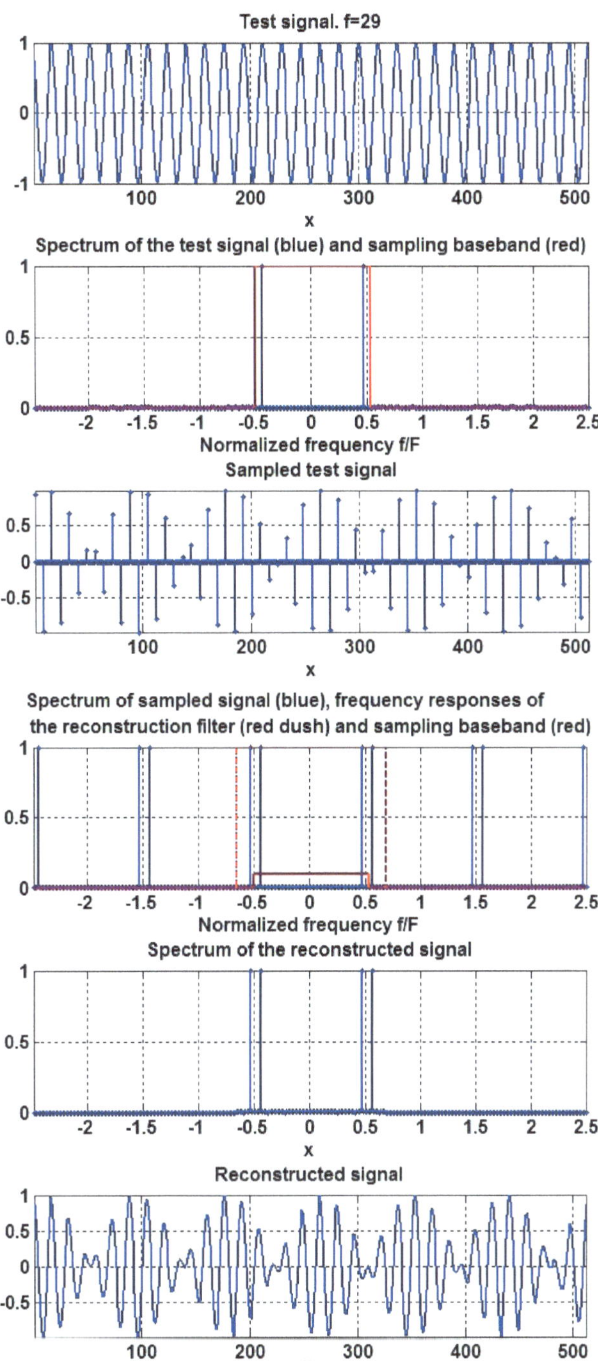

Fig. (2.17). Moiré effect for 1D signals in the reconstruction of a sampled sinusoidal signal using a reconstruction low-pass filter with a bandwidth that exceeds the sampling baseband.

2.5. EXERCISES

- **Strobe_Moire_Effects_BNTM.m**

Demonstration, in the form of a movie, of sampling aliasing effects: strobe and moiré effects for 1D signals. Displayed are: test sinusoidal signals of frequencies that linearly grow from frame to frame, their corresponding Fourier spectra at a fixed sampling rate, corresponding signals reconstructed from their samples and their Fourier spectra, and frequency response of the reconstruction filter

- **Aliasing_2D_BNTM.m**

Demonstration, in the form of a movie, of aliasing effects in sampling 2D signals. As test signals, 2D sinusoidal signals with different spatial frequencies that linearly grow from movie frame to frame are used. Displayed are test images, corresponding images reconstructed from their samples, and their Fourier spectra

- **Fringe_aliasing_demo_BNTM.m**

Demonstration, in the form of a movie, of strobe effect in sampling and reconstruction of 2D chirp signals with different speed of growth of spatial frequencies.

- **StrobEffect3D_BNTM.m**

Demonstration, in the form of a movie, of 3D strobe effect in image sampling and reconstruction on an example of a row-wise readout of a rotating image.

CHAPTER 3

Sampling Real Not Band-Limited Signals

3.1. MATHEMATICAL MODELS OF IMAGE SAMPLING AND RECON-STRUCTION DEVICES

The classic sampling theorem is based on the idealized concept of band-limited signals. However, in reality, signals are never band-limited. This chapter suggests an alternative formulation of the sampling theorem that does not engage the concept of signal band-limitedness and is based on mathematical models of real signal sampling and reconstruction devices.

Consider how image digitizers and displays are designed. Most of the modern cameras use for image acquisition arrays of CCD or CMOS light sensitive cells arranged over the rectangular sampling lattices (Fig. **3.1**).

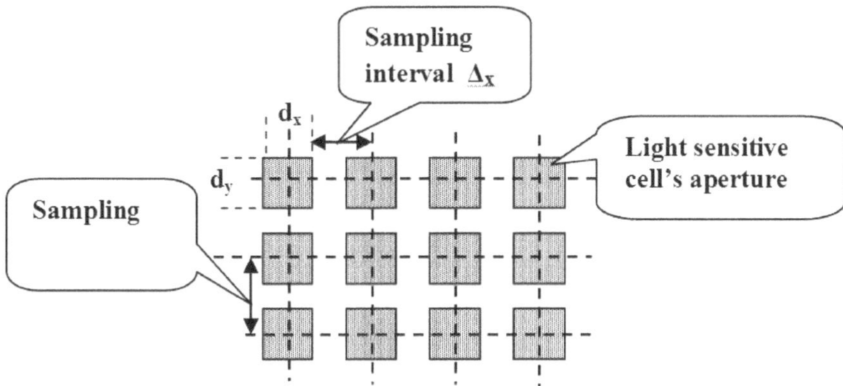

Fig (3.1). Arrangement of arrays of light-sensitive cells in image sampling devices.

Each cell measures the intensity of the incident light averaged over its aperture. This means that they generate image samples (*pixels*) as

$$\tilde{a}_{k,l} = \int\limits_{X}\int\limits_{Y} a(x,y) PSF^{(s)}\left(k\Delta_x - x, l\Delta_y - y\right) dx dy , \qquad (3.1)$$

where $a(x,y)$ is an image signal, $PSF^{(s)}(x,y)$ is the point spread function of the light-sensitive cells, (k,l) are 2D indices of the nodes of the rectangular sampling lattice, $\widetilde{a}_{k,l}$ is the value of (k,l)-th pixel and (X,Y) are dimensions of the array. For the light-sensitive array depicted in Fig. (**3.1**).

$$PSF^{(s)}(x,y) = \mathrm{rect}(x/d_x)\,\mathrm{rect}(y/d_y) \tag{3. 2}$$

where **rect(x)** is the rectangular window function defined by Eq. (2. 3).

As an example of the design of the modern image display devices, the family of LED monitors can be considered. They are implemented as arrays of light-emitting diodes (LED) arranged over the rectangular lattice in Cartesian coordinates (Fig. **3.2**). The diodes reproduce luminosity of their corresponding pixels.

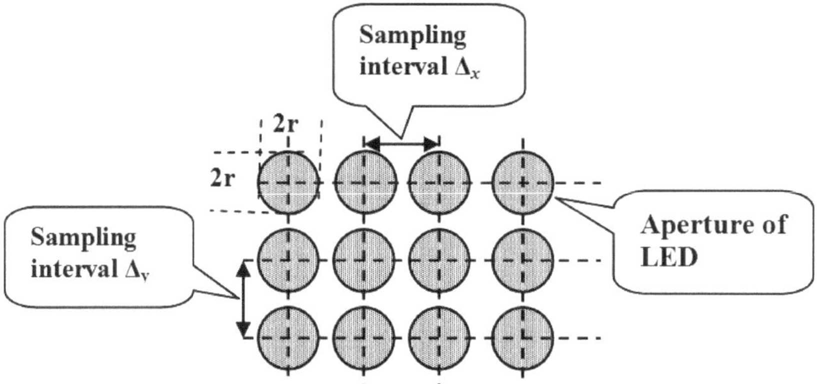

Fig. (3.2). Arrangement of light emitting cells in image display devices.

From the image sampled representation $\{\widetilde{a}_{k,l}\}$, these arrays generate a reconstructed image $a^{(r)}(x,y)$ that can mathematically be modeled as

$$\hat{a}(x,y) = \sum_{k=0}^{K-1}\sum_{l=0}^{L-1}\widetilde{a}_{k,l}\,PSF^{(r)}(x - k\Delta_x, y - l\Delta_y) \tag{3. 3}$$

where $K \times L$ is the number of image pixels, $PSF^{(r)}(x,y)$ is the point spread function of the LEDs, a function that describes the distribution of the luminosity over the LED's aperture. Typically, the light-emitting cells have circular apertures:

$$PSF^{(r)}(x,y)= circ\left(\frac{x - k\Delta_x}{r}, \frac{y - l\Delta_y}{r}\right),$$

(3. 4)

where $circ(x,y)$ is the *circular window function*

$$circ(x,y)= \begin{cases} 1, & \sqrt{x^2 + y^2} \leq 1 \\ 0, & otherwise \end{cases}.$$

(3. 5)

Similar models characterized by their PSFs describe all types of image display devices.

3.2. A REALISTIC RE-FORMULATION OF THE SAMPLING THEOREM

A link between image samples generated by the image sampling device and the reconstructed image is established using Eqs. (3. 1) and (3. 3). First, the summation limits in Eq. (3. 3) can be replaced by infinities assuming that image samples are equal to zero for indices less than zero and larger than, correspondingly, $K - 1$ and $L - 1$:

$$\hat{a}(x,y)= \sum_{k=-\infty}^{\infty} \sum_{l=-\infty}^{\infty} \tilde{a}_{k,l} PSF^{(r)}\left(x - k\Delta_x, y - l\Delta_y\right).$$

(3. 6)

Now, we can treat Eq.(3. 6) as a convolution

$$\tilde{a}(x,y)= \int_{-\infty}^{\infty}\int_{-\infty}^{\infty} PSF^{(r)}(x - \xi, y - \eta)\sum_{k=-\infty}^{\infty} \sum_{l=-\infty}^{\infty} \tilde{a}_{k,l}\delta\left(\xi - k\Delta_x, \eta - l\Delta_y\right)d\xi d\eta$$

(3. 7)

of a virtual sampled signal

$$\tilde{\tilde{a}}(x,y)= \sum_{k=-\infty}^{\infty} \sum_{l=-\infty}^{\infty} \tilde{a}_{k,l}\delta\left(x - k\Delta_x, y - l\Delta_y\right)$$

(3. 8)

with point spread function $PSF^{(r)}(x,y)$ of the image display device, which can be interpreted as passing the virtual sampled signal through a linear filter with this point spread function.

Second, Eq. (3. 1) for image samples $\{\tilde{a}_{k,l}\}$ can be transformed to represent them as

$$\tilde{a}_{k,l} = \int\limits_{-\infty}^{\infty}\int\limits_{-\infty}^{\infty} a(x,y)PSF^{(s)}\big(k\Delta_x - x, l\Delta_y - y\big)dxdy =$$

$$\int\limits_{-\infty}^{\infty}\int\limits_{-\infty}^{\infty} a(x,y)\left[\int\limits_{-\infty}^{\infty}\int\limits_{-\infty}^{\infty} PSF^{(s)}(\xi - x, \eta - y)\delta(\xi - k\Delta_x)\delta(\eta - l\Delta_y)d\xi d\eta\right]dxdy =$$

$$\int\limits_{-\infty}^{\infty}\int\limits_{-\infty}^{\infty}\left[\left[\int\limits_{-\infty}^{\infty}\int\limits_{-\infty}^{\infty} a(x,y)PSF^{(s)}(\xi - x, \eta - y)dxdy\right]\right]\delta(\xi - k\Delta_x)\delta(\eta - l\Delta_y)d\xi d\eta =$$

$$\int\limits_{-\infty}^{\infty}\int\limits_{-\infty}^{\infty}\tilde{a}(\xi,\eta)\delta(\xi - k\Delta_x)\delta(\eta - l\Delta_y)d\xi d\eta , \qquad\qquad (3.\,9)$$

where

$$\tilde{a}(\xi,\eta) = \int\limits_{-\infty}^{\infty}\int\limits_{-\infty}^{\infty} a(x,y)PSF^{(s)}(\xi - x, \eta - y)dxdy . \qquad\qquad (3.\,10)$$

$\tilde{a}(\xi,\eta)$ is a virtual pre-filtered signal $\tilde{a}(x,y)$ obtained by passing the image $a(x,y)$ through a linear filter with point spread function $PSF^{(s)}(x,y)$ of the image sampling device. By the convolution theorem of the Fourier Transform, Fourier spectrum

$$\tilde{\alpha}(f_x, f_y) = \int\limits_{-\infty}^{\infty}\int\limits_{-\infty}^{\infty} \tilde{a}(x,y)\exp\big[i2\pi(f_x x + f_x y)\big]dxdy \qquad\qquad (3.\,11)$$

of the signal $\tilde{a}(x,y)$ is a product

$$\tilde{\alpha}(f_x, f_y) = FR^{(s)}(f_x, f_y)\alpha(f_x, f_y) \qquad\qquad (3.\,12)$$

of the spectrum

$$\alpha(f_x, f_y) = \int\limits_{-\infty}^{\infty}\int\limits_{-\infty}^{\infty} a(x,y)\exp\big[i2\pi(f_x x + f_x y)\big]dxdy \qquad\qquad (3.\,13)$$

of the image signal $a(x,y)$ and the frequency response of the pre-filter

$$FR^{(s)}\left(f_x, f_y\right) = \int\limits_{-\infty}^{\infty}\int\limits_{-\infty}^{\infty} PSF^{(s)}(x, y)\exp\left[i2\pi\left(f_x x + f_x y\right)\right]dxdy \qquad (3.14)$$

The virtual sampled signal $\widetilde{\widetilde{a}}(x, y)$ is a periodical function in the Cartesian coordinate system (x, y). Its spectrum is

$$\widetilde{\widetilde{\alpha}}\left(f_x, f_y\right) = \int\limits_{-\infty}^{\infty}\int\limits_{-\infty}^{\infty}\widetilde{\widetilde{a}}(x, y)\exp\left[i2\pi\left(f_x x + f_y y\right)\right]dxdy =$$

$$\int\limits_{-\infty}^{\infty}\int\limits_{-\infty}^{\infty}\left[\sum\limits_{k=-\infty}^{\infty}\sum\limits_{l=-\infty}^{\infty}\widetilde{a}_{k,l}\delta\left(x - k\Delta_x, y - l\Delta_y\right)\right]\exp\left[i2\pi\left(f_x x + f_y y\right)\right]dxdy =$$

$$\sum\limits_{k=-\infty}^{\infty}\sum\limits_{l=-\infty}^{\infty}\widetilde{a}_{k,l}\exp\left[i2\pi\left(f_x k\Delta_x + f_y l\Delta_y\right)\right] \qquad (3.15)$$

Point values $\widetilde{a}\left(k\Delta_x, l\Delta_y\right)$ of the signal $\widetilde{a}(x, y)$ at the nodes (k, l) of the rectangular sampling lattice can be found by the inverse Fourier Transform of the spectrum $\widetilde{\alpha}\left(f_x, f_y\right)$ of the signal $\widetilde{a}(x, y)$ at points $\left(k\Delta_x, l\Delta_y\right)$:

$$\widetilde{a}_{k,l} = \int\limits_{-\infty}^{\infty}\widetilde{\alpha}\left(p_x, p_y\right)\exp\left[-i2\pi\left(p_x k\Delta_x + p_y l\Delta_y\right)\right]dp_x dp_y \qquad (3.16)$$

Insert Eq.(3.16) into Eq. (3.15) and obtain

$$\widetilde{\widetilde{\alpha}}\left(f_x, f_y\right) = \sum\limits_{k=-\infty}^{\infty}\sum\limits_{l=-\infty}^{\infty}\int\limits_{-\infty}^{\infty}\widetilde{\alpha}\left(p_x, p_y\right)\exp\left[-i2\pi\left(\left(f_x - p_x\right)k\Delta_x + \left(f_y - p_y\right)l\Delta_y\right)\right]dp_x dp_y =$$

$$\sum\limits_{k=-\infty}^{\infty}\sum\limits_{l=-\infty}^{\infty}\int\limits_{-\infty}^{\infty}\widetilde{\alpha}\left(p_x, p_y\right)\exp\left[-i2\pi\left(\left(f_x - p_x\right)k\Delta_x + \left(f_y - p_y\right)l\Delta_y\right)\right]dp_x dp_y =$$

$$\int\limits_{-\infty}^{\infty}\widetilde{\alpha}\left(p_x, p_y\right)_y\sum\limits_{k=-\infty}^{\infty}\sum\limits_{l=-\infty}^{\infty}\exp\left[-i2\pi\left(\left(f_x - p_x\right)k\Delta_x + \left(f_y - p_y\right)l\Delta_y\right)\right]dp_x dp . \qquad (3.17)$$

The double sum in Eq. (3. 17) is a Fourier series of a periodical function. To find this function, introduce a periodical function $\sum\limits_{k=-\infty}^{\infty}\sum\limits_{l=-\infty}^{\infty}\delta\left(f_x-\dfrac{k}{\Delta_x},f_y-\dfrac{l}{\Delta_y}\right)$ with a 2D period $\left[1/\Delta_x,1/\Delta_y\right]$ and represent it as a Fourier series:

$$\sum_{k=-\infty}^{\infty}\sum_{l=-\infty}^{\infty}\delta\left(f_x-\frac{k}{\Delta_x},f_y-\frac{l}{\Delta_y}\right)=\sum_{m=-\infty}^{\infty}\sum_{n=-\infty}^{\infty}D_{m,n}\exp\left[i2\pi\left(f_x m\Delta_x+f_y n\Delta_y\right)\right]. \quad (3.18)$$

Coefficients $D_{m,n}$ can be found as

$$D_{m,n}=\Delta_x\Delta_y\int_{-1/2\Delta_x}^{1/2\Delta_x}\int_{-1/2\Delta_y}^{1/2\Delta_y}\sum_{k=-\infty}^{\infty}\sum_{l=-\infty}^{\infty}\delta\left(f_x-\frac{k}{\Delta_x},f_y-\frac{l}{\Delta_y}\right)\exp\left[-i2\pi\left(f_x m\Delta_x+f_y n\Delta_y\right)\right]df_x df_y \quad (3.19)$$

As only one period with indices $\left(k=0,l=0\right)$ falls within the integration limits

$$\left[-1/\Delta_x,1/\Delta_x;-1/\Delta_y,1/\Delta_y\right].$$

$$D_{m,n}=\Delta_x\Delta_y\int_{-1/2\Delta_x}^{1/2\Delta_x}\int_{-1/2\Delta_y}^{1/2\Delta_y}\sum_{k=-\infty}^{\infty}\sum_{l=-\infty}^{\infty}\delta\left(f_x,f_y\right)\exp\left[-i2\pi\left(f_x m\Delta_x+f_y n\Delta_y\right)\right]df_x df_y. \quad (3.20)$$

By the definition (Eq. 2.15) of the delta-function,

$$\int_{-1/2\Delta_x}^{1/2\Delta_x}\int_{-1/2\Delta_y}^{1/2\Delta_y}\sum_{k=-\infty}^{\infty}\sum_{l=-\infty}^{\infty}\delta\left(f_x,f_y\right)\exp\left[-i2\pi\left(f_x m\Delta_x+f_y m\Delta_y\right)\right]df_x df_y=1$$

Therefore

$$\sum_{k=-\infty}^{\infty}\sum_{l=-\infty}^{\infty}\delta\left(f_x-\frac{k}{\Delta_x},f_y-\frac{l}{\Delta_y}\right)=\Delta_x\Delta_y\sum_{m=-\infty}^{\infty}\sum_{n=-\infty}^{\infty}\exp\left[i2\pi\left(f_x m\Delta_x+f_y n\Delta_y\right)\right] \quad (3.21)$$

This identity is called the *Poisson summation formula*. Using this formula in Eq. (3. 17), obtain that:

$$\widetilde{\widetilde{\alpha}}\left(f_x,f_y\right)=\int\limits_{-\infty}^{\infty}\widetilde{\alpha}\left(p_x,p_y\right)_y\sum_{k=-\infty}^{\infty}\sum_{l=-\infty}^{\infty}\exp\left[-i2\pi\left(\left(f_x-p_x\right)k\Delta_x+\left(f_y-p_y\right)l\Delta_y\right)\right]dp_xdp=$$

$$\frac{1}{\Delta_x\Delta_y}\int\limits_{-\infty}^{\infty}\widetilde{\alpha}\left(p_x,p_y\right)\sum_{k=-\infty}^{\infty}\sum_{l=-\infty}^{\infty}\delta\left(f_x-p_x-\frac{k}{\Delta_x},f_y-p_y-\frac{l}{\Delta_y}\right)dp_xdp_y=$$

$$\frac{1}{\Delta_x\Delta_y}\int\limits_{-\infty}^{\infty}\widetilde{\alpha}\left(p_x,p_y\right)\sum_{k=-\infty}^{\infty}\sum_{l=-\infty}^{\infty}\delta\left(f_x-p_x-\frac{k}{\Delta_x},f_y-p_y-\frac{l}{\Delta_y}\right)dp_xdp_y=$$

$$\frac{1}{\Delta_x\Delta_y}\sum_{k=-\infty}^{\infty}\sum_{l=-\infty}^{\infty}\int\limits_{-\infty}^{\infty}\int\limits_{-\infty}^{\infty}\widetilde{\alpha}\left(p_x,p_y\right)\delta\left(f_x-p_x-\frac{k}{\Delta_x},f_y-p_y-\frac{l}{\Delta_y}\right)dp_xdp_y=$$

$$\frac{1}{\Delta_x\Delta_y}\sum_{k=-\infty}^{\infty}\sum_{l=-\infty}^{\infty}\widetilde{\alpha}\left(f_x-\frac{k}{\Delta_x},f_y-\frac{l}{\Delta_y}\right),\tag{3.22}$$

i.e., that spectrum $\widetilde{\widetilde{\alpha}}\left(f_x,f_y\right)$ of the virtual sampled signal $\widetilde{\widetilde{a}}(x,y)$ (Eq. (3. 8)) is periodically replicated (in Cartesian coordinates (x,y) with a 2D period $\left[1/\Delta_x,1/\Delta_y\right]$) spectrum $\widetilde{\alpha}\left(f_x,f_y\right)$ of the virtual pre-filtered signal (Eq. (3. 10)). The interval $\left[-1/2\Delta_x,1/2\Delta_x;-1/2\Delta_y,1/2\Delta_y\right]$ in the Fourier domain represents the image *sampling baseband*. The said is illustrated in Fig. (**3.3**) in a 1D interpretation.

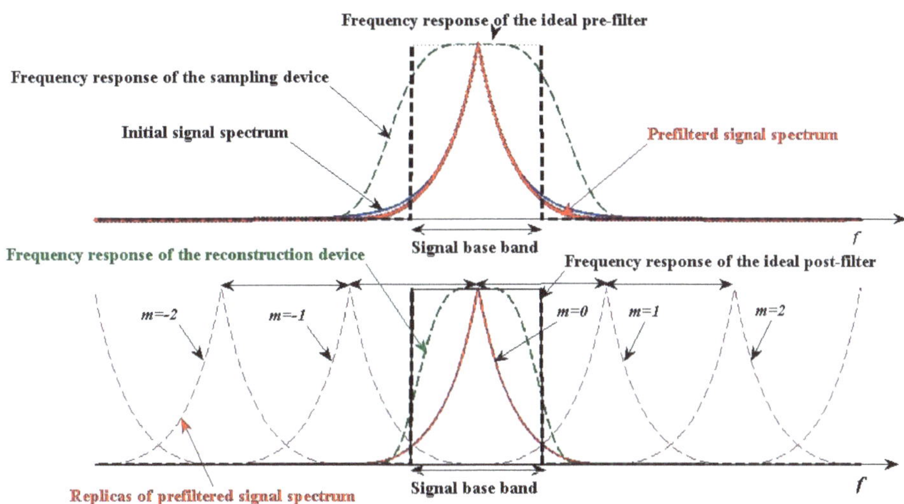

Fig. (3.3). 1D interpretation of sampling not band-limited signals. Upper plot: Fourier domain representation of signal pre-sampling filtering; bottom plots: Fourier domain representation of signal filtering in the process of its reconstruction from samples.

This analysis reveals that:

- The result of sampling an image $a(x, y)$ in a sampling device with point spread function $PSF^{(s)}(x, y)$ is a set of instantaneous values $\{\tilde{a}_{k,l} = \tilde{a}(k\Delta_x, l\Delta_y)\}$ of a virtual image $\tilde{a}(x.y)$ obtained from the image $a(x, y)$ by its "pre-filtering" in the sampling device.

- Signal sampling can be interpreted as converting a pre-filtered signal $\tilde{a}(x.y)$ into a virtual sampled signal $\tilde{\tilde{a}}(x, y)$ (Eq. (3. 8)), whose Fourier spectrum is composed of periodically replicated, in Cartesian coordinates with a 2D replication period $\left[1/\Delta_x, 1/\Delta_y\right]$, replicas of the initial image spectrum $\alpha(f_x, f_y)$ modified by the frequency response $FR^{(s)}(f_x, f_y)$ of a signal sampling device (Eq. (3. 14)). The sampling interval $\left[1/\Delta_x, 1/\Delta_y\right]$ defines the *sampling baseband*
$$BB = \left[-1/2\Delta_x, 1/2\Delta_x; -1/2\Delta_y, 1/2\Delta_y\right].$$

- Image reconstruction from its sampled representation can be treated as a "post-filtering" of the virtual discrete signal $\tilde{\tilde{a}}(x, y)$ (Eq. (3. 8)) in the display device with point spread function $PSF^{(r)}(x, y)$.

This "post-filtering" is described in the Fourier Transform domain as the multiplication of the periodical spectrum $\tilde{\tilde{\alpha}}(f_x, f_y)$ of the virtual signal $\tilde{\tilde{a}}(x, y)$ by the frequency response $FR^{(r)}(f_x, f_y)$ of the image display device:

$$\hat{\alpha}(f_x, f_y) = \tilde{\tilde{\alpha}}(f_x, f_y) FR^{(r)}(f_x, f_y) \tag{3. 23}$$

$$FR^{(r)}(f_x, f_y) = \int_{-\infty}^{\infty} \int_{-\infty}^{\infty} PSF^{(r)}(x, y) \exp\left[i2\pi(f_x x + f_y y)\right] dx dy . \tag{3. 24}$$

- A precise reconstruction of sampled not band-limited images is impossible due to the inevitable image distortions by their pre-filtering in the sampling devices and post-filtering in the display devices. The minimal distortions are achieved when the image pre- and post-filtering are performed by the ideal low-pass filters with passbands equal the sampling baseband $BB = \left[-1/2\Delta_x, 1/2\Delta_x; -1/2\Delta_y, 1/2\Delta_y\right]$. In this case, the only image distortions are losses of the image spectral components outside the sampling baseband. According to the Parseval's relationship (Eq. 2.31), the minimum mean squared error (MSE) of the image reconstruction from their sampled representation is

$$MSE_{\min}^{reconstr} = \int\limits_{-\infty}^{\infty}\int\limits_{-\infty}^{\infty}\left|a(x,y)-\hat{a}(x,y)\right|^2 dxdy=$$

$$\int\limits_{-\infty}^{\infty}\int\limits_{-\infty}^{\infty}\left|\alpha\left(f_x,f_y\right)\right|^2 df_x df_y - \int\limits_{-1/2\Delta_x}^{1/2\Delta_x}\int\limits_{-1/2\Delta_y}^{1/2\Delta_y}\left|\alpha\left(f_x,f_y\right)\right|^2 df_x df_y . \qquad (3.\,25)$$

- In the idealized special case of band-limited images with no spectral components outside the sampling baseband, the images are reconstructed precisely ($MSE_{\min}^{reconstr}=0$).

These statements constitute the sampling theorem in its realistic re-formulation.

3.3. SAMPLING DISTORTIONS OF REAL, NOT BANDLIMITED SIGNALS: ILLUSTRATIONS

From the above analysis of sampling and reconstruction of real not bandlimited images one can see that distortions of the reconstructed signal compared to the initial non-sampled signal are due to the following reasons (Fig. **3.3**):

- Distortions of the signal spectrum by its pre-filtering in the sampling device (Eq. (3. 1).
- Penetration of the fragments of the periodical replicas of the pre-filtered signal spectrum into the signal baseband, which causes the strobe effects.
- Getting into the reconstructed image spectrum fragments of the signal spectrum periodical replicas outside the sampling baseband that was not perfectly filtered out by the "post-filtering" in the reconstruction device, which causes the moiré effects.

Figs. (**3.4**-**3.6**), illustrate these phenomena. Fig. (**3.4**) presents a full-resolution test image and its Fourier spectrum centered at zero spatial frequencies $\left(f_x,f_y\right)$. As one can see, periodical components, which are present in the test image manifest themselves in the left and the right halves of the spectrum.

Fig. (**3.5**) demonstrates two examples of the results of sampling and reconstruction of a full-resolution test image presented in Fig. (3.4).

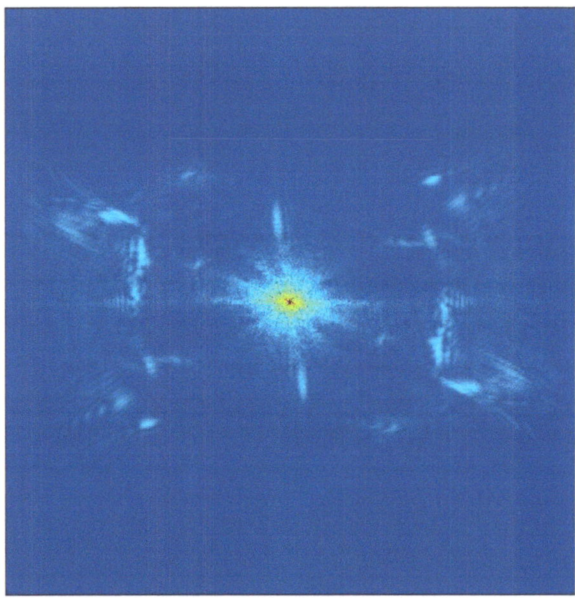

Fig. (3.4). A full resolution test image (upper) and module of its Fourier spectrum centered at zero spatial frequencies $\left(f_x, f_y\right)$ and displayed in false colors (MATLAB$^{\copyright}$ color map "jet") for better visibility of its high-frequency components (bottom).

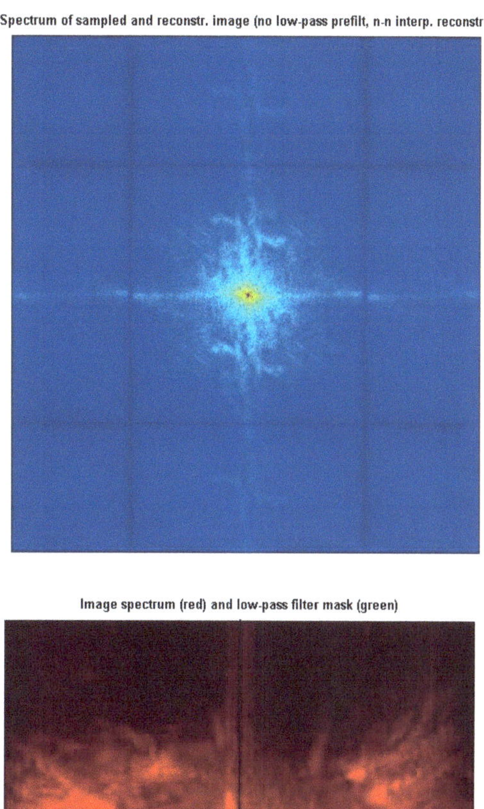

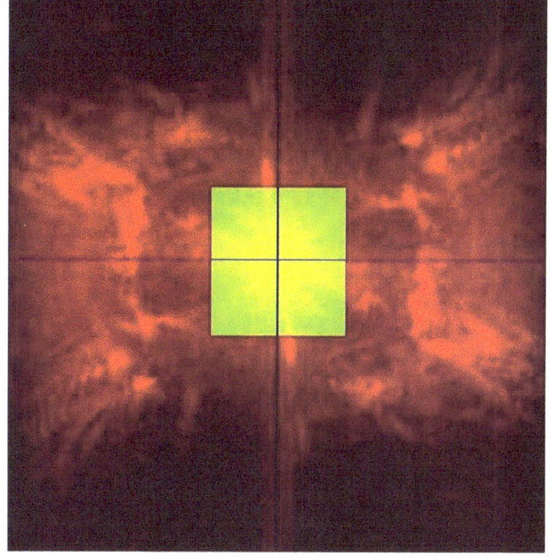

Fig. (3.5). Upper left: image reconstructed using the nearest neighbor interpolation from samples of the test image obtained without image pre-filtering. Upper right: module of Fourier spectrum of this image displayed for better visibility in false colors ((MATLAB$^©$ color map "jet")) and centered at zeros spatial frequencies. Bottom left: image reconstructed using sinc interpolation of samples of the test image sampled after its pre-filtering by the ideal low-pass filter. Bottom right: the module of the Fourier spectrum of the test full resolution image (red) and the sampling baseband (yellow-green).

The upper left image is sampled without pre-filtering and reconstructed using the nearest neighbor interpolation of samples, *i.e.*, a reconstruction filter with a rectangular point spread function:

$$PSF^{(r)}(x, y) = \mathrm{rect}(x/\Delta_x)\mathrm{rect}(y/\Delta_y) \tag{3.26}$$

and frequency response

$$FR^{(r)}(f_x, f_y) = \int_{-\infty}^{\infty} \int_{-\infty}^{\infty} \mathrm{rect}(x/\Delta_x)\mathrm{rect}(y/\Delta_y)\exp[i2\pi(f_x x + f_y y)]dxdy =$$

$$FR^{(r)}(f_x, f_y) = \int_{-\Delta_x/2}^{\Delta_x/2} \int_{-\Delta_y/2}^{\Delta_y/2} \exp[i2\pi(f_x x + f_y y)]dxdy =$$

$$\frac{\exp(i\pi f_x\Delta_x)-\exp(-i\pi f_x\Delta_x)}{i2\pi f_x}\frac{\exp(i\pi f_y\Delta_y)-\exp(-i\pi f_y\Delta_y)}{i2\pi f_y} = \frac{\sin(\pi f_x\Delta_x)}{\pi f_x\Delta_x}\frac{\sin(\pi f_y\Delta_y)}{\pi f_y\Delta_u} =$$

$$\mathrm{sinc}(\pi f_x\Delta_x)\mathrm{sinc}(\pi f_y\Delta_y), \tag{3.27}$$

where Δ_x Δ_y and are sampling intervals. This image demonstrates severe strobe effects on image periodical components. One can also see in the reconstructed image, especially in the vicinities of image edges, pixilation effects caused by the rectangular point spread function of the reconstruction filter that implements the nearest neighbor interpolation of image samples. The right upper image represents the module of the spectrum of this reconstructed image, in which one can see zeros of the sinc-functions (Eq. (3.27)) of the reconstruction filter frequency response (dark vertical and horizontal lines).

The bottom left image is sampled using the ideal low-pass pre-filtering and reconstructed using the ideal low-pass reconstruction filter, *i.e.*, by sinc interpolation of its samples. This image is, naturally, a blurred to a certain degree copy of the test image and it does not contain its periodical patterns. These patterns are completely filtered out by the ideal low-pass pre-sampling filter, which can be seen in the right bottom image that represents a module of the spectrum of the test image (red) and module of the pre-sampling filter frequency response (yellow-green).

Fig. (**3.6**) obtained using the program IdealVsNonidealSampling_BNTM provided in exercises demonstrates that for some images appropriate pre-sampling filtering might be of a crucial importance for image readability. The upper left image presents a full resolution image of a text. The bottom left image is reconstructed using a reconstruction filter with the rectangular PSF (Eq. (3. 26)) from samples of this test image obtained without using any pre-sampling filter. The bottom right image is reconstructed using the ideal low-pass filtering (sinc interpolation) of the test image samples obtained after its pre-sampling filtering by the ideal low-pass filter. The module of the frequency response of this filter is displayed yellow-green in the upper right image of the figure on the background of the module of the test image Fourier spectrum (red). As one can see, not properly sampled and reconstructed image (bottom left corner) is completely not readable whereas the properly sampled and reconstructed image is still readable, though it, naturally, is blurred due to the losses of the test image high-frequency components outside the sampling baseband.

Full resolution test image

Image spectrum(red) and low pass filter mask (green)

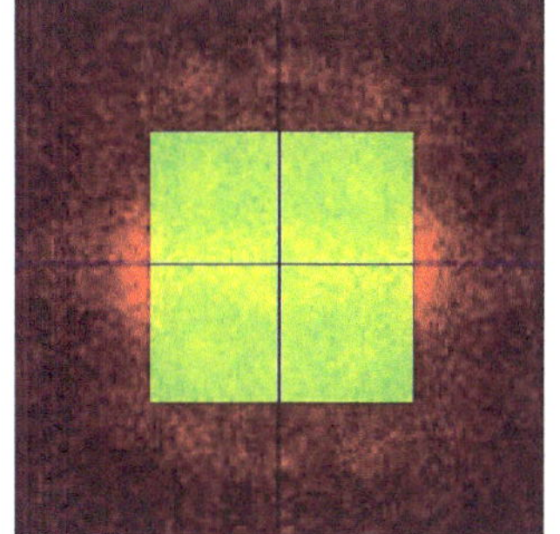

Sampled and reconstructed image
(no pre-filtering; n-n interp. reconstr.)

Sampled and reconstructed image
(ideal lowpass pre-filteing and post-filtering)

Fig. (3.6). An example of sampling and reconstruction of a test image (upper left) without pre-filtering before sampling and reconstruction using nearest-neighbor interpolation of its samples (bottom left) and that of sampling using the ideal low-pass filter and sinc interpolation of image samples at its reconstruction (bottom right). In the upper right image module of the Fourier spectrum of the test image is displayed in red and sampling baseband is displayed yellow-green.

3.4. EXERCISES

- **IdealVsNonidealSampling_BNTM.m**

Demonstration of visual effects of image sampling and reconstruction using pre-sampling and reconstruction filters with rect-functions and sinc-functions as filter point spread functions. Five pre-prepared test images are provided; using any other image from an image database as test images is also possible.

Three down-sampling rates can be chosen: 1/2, 1/3, and 1/4 of the sampling rate of test images.

Displayed are:

- the chosen test image;
- the image reconstructed by the nearest-neighbor interpolation (the rect-function as the reconstruction filter PSF) from the result of down-sampling the test image with the chosen sampling rate;
- the image reconstructed by the nearest-neighbor interpolation (the rect-function as the reconstruction filter PSF) from the result of test image down-sampling with the chosen sampling rate after its pre-filtering by the filter with the rect-function of the width equals the inverse of the sub-sampling rate as the filter PSF;
- the image reconstructed by the sinc interpolation (the sinc-function as the reconstruction filter PSF) from the result of test image down-sampling with the chosen sampling rate after its pre-filtering by the ideal low-pass filter of the corresponding bandwidth.

An option of displaying Fourier spectra of tested and reconstructed images is also provided.

CHAPTER 4

The General Sampling Theorem

4.1. THE DISCRETE SAMPLING THEOREM

Sampling is a special case of signal discretization methods [4]. In general, the discrete representation of a signal $a(x)$ is obtained as a set of coefficients $\{\alpha_k\}$ of signal expansion over a set of discretization basis functions $\{\varphi_k^{(d)}(x)\}$:

$$\alpha_k = \int_{-\infty}^{\infty} a(x)\varphi_k^{(d)}(x)dx \quad k = 0,1,\dots, N-1 \tag{4. 1}$$

and signal reconstruction from its discrete representation is performed using the reconstruction basis functions $\{\varphi_k^{(r)}(x)\}$ reciprocal to the discretization ones:

$$\hat{a}(x) = \sum_{k=0}^{N-1} \alpha_k \, \varphi_k^{(r)}(x) \tag{4. 2}$$

In the case of the sampling, discretization basis functions are "*shift basis functions*", $\{\varphi_k^{(d)}(x) = \varphi^{(d)}(x - k\Delta)\}$ and $\{\varphi_k^{(r)}(x) = \varphi^{(r)}(x - k\Delta)\}$, *i.e.*, they are formed from a certain "*mother function*" by means of its shifting. Among other basis functions for signal discretization, one can mention sinusoidal functions used for signal expansion in Fourier series, Walsh functions and wavelets. The sinusoidal basis functions, as well as Walsh functions, belong to the family of *multiplicative basis functions*, in which the sample's index k multiplies the mother function argument x, *i.e.*, changes the mother function's scale. The wavelets combine the concepts of the mother function shifting and scaling.

This chapter treats the signal sampling from this more general point of view. Assume that the accuracy of signal reconstruction from its samples is evaluated in terms of the mean squared reconstruction error (MSE) and consider the following discrete model.

Let $\mathbf{A}_N$ be a vector of N samples $\{a_n\}_{k=0,\dots,N-1}$ of a discrete signal, $\mathbf{\Phi}_N$ be an $N \times N$ orthonormal transform matrix, composed of orthonormal basis functions

$$\{\varphi_r(k)\}$$

$$\Phi_N = \{\varphi_r(k)\}_{r=0,1,\ldots,N-1} \ , \ k=0,1,\ldots,N-1 \ , \ r=0,1,\ldots,N-1 \tag{4.3}$$

and Γ_N be a vector of signal transform coefficients $\{\gamma_r\}$ such that:

$$\mathbf{A}_N = \Phi_N \Gamma_N = \left\{ \sum_{r=0}^{N-1} \gamma_r \varphi_r(k) \right\}, \tag{4.4}$$

Assume that only $K < N$ signal samples $\{a_{\tilde{k}}\}_{\{\tilde{k}\}\in\tilde{K}}$ are available, where $\tilde{\mathbf{K}}$ is a K -size subset $\{\tilde{k}\}$ of indices from the set $\{0,1,\ldots,N-1\}$. These available K signal samples define a system of K equations:

$$\left\{ a_{\tilde{k}} = \sum_{r=0}^{N-1} \gamma_r \varphi_r(\tilde{k}) \right\} , \{\tilde{k}\} \in \tilde{K} \tag{4.5}$$

for K signal transform coefficients $\{\gamma_r\}$ of certain K indices r.

Select a subset $\tilde{\mathbf{R}}$ of K transform coefficients indices $\{\tilde{r} \in \tilde{\mathbf{R}}\}$ and define a " $\mathbf{K}$ *of* $\mathbf{N}$"-bounded spectrum (BS) approximation $\hat{A}_N^{(BS)}$ to the signal $\mathbf{A}_N$ as:

$$\hat{\mathbf{A}}_N^{(BS)} = \left\{ \hat{a}_k = \sum_{\tilde{r}\in R} \gamma_{\tilde{r}} \varphi_{\tilde{r}}(k) \right\}. \tag{4.6}$$

Rewrite this equation in a more general form that involves all transform coefficients:

$$\hat{\mathbf{A}}_N^{BS} = \left\{ \hat{a}_k = \sum_{r=0}^{N-1} \tilde{\gamma}_r \varphi_r(k) \right\} \tag{4.7}$$

assuming that all transform coefficients with indices $r \notin \tilde{\mathbf{R}}$ are set to zero:

$$\tilde{\gamma}_r = \begin{cases} \gamma_r, & r \in \tilde{R} \\ 0, & otherwise \end{cases}. \tag{4.8}$$

Then the vector $\widetilde{\mathbf{A}}_K$ of available signal samples $\left\{a_{\widetilde{k}}\right\}$ can be expressed in terms of the basis functions $\left\{\varphi_r(k)\right\}$ of the transform Φ_N as:

$$\widetilde{\mathbf{A}}_K = \mathbf{K}\mathbf{o}\mathbf{f}\mathbf{N}_\Phi \cdot \widetilde{\Gamma}_K = \left\{ a_{\widetilde{k}} = \sum_{\widetilde{r} \in R} \gamma_{\widetilde{r}} \varphi_{\widetilde{r}}\left(\widetilde{k}\right) \right\} , \tag{4.9}$$

where $K \times K$ sub-transform matrix $\mathbf{K}\mathbf{o}\mathbf{f}\mathbf{N}_\Phi$ is composed of samples $\varphi_{\widetilde{r}}\left(\widetilde{k}\right)$ of the basis functions with indices $\left\{\widetilde{r} \in \widetilde{\mathbf{R}}\right\}$ for signal sample indices $\widetilde{k} \in \widetilde{\mathbf{K}}$, and $\widetilde{\Gamma}_K$ is a vector composed of the corresponding subset $\left\{\gamma_{\widetilde{r}}\right\}$ of the signal transform coefficients supposed to be non-zero. This subset of the coefficients can be found by inverting the matrix $\mathbf{K}\mathbf{o}\mathbf{f}\mathbf{N}_\Phi$ as

$$\widetilde{\Gamma}_K = \left\{\gamma_{\widetilde{r}}\right\} = \mathbf{K}\mathbf{o}\mathbf{f}\mathbf{N}_\Phi^{-1} \cdot \widetilde{\mathbf{A}}_K \tag{4.10}$$

provided that the matrix $\mathbf{K}\mathbf{o}\mathbf{f}\mathbf{N}_\Phi^{-1}$ inverse to the matrix $\mathbf{K}\mathbf{o}\mathbf{f}\mathbf{N}_\Phi$ exists, which, in general, is conditioned, for a specific transform, by positions $\widetilde{k} \in \widetilde{\mathbf{K}}$ of available signal samples and by the selection of the subset $\left\{\widetilde{R}\right\}$ of transform basis functions that correspond to the non-zero transform coefficients.

By virtue of the Parseval's relationship for orthonormal transforms

$$\sum_{k=0}^{N-1} \left|a_k\right|^2 = \sum_{r=1}^{N-1} \left|\gamma_r\right|^2 , \tag{4.11}$$

the bounded spectrum signal $\hat{\mathbf{A}}_N^{BS}$ approximates the complete signal $\mathbf{A}_N$ with the mean squared error:

$$MSE = \left\| A_N - \hat{A}_N \right\|^2 = \sum_{k=0}^{N-1} \left|a_k - \hat{a}_k\right|^2 = \sum_{r \notin R} \left|\gamma_{\widetilde{r}}\right|^2 \tag{4.12}$$

This error can be minimized by an appropriate selection of K basis functions of the sub-transform $\mathbf{K}\mathbf{o}\mathbf{f}\mathbf{N}_\Phi$. In order to do so, one must know the *energy compaction ordering* of the basis functions of the transform Φ_N, *i.e.*, the order of basis functions, in which the energy (squared module) of their corresponding signal representation coefficients decays with their indices. If, in addition, one knows, for a class of signals, a transform that features the best *energy compaction* into the smallest number of the transform coefficients, one can, by choosing this transform, secure the best minimum mean squared error (MSE) bounded spectrum approximation of the signal $\{a_k\}$ for the given subset $\{\tilde{a}_k\}$ of its samples. The subset Ω_{MSE} of indices $\{\tilde{r}\}$ of the largest transform coefficients with total energy

$$\sum_{k=0}^{N-1}|a_k|^2 - MSE$$, which reconstruct signal $\{a_k\}$ with mean squared error *MSE*

will be called the signal spectrum's *energy compaction zone* (EC- zone) for the given signal reconstruction mean square error *MSE* .

With the above reasoning, the following *Discrete Sampling Theorem* can be formulated in these two statements:

<u>*Statement 1.*</u> *For any discrete signal of* N *samples defined by its* $K \leq N$ *samples, its bounded spectrum, in terms of a certain transform* Φ_N *, approximation defined by Eq.(4.6), can be obtained with mean squared error defined by Eq. (4. 12) provided positions of the samples secure the existence of the matrix* $\mathbf{KofN}_\Phi^{-1}$ *inverse to the sub-transform matrix* $\mathbf{KofN}_\Phi$ *that corresponds to the spectrum bounding. The approximation error can be minimized by using a transform with the best capability of compacting signal energy in a small number of signal transform coefficients (energy compaction capability).*

<u>*Statement 2.*</u> *Any signal of* N *samples that is known to have only* $K \leq N$ *non-zero transform coefficients for a certain transform* Φ_N *(*Φ_N *- transform "bounded spectrum" signal) can be precisely reconstructed from exactly* K *its samples provided positions of the samples secure the existence of the matrix* $\mathbf{KofN}_\Phi^{-1}$ *inverse to the sub-transform matrix* $\mathbf{KofN}_\Phi$ *that corresponds to the spectrum bounding.*

In this formulation, the discrete sampling theorem is applicable to signals of any dimensionality. Neither it requires any assumption regarding compactness of signal energy compaction zone in the transform domain. The signal dimensionality affects only the formulation of the signal spectrum bounding.

4.2. DISCRETE SAMPLING THEOREM FORMULATIONS FOR SPECIFIC TRANSFORMS

The applicability of the particular transforms for the bounded spectrum signal approximation from its given K samples depends on whether the $KofN$ matrix for this transform is invertible, *i.e.*, on whether the placement of the available signal samples is compatible with the type of the signal spectrum bounding chosen for this transform. This section addresses the invertibility conditions for the most widely used in applications Discrete Fourier transform (DFT), Discrete Cosine transform (DCT), Walsh transform, and Wavelet transform.

4.2.1. Discrete Fourier and Discrete Cosine Transforms

The discrete Fourier transform (DFT) of a signal $\{a_k\}$ of N samples is defined as

$$\alpha_r^{DFT} = \frac{1}{\sqrt{N}} \sum_{k=0}^{N-1} a_k \exp\left(i2\pi \frac{kr}{N} \right). \tag{4.13}$$

The discrete Cosine transform (DCT) of a signal $\{a_k\}$ of N samples is defined as

$$\alpha_r^{DCT} = \frac{2}{\sqrt{2N}} \sum_{k=0}^{N-1} a_k \cos\left(\pi \frac{k+1/2}{N} r \right). \tag{4.14}$$

Their inverse transforms are correspondingly

$$a_k = \frac{1}{\sqrt{N}} \sum_{k=0}^{N-1} \alpha_r^{DFT} \exp\left(-i2\pi \frac{kr}{N} \right). \tag{4.15}$$

and

$$a_k = \frac{1}{\sqrt{2N}} \left[\alpha_0^{DCT} + 2\sum_{r=0}^{N-1} \alpha_r^{DCT} \cos\left(\pi \frac{k+1/2}{N} r \right) \right] \tag{4.16}$$

These transforms are closely related. As one can easily verify, the DCT is the "Shifted" DFT [4]

$$\alpha_r^{DCT} = \frac{1}{\sqrt{N}} \sum_{k=0}^{2N-1} \widetilde{a}_k \exp\left(i2\pi \frac{k+1/2}{2N} \right) = \frac{2}{\sqrt{2N}} \sum_{k=0}^{N-1} a_k \cos\left(\pi \frac{k+1/2}{N} r \right) \qquad (4.\,17)$$

of a signal $\{\widetilde{a}_k\}$ of $2N$ samples obtained by an even extension of a signal $\{a_k\}$ of N samples by its mirror reflection from its borders:

$$\widetilde{a}_k = \begin{cases} a_k, & k = 0,1,\ldots, N-1 \\ a_{2N-1-k}, & k = N, N = 1,\ldots, 2N-1 \end{cases}. \qquad (4.\,18)$$

For 2D signals, the DFT and DCT are defined as separable transforms over the signal two coordinates:

$$\alpha_{r,s}^{DFT} = \frac{1}{\sqrt{N_x N_y}} \sum_{k=0}^{N_y-1}\sum_{l=0}^{N_x-1} a_{k,l} \exp\left[i2\pi\left(\frac{kr}{N_x} + \frac{ls}{N_y} \right) \right] =$$

$$\frac{1}{\sqrt{N_x N_y}} \sum_{k=0}^{N_y-1} \exp\left(i2\pi \frac{kr}{N_x} \right) \sum_{l=0}^{N_x-1} a_{k,l} \exp\left[i2\pi\left(\frac{ls}{N_y} \right) \right],$$

(4.\,19)

$$\alpha_{r,s}^{DFT} = \frac{1}{\sqrt{N_x N_y}} \sum_{k=0}^{N_y-1}\sum_{l=0}^{N_x-1} a_{k,l} \cos\left(\pi \frac{k+1/2}{N_x} r \right) \cos\left(\pi \frac{l+1/2}{N_y} s \right) =$$

$$\frac{1}{\sqrt{N_x N_y}} \sum_{k=0}^{N_y-1} \cos\left(\pi \frac{k+1/2}{N_x} r \right) \sum_{l=0}^{N_x-1} a_{k,l} \cos\left(\pi \frac{l+1/2}{N_y} s \right) \qquad (4.\,20)$$

For the discrete Fourier and discrete cosine transforms, the following statements hold:

<u>Statement 3.</u> *For any discrete signal of N samples, its bounded DFT (DCT) spectrum approximation with $K \le N$ non-zero spectral coefficients defined by Eq. (4. 6) can be obtained with mean squared approximation error defined by Eq. (4. 12) from exactly K of its samples taken in arbitrary positions.*

<u>Statement 4.</u> *Any discrete signal of N samples with an arbitrarily bounded DFT (DCT) spectrum with $K \le N$ non-zero spectral coefficients can be precisely reconstructed from exactly K of its samples taken in arbitrary positions.*

These statements constitute the *Discrete Sampling Theorem* for the discrete Fourier and discrete cosine transforms. To rigorously prove this theorem, one should prove that any trimmed $\;\;$ sub-matrix $\mathbf{KofN}_{DFT}$ of DFT has its inverse $\mathbf{KofN}_{DFT}^{-1}$ or correspondingly any trimmed $\;\;$ sub-matrix $\mathbf{KofN}_{DCT}$ of DCT has its inverse $\mathbf{KofN}_{DCT}^{-1}$ for arbitrary placed subset $\left\{a_{\tilde{k}}\right\}_{\{\tilde{k}\}\in\tilde{K}}$ of K signal samples. For the case of compact sets of the transform non-zero coefficients, this theorem has been proved in a study [5]. Although the full proof for the general case is yet to be done, there is considerable experimental evidence of the validity of these theorems. Some results of the experimental verification of the validity of the discrete sampling theorem for the discrete Fourier and discrete cosine transforms are presented below.

Fig. (**4.1**), left column, presents results of the precise reconstruction of a realization of a pseudo-random 1D low-pass band-limited test signal from its samples, carried out by the direct matrix inversion for two cases of the placement of signal samples: compact, (Fig. (**4.1**) upper left plot) and random (left bottom). The experiment was conducted for test signals of 64 samples and the first 13 low-frequency nonzero DFT coefficients (the signal base band).

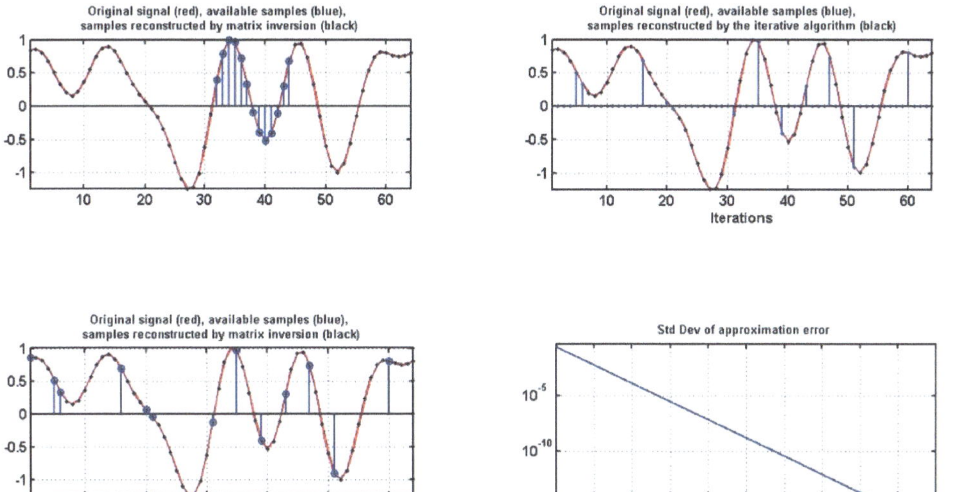

Fig. (4.1). Reconstruction of a DFT low pass band-limited signal by the matrix inversion for the cases of compactly placed signal samples (left column, upper plot) and random (left column, bottom plot) and by the iterative algorithm (right column). Bottom right plot represents root mean squared (RMS) of the signal reconstruction error *vs.* the number of iterations.

Matrix inversion is a very hard computational task for large matrices. A good practical alternative is a Gerchberg-Papoulis type iterative algorithm for signal reconstruction from their sparse samples. A flow-diagram of the algorithm is shown in Fig. (**4.2**).

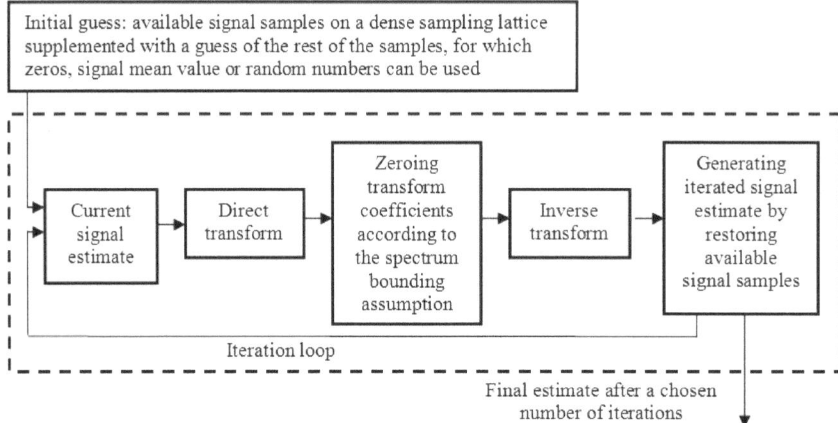

Fig. (4.2). Flow diagram of the Gerchberg-Papoulis type algorithm for signal reconstruction from their sparse samples.

According to the algorithm, at each iteration step the signal spectrum found by the direct DFT (DCT) is computed, spectral coefficients that are supposed to be zero are zeroed, and then the modified in this way spectrum is inverse transformed, after which the available signal samples are restored in their known position producing a reconstructed signal estimate for the next iteration step.

Fig. (**4.1**), right column, presents a result of reconstruction of the same test signal as that in the left column from its randomly placed samples using the iterative algorithm (upper right) and a plot of the mean squared reconstruction error *vs.* the number of iterations normalized to signal maximum. As one can see, the reconstruction error RMS reaches the level of the machine zero after about 8000 iterations.

Figs. (**4.3** and **4.4**) present similar results for 2D pseudo-random test signals with DCT spectra bounded by five different shapes shown in the left column of (Fig. **4.3**).

The test signals were sampled at K randomly chosen positions, where K is the area of the spectra shapes (the number of their non-zero samples) as it is dictated by the Discrete sampling theorem. The results were obtained using the iterative reconstruction algorithm. The right column in Fig. (**4.3**) contains plots of the RMS reconstruction errors normalized to the signal maximum *vs.* the number of iterations. They show that the 2D iterative reconstruction converges to the right result much slower than the 1D one: achievable normalized RMS of the reconstruction error after 10^5 iterations is of the order of 10^{-4}.

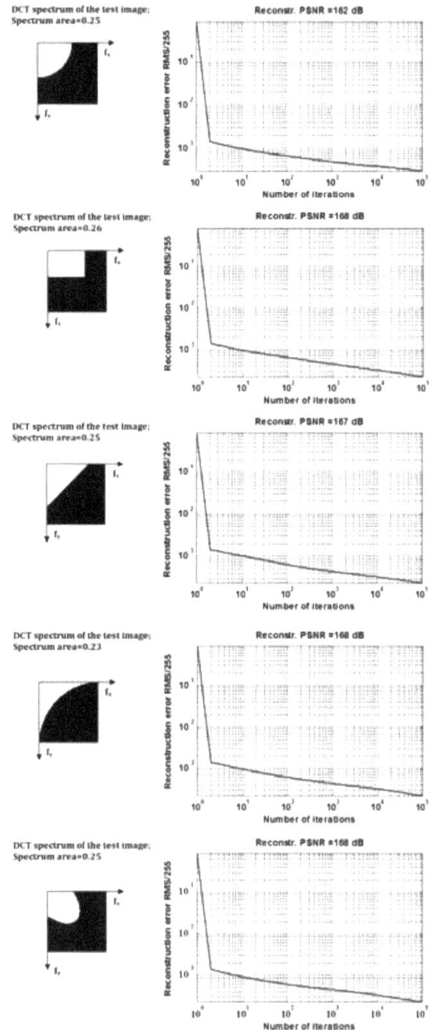

Fig. (4.3). Plots of the RMS of the reconstruction errors (right column) for different shapes of the test image spectra (left column). White in the images of the shape represents ones, black represents zeros.

Note that the convergence of iteration is very non-uniform over image area. Bottom right image in Fig. (**4.4**) is a pattern of the reconstruction error obtained as a difference between the initial test image (upper left image) and the reconstructed image (bottom right image). Comparing sampled image (Fig. **4.4**, upper right) and the pattern of the error, one can easily see that large errors are quite rare in the image and occur mostly in the places in the image area, where samples happen to be sparser than on the other parts of the image. Similar results obtained for real life images will be presented and discussed in Chapter 6.

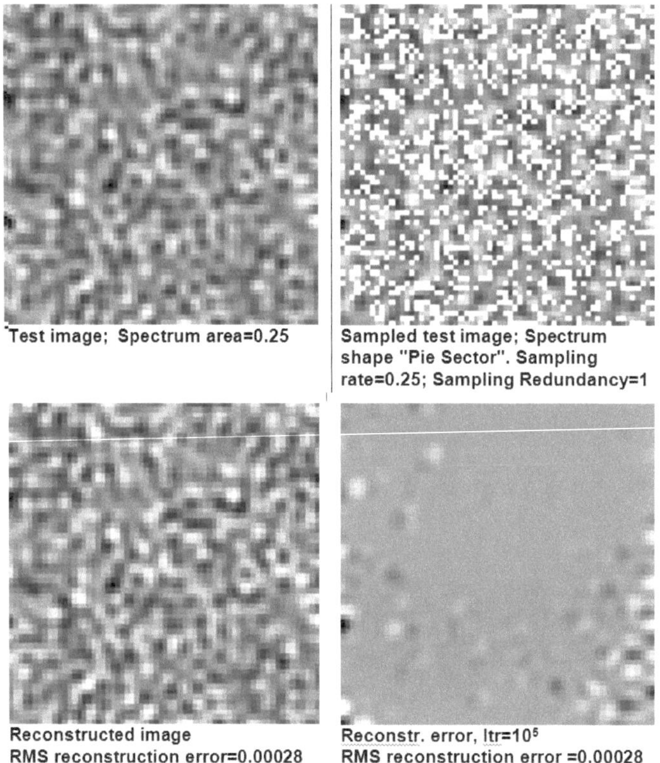

Fig. (4.4). A test image (upper left), a sampled test image (upper right), a reconstructed test image after 10^5 iteration (bottom left) and a pattern of the reconstruction errors (bottom right). In the latter, grey color represents zero errors, bright color represents large positive errors; dark color represents large negative errors).

4.2.2. Wavelets and Other Transforms

Among other transforms, the most feasible and usable are Walsh-Hadamard Transform and wavelet transforms. In the processing sampled signals they conventionally are defined for signals with the number of samples N equal to an integer power n of 2:

$$N = 2^n \tag{4.21}$$

Basis functions of the Walsh-Hadamard transform of size $N = 2^n$ are introduced as n-dimensional DFT, in which signal sample indices k and basis function indices r are treated as n-dimensional vectors represented by binary digits $\{k_m\}$ and, correspondingly, $\{r_m\}$ of their binary codes:

$$k = \sum_{m=0}^{n-1} k_m 2^m ,$$
(4. 22)

$$r = \sum_{m=0}^{n-1} r_m 2^m$$
(4. 23)

As the size of these vectors in each dimension equals 2, the DFT basis functions (Eq. **(4. 13)** convert to

$$had_r(k) = 2^{-(n-1)} \prod_{m=0}^{n-1} \exp\left(i2\pi \frac{k_m r_m}{2} \right) = 2^{-(n-1)} \prod_{m=0}^{n-1} \exp(i\pi k_m r_m) = 2^{-(n-1)} \prod_{m=0}^{n-1} \exp(-1)^{k_m r_m}$$
(4. 24)

These binary functions are rows of the so-called *Hadamard matrix*.

Rows of Hadamard matrix are ordered in the order of the direct binary code of their indices. In applications, it is much more convenient to order them according to the number of function's zero crossing, called "*sequency*". It is an analog of frequency for the Fourier transform basis functions. This ordering is achieved when indices $\{r\}$ of the functions are rewritten from the direct binary code (Eq. (4. 23) into the so-called "*Grey code*" according to the rule:

$$r_m^{GC} = r_m \oplus r_{m+1} .$$
(4. 25)

where $\oplus$ denotes modulo 2 addition:

$$0 \oplus 0 = 1 \oplus 1 = 0; \ 1 \oplus 0 = 1 \oplus 0 = 1 .$$
(4. 26)

Indexed in this way functions

$$walsh_r(k) = 2^{-(n-1)} 2^{-(n-1)} \prod_{m=0}^{n-1} \exp(-1)^{k_m r_m^{GC}}$$
(4. 27)

are called the *Walsh functions* and the transform with these basis functions is called the *Walsh-Hadamard transform*.

The first eight Walsh functions are shown in Fig. (**4.5**) (left column) in collation with the cosinusoidal and sinusoidal functions of the Fourier Transform (middle column), for which the sequency index of Walsh functions translates into their frequency index.

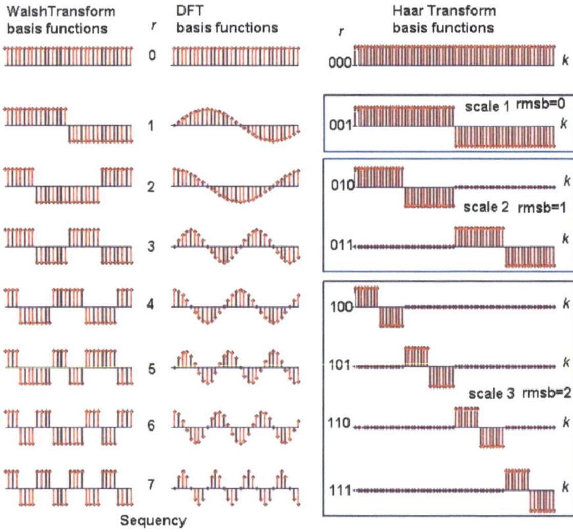

Fig. (4.5). Basis functions of the Walsh, DFT, and Haar transforms.

Thanks to the ordering of the Walsh functions according to their sequency, transform coefficients' energy decays with their index for many real signals similarly to Fourier transform coefficients. Therefore, for the Walsh transform, the concept of the signal band-limited approximation similar to that for DFT can be used.

Walsh functions are binary peace-wise constant functions. Signals with $N = 2^n$ samples and band-limitation of K Walsh-Hadamard transform coefficients have the shortest intervals of the signal constancy of $2^{n-\tilde{s}}$ samples, where $\tilde{s} = \left(\lfloor \log_2 (K-1) \rfloor + 1 \right)$ and symbol $\lfloor \sigma \rfloor$ denotes the integer part of σ. A necessary condition for the perfect reconstruction is to have K signal samples taken at different intervals. Not all the intervals are needed to be sampled, but only K intervals out of the total number of intervals. For a special case of K equals a power of 2, there are K intervals, each of which has to be sampled to secure the possibility of the perfect reconstruction.

An example of the perfect reconstruction of a Walsh transform domain "band-limited" signal of N=512 and band limitation K=5 is illustrated in Fig. (**4.6**). In this example, the resulted from available samples $KofN^{Walsh}$ matrix is:

$$KofN^{Walsh}\Big|_{K=5} = \begin{vmatrix} 1 & -1 & 1 & -1 & -1 \\ 1 & -1 & -1 & 1 & 1 \\ 1 & 1 & 1 & 1 & 1 \\ 1 & 1 & -1 & -1 & -1 \\ 1 & 1 & 1 & 1 & -1 \end{vmatrix}. \tag{4.28}$$

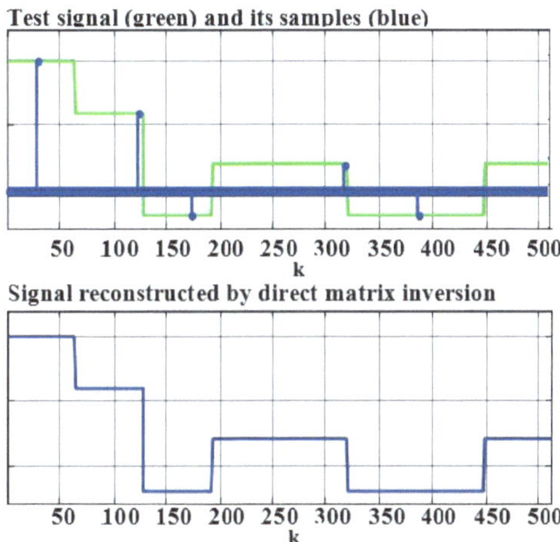

Fig. (4.6). An example (bottom plot) of the perfect reconstruction of a test signal of 512 samples (upper plot, solid green) by the direct matix invesrsion from its 5 samples (upper plot, blue stems) in the Walsh transform domain.

As was mentioned in Sect.4.1, basis functions of Wavelet transforms are built on the idea of combining shifting and scaling mother functions. The wavelet basis functions are most naturally ordered in terms of two parameters: scale and position within the scale. Scale index is analogous to the frequency index for DFT and DCT. Position index tells only of the shift of the same basis function within the signal extent on each scale. Therefore, the band-limitation for the DFT translates to scale limitation for the wavelets. The limitation in terms of position is trivial: it simply means that some parts of the signal are not relevant.

Commonly, discrete wavelets are designed for signals whose length N is an integer power of 2 ($N = 2^n$). For such signals, there are $s \leq n$ scales and possible "band-limitations".

The simplest wavelet transform is the *Haar transform*. Basis functions of the the Haar transform are defined as

$$haar_r(k) = 2^{(rmsb-n)}(-1)^{k_{n-rmsb-1}} \delta\left(\lfloor k/2^{n-msb} \rfloor \oplus (r)\bmod 2^{rmsb}\right), \tag{4.29}$$

where **rmsb** is the index of the most significant non-zero digit (bit) in the binary representation of r (Eq. 4.23), $(r)\bmod 2^{rmsb}$ is modulo 2^{rmsb} value of r (a residual from division of r by 2^{rmsb}), $\lfloor k/2^{n-msb} \rfloor$ is an integer part of division of k by 2^{n-msb}, and $\oplus$ denotes modulo 2 addition of binary numbers (Eq. (4.26). The index **rmsb** defines the scale of the basis function.

Plots of the first eight Haar functions are presented in the right column of (Fig. **4.5**). Blue rectangles in the figure outline the groups of functions with the same **rmsb** that belong to the same scale. Signals of $N = 2^n$ samples and with only K non-zero transform coefficients with indices $\{0,1..,K-1\}$ are ($\tilde{s} = (\lfloor \log_2(K-1) \rfloor + 1)$) - "band-limited", where $\lfloor x \rfloor$ is an integer part of x.

Haar basis functions are piecewise constant. The shortest interval of the function constancy contains $2^{n-rsmb-1}$ samples. As one can see on the plots of the Haar basis functions, for any two samples located within the same interval all Haar basis functions on this and lower scales have the same value. Therefore, having more than one sample per interval of the constancy of the function does not change the rank of the trimmed Haar transform matrix **K of N**. The condition for perfect reconstruction is, therefore, to have at least one sample on each of those intervals. Fig. (**4.7**) illustrates this by two examples of arrangements of sparse samples: one, for which the signal is not recoverable in Haar transform (left), and another, for which signal recovery is possible (right).

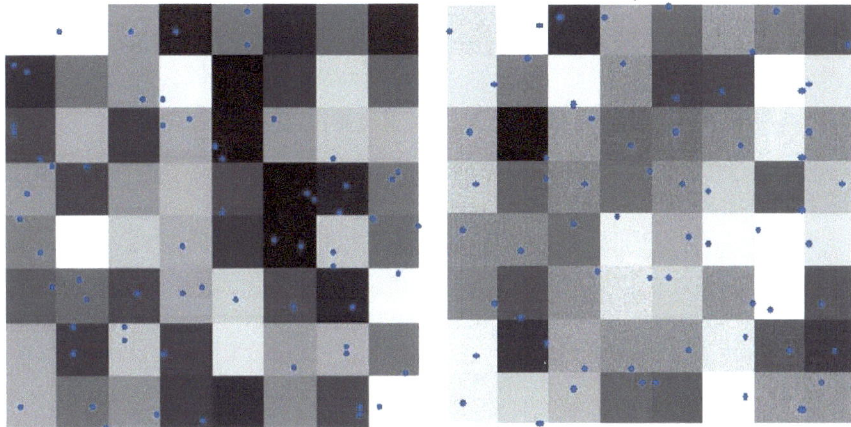

Fig. (4.7). Two cases of the sparse sampling of an image band-limited in the Haar Transform: the not recoverable case (**a**), and the recoverable case (**b**). Sample points are marked with the blue dots. Image size is 64x64 pixels; the scale 3 band-limitation; the number of samples is 64.

4.3. THE GENERAL SAMPLING THEOREM

In the limit, when the number of samples N in our discrete model tends to the infinity, the considered discrete model converts to a continuous one. In particular, if the Discrete Fourier transform is chosen as the image transform, it converts to the integral Fourier transform and the Discrete Sampling Theorem for the DFT converts to the *General Sampling Theorem* that refers to signal Fourier spectra and states:

Statement 1: The minimal number of signal samples per unit of the signal area (sampling rate) sufficient for signal reconstruction from their arbitrarily placed samples with mean square reconstruction error **MSE** *equals the area* B_Ω *of the spectrum EC-zone* Ω_{MSE} *in the signal Fourier domain that contains* $(E - MSE)/E$ *-th fraction of the image signal energy* E .

Statement 2: Signals known to have the Fourier spectrum bounded by a figure Ω *of an arbitrary shape can be precisely reconstructed from their arbitrarily placed samples taken with the density per unit of the signal area equals the area* B_Ω *of the spectrum bounding figure* Ω .

The next two chapters address the problem of reaching this theoretical minimum.

CHAPTER 5

Compressed Sensing: A Method of Reconstruction of Signals Sampled With Aliasing

5.1. THE UBIQUITOUS REDUNDANCY OF IMAGES SAMPLED OVER REGULAR RECTANGULAR SAMPLING LATTICES

As indicated earlier, sampling images over the regular rectangular sampling lattices at equidistant positions is accepted as the standard in imaging engineering, and such sampling is assumed, by default, by the image processing software and image display devices. This, by the necessity, implies that in order to avoid image distortions additional to those that define the image EC-zone, image EC-zone must be inscribed into the sampling base-band rectangle, defined by the image sampling rate. Therefore, sampling images over the rectangular sampling lattices always requires a sampling rate that exceeds the minimal one defined by the area of the image spectrum EC-zone, *i.e.*, images sampled in the standard way are always oversampled. The degree of the oversampling or the oversampling redundancy is inverse to the ratio of the EC-zone area to the area of the image base-band called the *image spectrum sparsity*. Data presented in Fig. (**5.1**) and Table **5.1** illustrate this ubiquitous redundancy of digital images acquired by the standard sampling technique.

Fig. (**5.1**) obtained using the program DFT_Spectr_sparsity_BNTM.m provided in the Exercises presents ten test images (the first and the third rows from the top) and their corresponding Fourier spectra centered around zero spatial frequencies (the second and the fourth rows). Spectra are displayed in artificial colors for better visibility. Highlighted in the spectra are image spectra EC-zones that contain image spectral components, which reconstruct images with MSE equals to that of the image JPEG encoding. Image base-band in these spectra is the entire area of image spectra. Fourier spectra of the images were estimated using Discrete Fourier Transform as a discrete representation of the integral Fourier transform and applying to images, before the spectral analysis, a circular apodization mask in order to smoothly bring images down to zero at the edges of the sampling region and in this way to avoid as much as possible spectrum estimation errors due to the boundary effects.

Estimates of the image spectra sparsities for these images are given in Table **5.1**. They indicate that these images are from 2.5 to 10 times oversampled. The experience shows that these figures of the sampling redundancy are typical for digital images acquired by digital cameras. The sampling redundancy is the fundamental reason for the image compressibility, which is usually removed by image compression after the sampling.

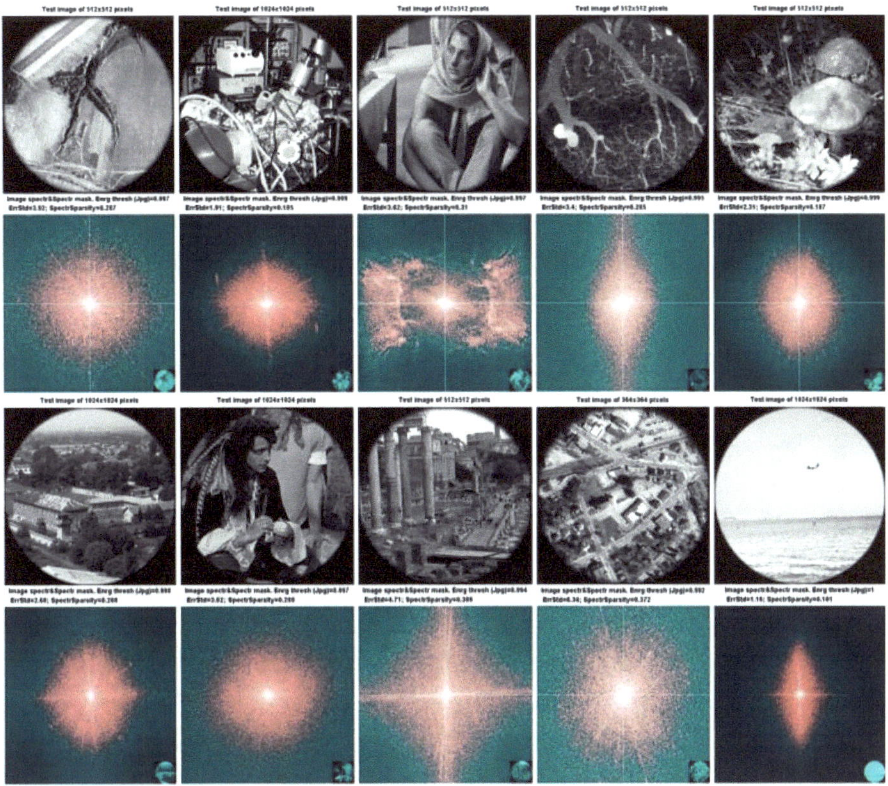

Fig. (5.1). A set of sampled test images (the first and the third rows) and their corresponding Fourier spectra centered at their DC component (the second and the fourth rows): "AerialPhoto512", "AFM512, "Barbara512", "BloodVessels512", "Mushrooms512", "Nish1024", "Pirate1024, "Rome512", "WestConcord364" and "Test4CS1024". Highlighted are the largest spectral components sufficient for image reconstruction with the same MSE as that of their JPEG compression (the image spectra EC-zones).

Table 5.1. Estimates of the image spectra sparsities for the test images presented in Fig. (5.1).

Test Images	Image Spectrum Sparsity
AerialPhoto512	0.29
AFM512	0.19
Barbara512	0.31
BloodVessels512	0.2
Mushrooms512	0.19

(Table 5.1) contd.....

Nish1024	0.21
Pirate1024	0.29
Rome512	0.39
WestConcord364	0.37
Test4CS1024	0.1

5.2. COMPRESSED SENSING AND RECONSTRUCTION OF SIGNALS SAMPLED WITH THE ALIASING

The phenomenon of the ubiquitous compressibility of images acquired by the conventional methods raises a very natural question: is it possible to just directly measure the minimal amount of data and to avoid the need in image compression? This question was apparently first posed by the inventors of the *compressed sensing* approach (also known under the name *"compressed sampling"*) as a solution to this problem [6,7].

The compressed sensing approach considers the signal sampling and reconstruction as an underdetermined inverse problem of recovering a signal of N samples from a fewer number $K < N$ of measurements. As the signal recovering problem is underdetermined, it might have an indefinite number of solutions unless there is a priori restriction on signals to be recovered that allows choosing from all possible solutions the only one that satisfied this restriction. In the compressed sensing approach, this restriction is an assumption that signals that can be recovered from an incomplete number of measurements, are signals whose spectrum in a certain chosen *"sparsifying" transform* is sparse, *i.e.*, contains less non-zero transform coefficients than the total number of the transform coefficients.

It was proven in the theory of the compressed sensing that if an image of N samples is known to have, in the domain of a "sparsifying" transform, only $K < N$ non-zero transform coefficients, the image can be precisely reconstructed from a certain number $K < M < N$ measurements by means of minimization of the amount of image non-zero spectral coefficients, *i.e.*, minimization of the **L0** norm in the image transform domain or, which turned out to be more practical in the algorithmic implementation of the minimization procedure, by minimization of the sum of the modules of image spectral coefficients, *i.e.*, by minimization of the **L1** norm, or the so-called *total variation,* of the image transform coefficients. This, in particular, means that the signal sampling rate, in distinction from the conventional sampling according to the sampling theorem, does not depend on the signal's highest frequency. This implies that the signal sampling rate can be lower than twice the signal highest frequency, *i.e.*, a kind of a "sub-Nyquist" sampling with aliasing is admissible.

False spectra aliasing components within the sampling base-band caused by the "sub-Nyquist" signal sampling can not, in principle, be filtered out by signal linear filtering as it is done in the signal conventional sampling and reconstruction. The minimization of L0 or L1 norms of image spectra suggested by the compressed sensing approach for separating signal spectrum components from the false aliasing components implements a kind of nonlinear filtering. The capability of the compressed sensing approach of reconstructing signals sampled with aliasing can be demystified using the following simple model.

Let a signal of N samples composed of a certain known number $K < N$ of sinusoidal components be sub-sampled in $M < N$ arbitrarily chosen points and it is required to precisely reconstruct all N signal samples from these M available samples. This would be achieved if one could determine amplitudes and frequencies of the known number of the signal sinusoidal components. Fig. (**5.2**) obtained using the program RandomSamplingSinusoids_BNTM.m provided in the Exercises illustrates, utilizing the results of a computer simulation, how and when this can be done. Plots in this figure are numbered from top to bottom.

A test signal presented in Fig. (**5.2**), 1st plot, is composed of five sinusoidal components ($K = 5, N = 512$) seen as five Kronecker deltas in the signal Discrete Cosine Transform (DCT) spectrum (2nd plot in Fig. **5.2**). When this signal is sub-sampled (the 3rd plot in Fig. **5.2**), the aliasing spectral components appear in the spectrum of the sub-sampled signal (the 4th plot in Fig. **5.2**). In our example, the signal is sub-sampled in random positions with a sampling rate equals 0.15 of the rate of the sampling according to the signal base-band ($M = 76$). In this spectrum, a lot of false aliasing components can be seen. However, in this particular example, five true spectral components signals exceed the aliasing ones and can be easily detected and separated by finding positions of the given number K (in this particular case $K = 5$) the largest spectral components. When this is the case, one can run the following iterative Gerchberg-Papoulis type signal reconstruction algorithm:

1. Compute the DCT of the current estimate of the reconstructed signal.
2. Detect the given number K - the largest spectral components.
3. Set to zero all spectral components except the detected ones.

4. Compute the inverse DCT of the modified in this way signal spectrum to get a next estimate of the reconstructed signal.
5. Replace samples of the obtained estimate of the reconstructed signal in the positions of the available signal samples by them and repeat the loop.

The plot of the reconstruction root mean squared error (RMSE) normalized to signal maximum *vs.* the number of reconstruction iterations (5th plot in Fig. **5.2**) and the plot of DCT spectrum of the reconstructed by the iterative algorithm signal (6th plot) illustrate this process and demonstrate that practically precise reconstruction of the signal is achieved: after 50 iterations reconstruction RMSE is as small as 4.37×10^{-5}.

In this example, the signal sparsity, *i.e.*, the ratio of the number of signal non-zero spectral coefficients to the total number of spectral coefficients, is $K/N = 5/512 \approx 10^{-2}$. According to the discrete sampling theorem, the minimal number of signal samples sufficient for its precise reconstruction is $K = 5$, whereas it took $M = 76$ samples. Therefore, the sampling redundancy, *i.e.*, the ratio of the actual number of signal samples to the number of the signal non-zero spectral coefficients, is $R = M/K = 76/5 \cong 15.2$.

When the signal sub-sampling rate is too low and the aliasing is severe, reliable detection of the signal spectral components in the spectrum of the sampled signal and, hence, signal reconstruction becomes impossible. This case is illustrated in Fig. (**5.3**) by the results of the same experiment and with the same parameters as in Fig. (**5.2**), but for another realization of positions of signal samples, when two of the signal spectrum peaks are not detected and false peaks are detected instead. As a result, signal reconstruction by the iterative algorithm failed.

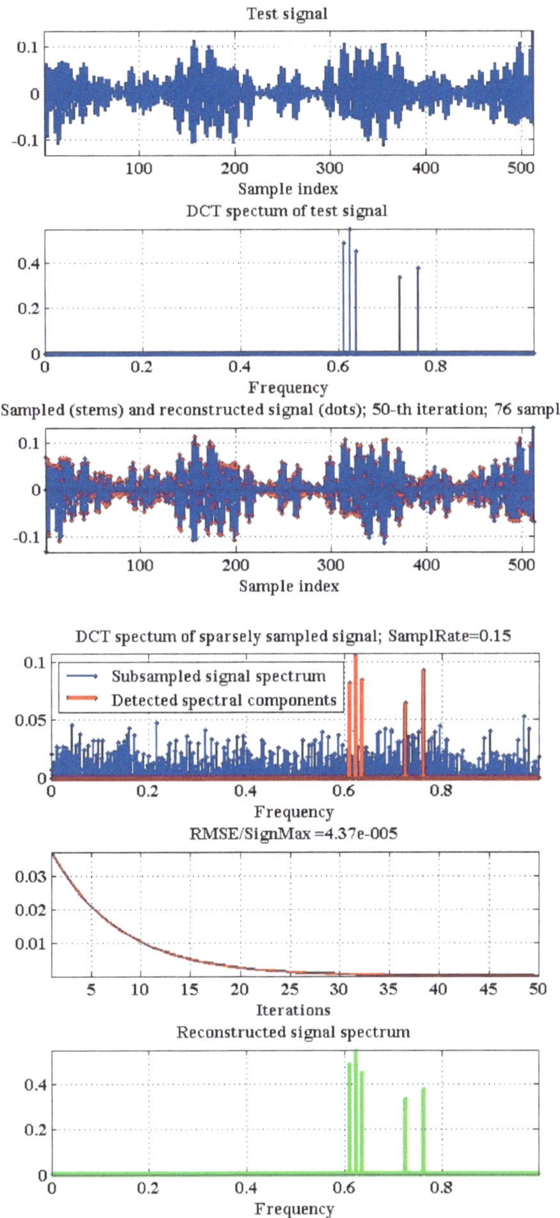

Fig. (5.2). Reconstruction of a test signal sampled with aliasing. From top to bottom: a test signal composed of five sinusoidal components; its DCT spectrum; this signal randomly sub-sampled and reconstructed; DCT spectrum of the sub-sampled signal; plot of the root mean square reconstruction error (RMSE) *vs.* the number of the reconstruction iterations; DCT spectrum of the reconstructed signal. Frequency in plots of spectra is given in fractions of the sampling baseband.

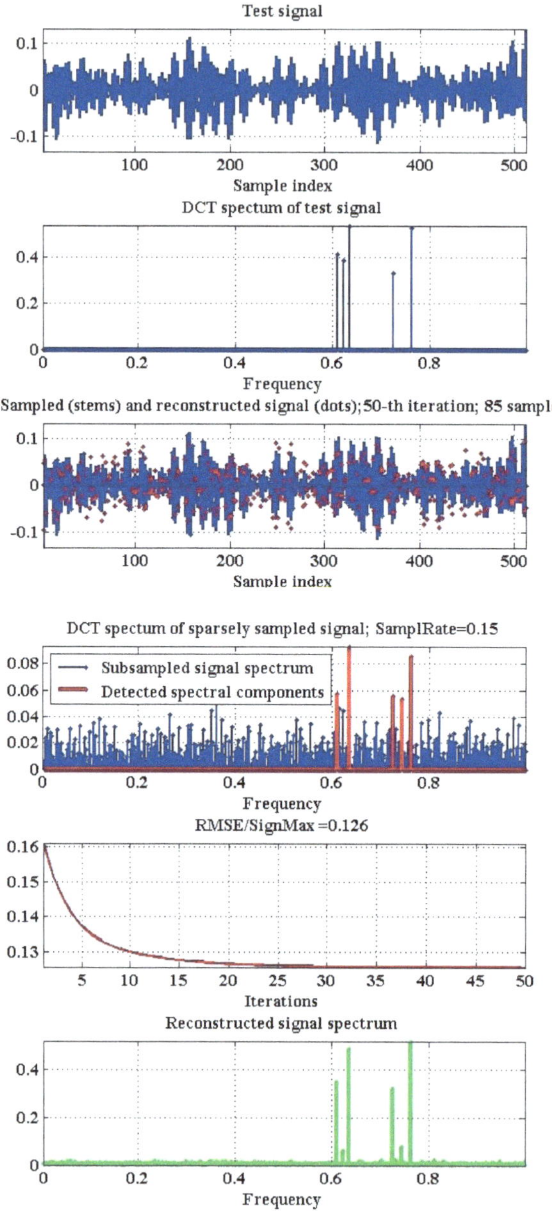

Fig. (5.3). Failure of reconstruction of a test signal sampled with aliasing. From top to bottom: a test signal composed of five sinusoidal components; its DCT spectrum; this signal randomly sub-sampled and reconstructed; DCT spectrum of the sub-sampled signal; plot of the root mean square reconstruction error (RMSE) *vs*. the number of the reconstruction iterations; DCT spectrum of the reconstructed signal. Frequency in plots of spectra is given in fractions of the sampling base-band.

From this model, it is also clear that the presence of noise in the sampled data hampers reliable detection of the signal spectral components and requires an additional sampling redundancy for reliable signal reconstruction.

When sampling is carried out in random positions, one can evaluate the performance of the described signal reconstruction method in terms of the probability of error in detecting signal spectral components. This probability depends on the sub-sampling rate and on the signal sparsity K/N. Fig. (**5.4**), left plot, presents results of an experimental evaluation of the probability of the frequency identification error as a function of the sub-sampling rate for a sinusoidal signal ($K=1$) of five different frequencies (0.9, 0.7, 0.5, 0.3 and 0.1 of the signal base-band), five different signal lengths N (128, 256, 512, 1024, 2048) and, correspondingly, of five different signal sparsities K/N. These results for each value of the signal sparsity are the averages over the results obtained for the different frequencies. The right plots in Fig. (**5.4**) show that sampling redundancies in the range of 14-32 times are required for the signal reconstruction by the above-described algorithm with the probability of the signal frequency identification error less than 10^{-4} , 10^{-3} and 10^{-2}. These results were obtained by a Monte-Carlo simulation of the algorithm with 5×10^{4} realizations of the random sampling for each individual experiment with a given sampling rate, signal frequency and signal length.

5.3. IS THE COMPRESSED SENSING A SOLUTION TO THE PROBLEM OF MINIMIZATION OF THE IMAGE SAMPLING RATE?

Potentials of the compressed sensing approach to the image sampling and reconstruction are widely advertised in the literature. Much less is known about its limitations. Particularly important is the question, how close is the amount of measurements required by the compressed sensing methods of signal and image acquisition to the theoretical minimum defined by the sampling theory.

According to the theory of the compressed sensing [8], for the precise reconstruction of a signal of N samples that has $K < N$ non-zero transform coefficients, it is required that the number of measurements M sufficient for signal reconstruction satisfies the following inequality

$$M/K > -2\log\left[(M/K)(K/N)\right] \qquad (5.\,1)$$

By virtue of the discrete sampling theorem, the signal sparsity $Ss = K/N$ is the theoretical lower bound of the sampling rate required for signal reconstruction. Therefore, the ratio $R = M/K$ of the number of the required measurements M to the number K of the signal non-zero transform coefficients represents the sampling redundancy with respect to the theoretical minimum. Inequality (5. 1) can be rewritten as a relationship between the signal sparsity $Ss = K/N$ and the sampling redundancy $R = M/K$ as

$$R > -2\log\left(R \times Ss\right) \qquad (5.\,2)$$

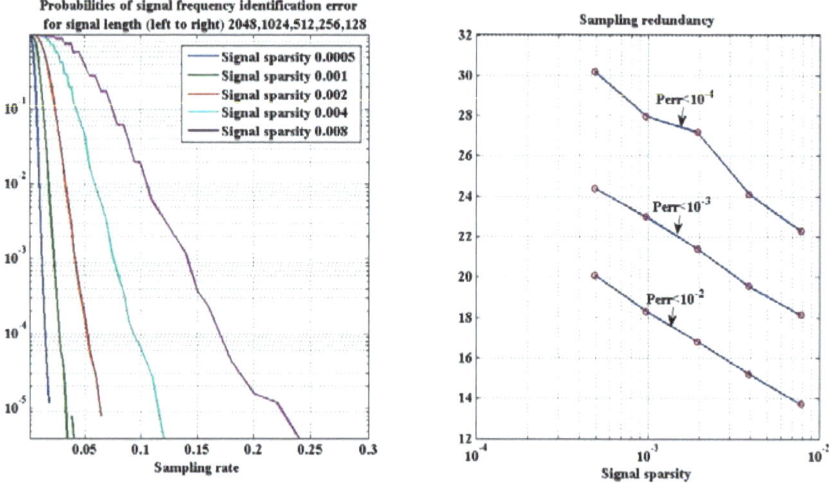

Fig. (5.4). Plots of the probabilities of error in identification of the signal frequency *vs* the sampling rate (left) and estimates of the sampling redundancy *vs.* the signal sparsity (right).

Numerical evaluation of this relationship between the sampling redundancy R and the signal sparsity Ss is presented in (Fig. **5.5**), by the dash-dot line. The solid line in this figure is plotted on the base of the experimental data collected in the literature [9].

It has been observed in Fig. (**5.5**) that in the range of the sparsities from 0.1 to 0.39 of the test images shown in Fig. (**5.1**), the sampling redundancy of the compressed sensing methods should theoretically be larger than 2 to 3 and, according to the experimental curve, it should be larger than 2.5 to 5. This means that the sampling redundancy required by the compressed sensing methods for this set of test images is not much lower than the sampling redundancy of their regular sampling (2.5 - 10), *i.e.*, the compressed sensing methods are far from reaching the theoretical minimum of signal sampling rates.

The substantial sampling redundancy required by the compressed sensing methods is not their only drawback. The applicability of the compressed sensing is also impeded by its vulnerability to noise in the sensed data and by the impossibility to predict and secure the resolving power of the reconstructed images. Resolving power of images is determined by the size and shape of the EC-zones of their spectra. EC-zones of spectra of images reconstructed by the methods of the compressed sensing are formed in the process of the image reconstruction, rather than are specified in advance from the requirements to the image resolving power. To summarize the said, the compressed sensing methods are, to a certain degree, capable of reconstructing sparse approximations of signals and images sampled with the aliasing. No knowledge regarding EC-zones of the image spectra is required for this. One has to only choose an image sparsifying transform and specify the desired spectrum sparsity. Not requiring any knowledge regarding image spectra EC-zones is an attractive feature of the compressed sensing methods. It, however, has its price. Due to this, the compressed sensing methods require a significant redundancy in the number of measurements sufficient for image reconstruction compared to the theoretical minimum.

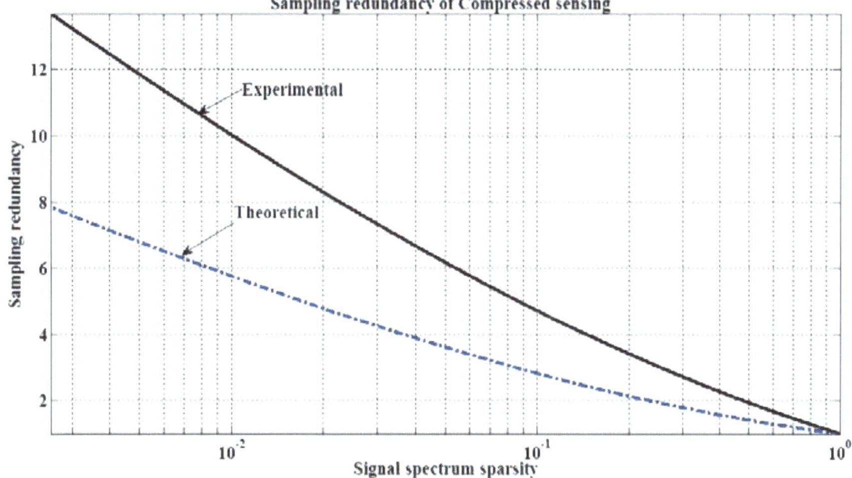

Fig. (5.5). Theoretical and experimental relationships between the signal sparsity and the sampling redundancy required by the compressed sensing approach. For sampling redundancies above the curves, signal reconstruction is possible, otherwise, it is not.

In many practical tasks of the digital image acquisition, the assumption of the complete uncertainty regarding the image spectra EC-zones has no justification. In fact, if one is ready, as it is supposed by the compressed sensing approach, to accept a sparse spectrum approximation to an image and has chosen an image sparsifying transform, one tacitly implies certain knowledge of the energy compaction capability of the chosen transform. The next chapter proves that making use of this in any way available a priori knowledge allows implementing image sampling with the rates close to the theoretical minimum.

5.4. EXERCISES

•DFT_Spectr_sparsity_BNTM.m

Visualization of Spectra EC-zones of INPIMG at the level that corresponds to the same image reconstruction error as that of JPEG compression.
Color images are replaced by their grey scale copies

•RandomSamplingSinusoids_BNTM.m

Demonstration on a discrete simulating model of the effects of sparse random sampling of signals composed of a given number of sinusoidal components; reconstruction by detection in the spectra of the sampled signals of the given number of the largest sinusoidal components; and subsequent determination of their intensities using an iterative Gerschberg-Papoulis type algorithm.

The frequencies of the sinusoidal components of the test signals are chosen randomly by a random number generator. The requested parameters are

• The number of samples of the signal discrete model,
• The number of signal sinusoidal spectral components, and
• The signal sampling rate (in a fraction of the width of the signal base-band).

CHAPTER 6

How One Can Sample Images with Sampling Rates Close To the Theoretical Minimum

6.1. A METHOD OF IMAGE SAMPLING AND RECONSTRUCTION WITH SAMPLING RATES CLOSE TO THE THEORETICAL MINIMUM

This chapter will show how one can implement image sampling and reconstruction according to the General sampling theorem. As outlined in Chapter 4, the general sampling theorem suggests the following principle of image sampling and reconstruction:

- Choose the required number N of image samples.
- Choose an image *sparsifying transform* that features the best, for the given image, energy compaction capability, *i.e.*, the capability to compact image energy into the smallest number of its transform coefficients.
- Specify the desired EC-zone of the image spectrum, *i.e.*, a set of $M \leq N$ transform coefficients to be used for image reconstruction.
- Take M image samples in arbitrary positions.
- Use the obtained M image samples for determining M transform coefficients that belong to the chosen EC-zone.
- Set the rest $N - M$ transform coefficients to zero and use the obtained spectrum for the reconstruction of the required N image samples by its inverse transform.

Consider possible ways for the implementation of this principle.

Choosing an Image Sparsifying Transform. The choice of the image sparsifying transform is governed by the transform energy compaction capability. An additional requirement is the availability of a fast transform algorithm. From this point of view, the discrete cosine (DCT), discrete Fourier (DFT) and wavelet transforms are among the primary candidates.

Specifying the Image EC-zone. Specification of the subset of image transform coefficients to be used for image reconstruction, *i.e.*, of the image spectrum EC-zone, can be made based on the known energy compaction capability of the chosen transform. In what follows, using the DCT as the image sparsifying transform is assumed. The DCT is known to efficiently compact the largest image transform coefficients into more or less compact groups in the area of low spatial frequencies around the DC component.

A considerable practical experience, including that obtained in the course of developing zonal quantization tables for the JPEG image compression standard, shows that although these groups of the DCT coefficients do not have sharp borders, they are quite well concentrated. This means that the groups can be, with a reasonably good accuracy in terms of the preservation of the group total energy, circumscribed by one of some standard shapes that encompass the area of image low spatial frequencies and can be specified by few parameters, such as area, aspect ratio, angular orientation, *etc*. Fig. (**6.1**) presents a set of five possible standard shapes well suited for the DCT as the sparsifying transform: rectangle, triangle, pie-sector, ellipse, and superellipse. In principle, each particular standard shape can be associated with a certain class of images, such as micrographs, aerial photographs, space photos, in-door and out-door scenes, *etc*.

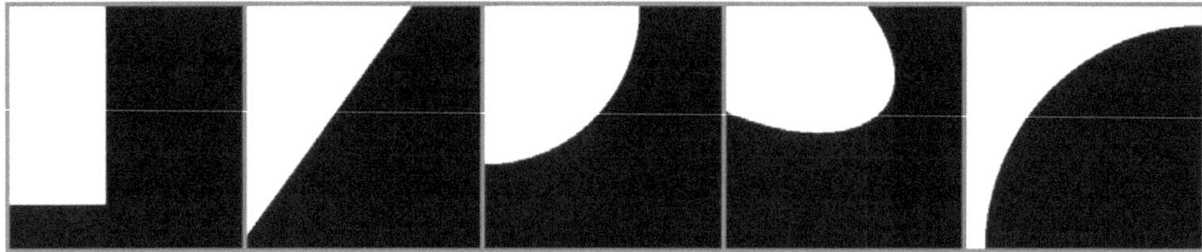

Fig. (6.1). Examples of the possible standard shapes for approximating the EC-zones of image DCT spectra. From left to right: rectangle, triangle, pie-sector, oval, and superellipse. Spectrum DC components are in the upper left corners of the shapes.

The experimental experience shows that no fine-tuning of the shape parameters is required for specifying the chosen shapes as approximations of the image spectra EC-zones. This property of sparse DCT spectra is illustrated in Fig. (**6.2**) in an example of the sparse DCT spectrum of the test image "BloodVessels512" (Fig. **5.1**). One can easily notice in the image a certain prevalence of horizontal edges. This causes anisotropy of image EC-zone seen in boxes b) – d) in Fig. (**6.2**), where white dots indicate positions of the largest DCT coefficients that reconstruct this image with root mean square error (RMSE) 3.85 gray levels of 255 levels. This RMSE has been chosen the same as the reconstruction RMSE of this image after its standard JPEG compression by the MATLAB© tools. This image EC-zone occupies 0.164 of the image baseband area. Additionally in boxes (b) – (e) shown are borders of the rectangular, triangular, and oval shapes that all have the same area (0.275 of the baseband area) and different aspect ratios (0.35, 0.25, 0.3 and 0.45, correspondingly). When used as spectrum bounding shapes that approximate the image spectrum EC-zone, they all reconstruct the test image with practically the same reconstruction RMSEs (4.1, 3.7, 3.8, and 3.8 of image gray levels, correspondingly) as that of the JPEG compression (3.85).

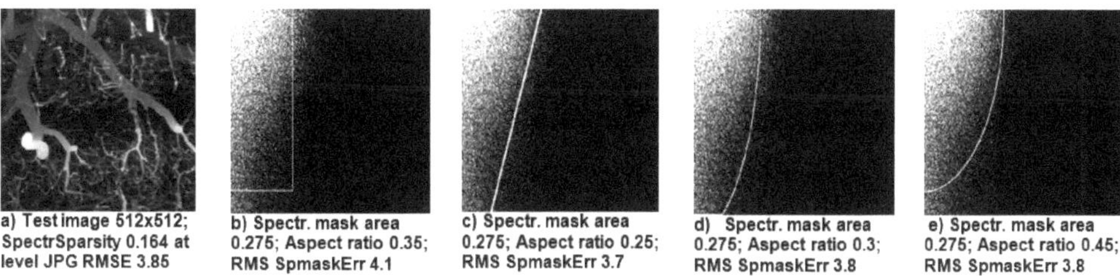

Fig. (6.2). Test image "BloodVessels512" with spectrum sparsity 0.164 at the level of JPEG encoding RMSE 3.85 of image gray levels (**a**), image EC-zones, *i.e.*, sets of image largest spectral components that reconstruct the image with RMSE 3.85 (white dots) and the borders (white lines) of the rectangular, triangular and oval shapes with different shape parameters that approximate the image EC-zone (**b-e**).

Images with spectra bounded by one of these shapes are visually indistinguishable from one another though patterns of the reconstruction errors look, naturally, a bit different. Two examples of such images obtained for the spectrum bounding by the rectangle as in Fig. (**6.2b**) and by the oval as in Fig. (**6.2d**) are shown in Fig. (**6.3a**) and Fig. (**6.3b**) along with the corresponding patterns of the reconstruction errors (Fig. **6.3c, d**). For display purposes, the reconstruction errors are shown 8 times contrasted).

As one can see in Fig. (**6.3**), the shapes that are chosen to approximate the image spectrum EC-zone do not include all spectral coefficients of the EC-zone. On the other side, they include some of the spectral components that do not belong to the EC-zone. Those components that do not belong to the EC-zone and happen to be inside of the chosen spectral shape have, by the definition, lower intensity than the components of the EC-zone that happen to be outside the shape. Therefore, given the energy of all spectral components encompassed by the chosen spectral shape, the number of these internal "no-EC-zone components" must exceed the number of the EC-zone components not encompassed by the shape. This means that the area of the shape that defines the number of samples to be taken will always exceed to a certain degree the number of the EC-zone coefficients, which, theoretically, is the minimal number of samples required. For instance redundancies of approximating EC-zone shapes of the image in Fig. (**6.2**) are 0.275/0.164=1.67. Experimental results reported in the next section show that redundancies of the standard EC-zones for natural images are, as a rule, of the same order of magnitude. This EC-zone shape's redundancy is the price one should pay for not knowing exact indices of the transform coefficients that form the image spectrum EC-zone.

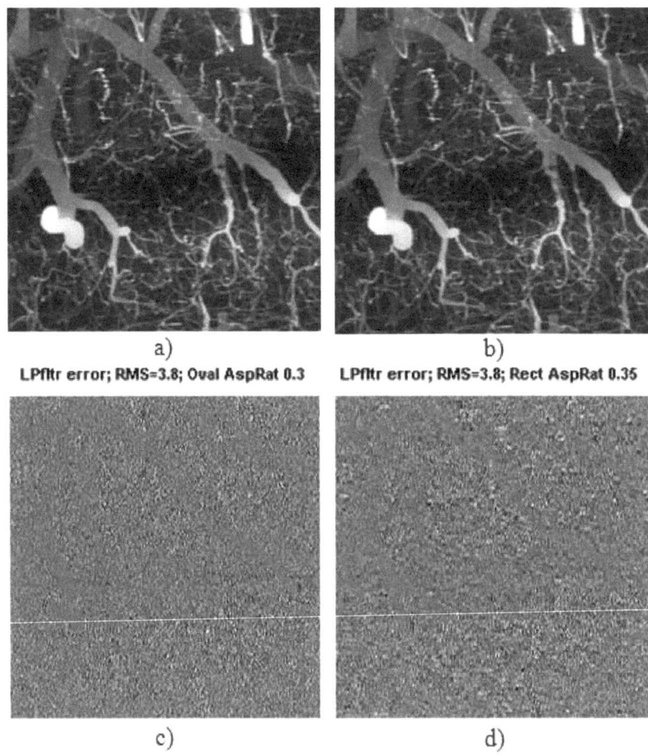

Fig. (6.3). (**a, b**): Images reconstructed after bounding the DCT spectrum of the test image of Fig. (**6.2a**) by the oval Fig. (**6.2d**) and by the rectangular Fig. (**6.2b**) spectral masks; (c), (d): patterns of the corresponding reconstruction errors, displayed 8 times contrasted for better readability.

Specifying positions of the image samples. Positions of the image samples should permit computation from the samples of the group of transform coefficients chosen for image reconstruction. As mentioned in Sect. 4.2, some image transforms, such as wavelets, impose a certain limitation on the positions of the image samples, whereas for the DFT and DCT positions of the image samples can be arbitrary. An additional advantage of using the DFT and DCT as the image sparsifying transforms is that they are discrete representations of the integral Fourier transform and, as such, they ideally concord with the characterization of imaging systems in terms of their frequency responses.

Methods of image reconstruction. For image reconstruction, there are two options:

- The direct inversion of the $M \times M$ transform sub-matrix that links M available samples and M transform coefficients specified by the chosen spectral EC-zone with the rest $N - M$ coefficients set to zero. Once the M chosen transform coefficients are found and the rest $N - M$ transform coefficients are set to zero, the inverse transform is applied to the found spectrum to reconstruct all required N samples. Generally, the matrix inversion is a very hard computational task and no fast matrix inversion algorithms are known. In our particular case, a trimmed fast transform matrix should be inverted. There exist pruned versions of the fast transforms for computing subsets of transform coefficients of signals with all samples except several ones equal to zero [10]), which is inverse to what is required in the given case. The question, whether these pruned algorithms can be inverted for computing a subset of transform non-zero coefficients from a subset of signal samples is open.

- The above described iterative Gerchberg-Papoulis type algorithm (Fig. **4.2**). As a zero-order approximation, from which the reconstruction iterations start, an image interpolated in one or another way from the available samples can be taken. A particular interpolation algorithm used in the verification experiments is detailed in the next section.

The above reasoning suggests the following protocol of image sampling and reconstruction assuming DCT as the image sparsifying transform:

Image Sampling

- Choose a required image spatial resolution SpR (in "dots per mm (inch)") in the same way as it is being done in the conventional image sampling.
- Based on the evaluation of the image, choose one of the standard spectral bounding shapes for bounding EC-zone of the DCT spectrum and set its shape parameters, such as the aspect ratio for the rectangle and triangle, the aspect ratio and the orientation angle for the ellipse, *etc.*
- Evaluate X and Y dimensions $ShSzX$ and $ShSzY$ of the chosen shape using SpR as the shape's largest diameter.
- Specify the number of pixels $N_x \geq ShSzX$ and $N_y \geq ShSzY$ "per mm (inch)" in X and Y dimensions of the image to be reconstructed.
- For the chosen image spectrum EC-zone approximating shape, evaluate fraction Fr of the area the shape occupies in the rectangle $N_x \times N_y$. This fraction times $SpR \times SpR$ determines spatial density $SpD = Fr \times SpR^2$ of samples to be taken (in "dots per square mm (inch)"). The number of

samples M to be taken can then be found as a product of SpD and the image area $ImgSzX \times ImgSzY$:

$$M = SpD \times ImgSzX \times ImgSzY \ . \tag{6.1}$$

- Sample the image in whatever M positions. The issue pre-sampling low-pass filtering will be discussed below in Sect. 6.3.

As one can see, the described sampling protocol does not essentially differ from the ordinary standard 2D sampling protocol. The only difference is that in the suggested method arbitrary sampling grids can be used and evaluation of the spectrum bounding shapes for approximating the image spectra EC-zones is required in addition to the specification of the desired image resolution, which anyway is required by the standard sampling protocol.

Image Reconstruction

Apply to the sampled image one of the above-described reconstruction options using for the image spectrum bounding the chosen spectrum EC-zone approximating shape. In this way, an image with spectrum bounded in the chosen transform by the chosen EC-zone approximating shape, or a bounded spectrum (BS-) image, will be obtained, which has the prescribed spatial resolution SpR .

As much as in the suggested method the sampling rate is equal to the area of the chosen spectrum bounding shape, which defines the minimum sampling rate, the method reaches this minimal rate for the given spectrum bounding shape. However, as mentioned previously, the latter is somewhat larger than the area occupied by the actual image spectrum EZ-zone, which the chosen spectrum bounding shape approximates. Therefore, for each particular image, the method has a residual sampling redundancy that is equal to the ratio of the area of the chosen spectrum bounding shape to the area of the actual image spectrum EC-zone. Practical estimates of this redundancy are discussed below in Sect. 6.2.

Because of the said the described image sampling and reconstruction method will be called the Arbitrary Sampling and Bounded Spectrum Reconstruction (ASBSR) method.

6.2. EXPERIMENTAL VERIFICATION OF THE WORKABILITY OF THE METHOD

This section presents the results of the experimental verification of the workability of the ASBSR method of image sampling and reconstruction. The experiments were conducted with ten real-life images presented in Fig. (**5.1**). These results supplement the experimental results conducted with pseudo-random test images presented in Sect. 4.2 in confirmation of the validity of the Discrete sampling theorem for DFT and DCT. In the given experiments, the above-described iterative Gerchberg-Papoulis type algorithm was used for image reconstruction from their samples and the following three types of sampling lattices were tested:

1) "quasi-uniform" sampling grid, in which M image samples are distributed uniformly with an appropriate rounding off their positions to the nearest nodes of the dense square sampling lattice of N samples;
2) uniform sampling lattice with jitter, in which horizontal and vertical positions of each of M samples are randomly chosen, independently in each of two image coordinates within the primary uniform sampling intervals;
3) pseudorandom sampling lattice, in which positions of M samples are uniformly distributed in a pseudo-random order over nodes of the dense sampling lattice of N samples.

As an image sparsifying transform that compacts the image spectrum, the Discrete Cosine Transform was used. As an admissible RMSE of approximation of test images by images with bounded DCT spectra, RMSE of image compression by the standard JPEG compression in MATLAB$^{©}$ implementation is taken. These RMSEs were used for choosing image spectrum EC-zone approximating shapes for each particular image. The chosen shapes were used for bounding image DCT spectra both for image pre-filtering before sampling to prevent aliasing distortions and in the process of image reconstruction.

A zero-order approximation to reconstructed images, from which the iterative reconstruction starts, was generated from the sampled image by interpolation of each not available image sample from three the nearest to it available samples taken with weights inversely proportional to its distances from them.

Figs. (**6.4 - 6.6**) obtained using the program Arbitr Sampling and BS Reconstr_ BNTM.m provided in the Exercises illustrate the results of the experiments with ten images of the tested set.

Fig. (**6.4**) shows:

(i) test image;
(ii) reconstructed image;
(iii) sampled test image;
(iv) the border of the chosen image EC-zone approximating shape (solid line) and positions of the image DCT spectrum largest coefficients (white dots), which reconstruct the image with RMSE equal to that of the image JPEG compression;
(v) plots of RMS of all reconstruction errors (the difference between the initial test image pre-filtered for bounding its spectrum before sampling and the reconstructed image) and of RMS of 90% of the smallest reconstruction errors *vs.* the iteration number.

Separate counting RMS of 90% of the smallest reconstruction errors is motivated by the observation that the iterative reconstruction converges not uniformly over the image area: most of the errors decay with iterations much more rapidly than few isolated large errors that occur in places where the density of samples happens to be too small. Reconstruction RMSE is given in units of image gray levels in the range 0-255.

Figs. (**6.5** and **6.6**) present:

(i) reconstructed images (left column),
(ii) test image spectra EC-zones (white dots) and borders (solid lines) of their chosen EC-zone approximating shapes (middle column), and
(iii) plots of reconstruction RMSE *vs.* the number of iterations (right column).

For all images, sampling over the uniform sampling lattices with jitter was used, for which RMS of the reconstruction errors decayed with iterations most rapidly. It was observed in the experiments that for the same number of iterations, reconstruction RMSE for a totally random sampling lattice was about 1.5-2 times and for "quasi-uniform" sampling lattice 2-2.5 times larger than that for the "uniform with jitter" sampling lattice. For "quasi-uniform" sampling lattices, stagnation of the iteration process was observed, which can be attributed to the presence of regular patterns of thickening and rarefication of sampling positions due to rounding off their coordinates to the positions of the nodes of the regular uniform sampling grid.

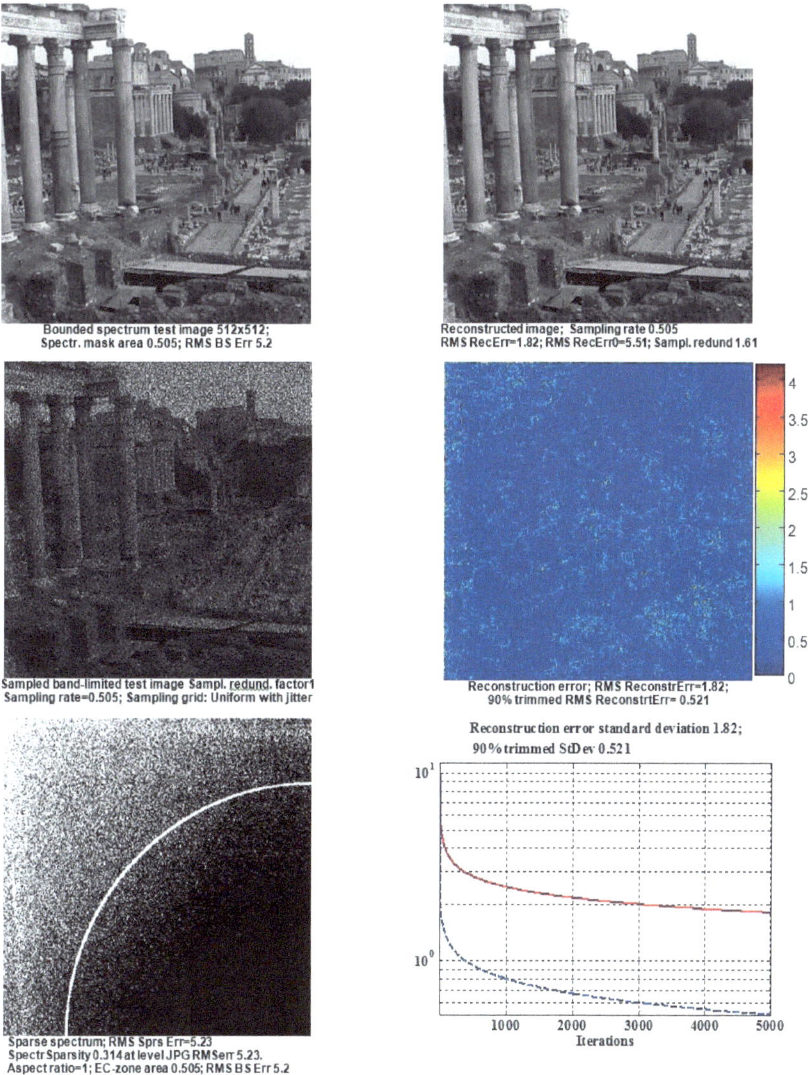

Fig. (6.4). Results of experiments on the sampling and BS-reconstruction of the test image "Rome512". From top to bottom, from left to right: test image; reconstructed BS-image; sampled test image; the pattern of reconstruction errors (absolute value of the difference between the initial test image and the reconstructed image displayed in MATLAB© color map "jet"); test image spectrum EC-zone (white dots) and the border of the chosen approximating the EC-zone shape (white solid line); plots of RMS of all (solid line) and of the smallest 90% (dash line) of reconstruction errors *vs.* the number of iterations.

Table **6.1** summarizes the numerical results obtained for all ten test images for the reconstruction accuracy, spectrum sparsity, sampling rate, redundancy of the chosen EC-zone approximating shapes (the ratio of fractions of the area they occupy in the sampling baseband to the spectrum sparsity), sampling redundancy (the ratio of the sampling rate to the relative area of the chosen EC-zone approximating shape, which is the theoretical minimum of the sampling rate for the given shape) and the overall sampling redundancy (the ratio of the sampling rate to the spectrum sparsity).

Table 6.1. Summary of experimental results.

Test image	Reconstruction RMSE (Peak signal to RMSE ratio)	Spectrum sparsity	Sampling rate	Sampling redundancy		
				Redundancy of the chosen EC-zone approximating shape	Sampling redundancy with respect to chosen EC-zone	Overall sampling redundancy
AerialPhoto512	1.26 (46.2 dB)	0.227	0.365	1.6	1	1.6
AFM1024	1.1 (47.3 dB)	0.154	0.226	1.46	1	1.46
Barbara512	4.02 (36.1 dB)	0.265	0.412	1.55	1	1.55
	0.69 (51.4 dB)	0.265	0.474	1.55	1.15	1.78
BloodVessels512	1.94 (42.4 dB)	0.164	0.257	1.56	1	1.56
Mushrooms512	1.46 (44.9 dB)	0.159	0.226	1.41	1	1.41
Nish1024	1.13 (47.1 dB)	0.17	0.25	1.47	1	1.47
Pirat1024	1.15 (46.9 dB)	0.245	0.42	1.61	1	1.61
Rome512	1.92 (42.5 dB)	0.314	0.5	1.59	1	1.59
Test4CS1024	1.06 (47.7 dB)	0.09	0.136	1.53	1	1.53
WestConcord	1.96 (42.3 dB)	0.314	0.521	1.73	1	1.73

Plots of the reconstruction RMSE *vs.* the number of iterations in Figs. (**6.4 - 6.6**) indicate that RMS of the reconstruction errors decay at the first couple of hundreds of iterations quite rapidly but after they reach the value of about 2-3 quantization intervals, the error decay slows down. It was found in the experiments that one can substantially accelerate the error decay, if the number of samples is taken with a certain small excess, *i.e.*, 10-20% larger than the minimal number equals the area of the chosen EC-zone approximating shape (see the results for the test image "Barbara512" in Table **6.1**).

To summarize, the experiments confirm that images sampled with sampling rates equal to the minimum rate for their chosen EC-zone approximating shapes can be reconstructed with sufficiently good accuracy. The redundancy in the number of the required samples associated with the redundancy of the standard shapes approximating the image spectra EC-zones is of the order 1.5-1.6; it never exceeded 2 in experiments with other images.

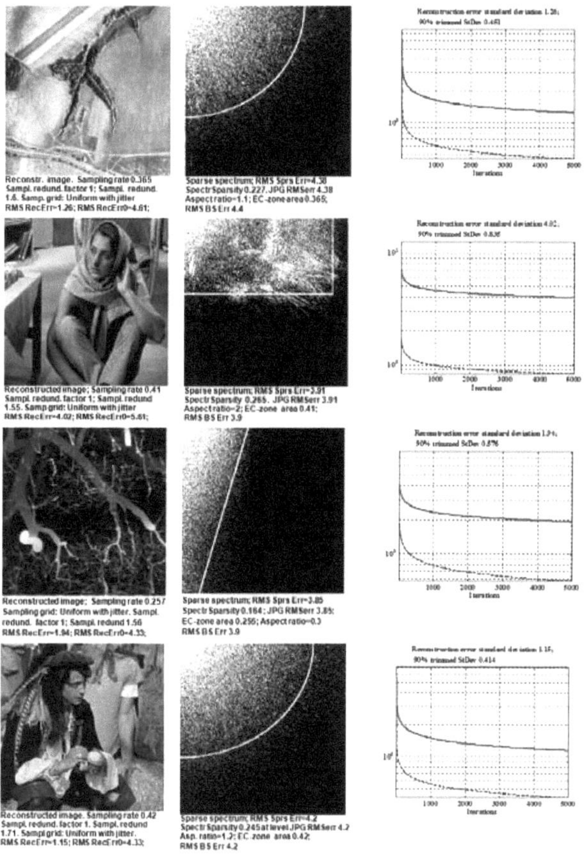

Fig. (6.5). Results of experiments on sampling and reconstruction of test images. From top to bottom: "AerialPhoto512" "Barbara512", "BloodVessels512" and "Pirat1024". From left to right: reconstructed images; image spectra EC-zones (white dots) and borders of the corresponding chosen approximating EC-zones shapes (white solid line); plots of RMS of all (red solid line) and of the smallest 90% of reconstruction errors (blue dash line) *vs.* the number of iterations.

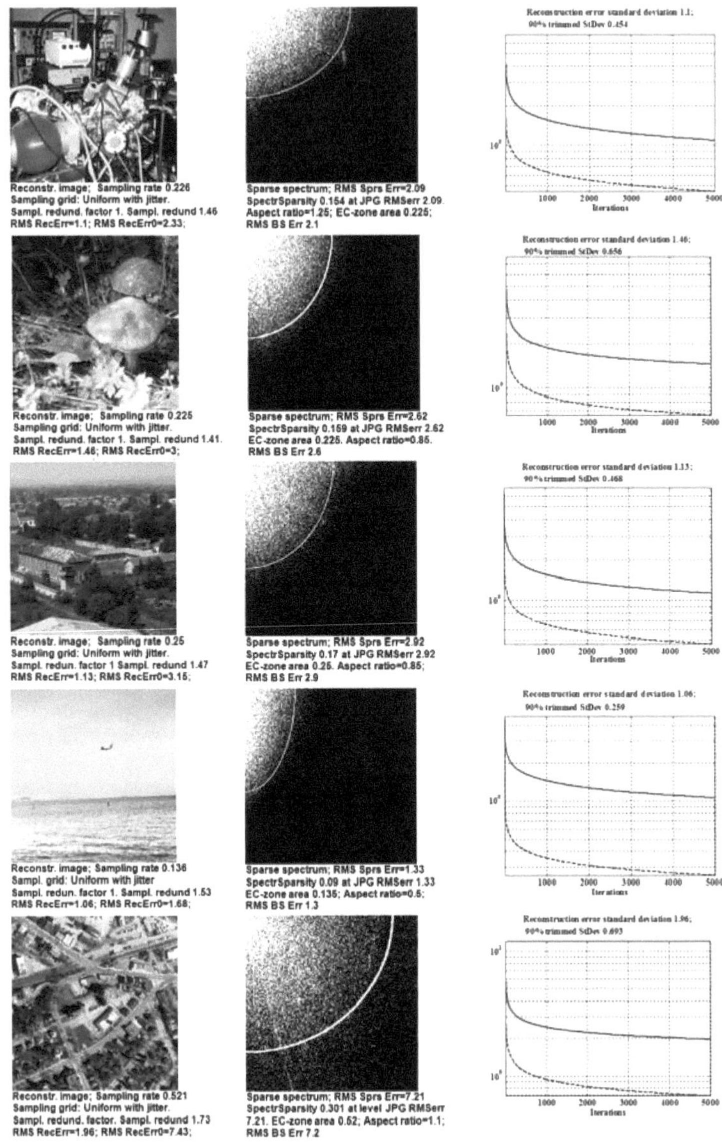

Fig. (6.6). Results of experiments on sampling and reconstruction of test images. From top to bottom: "AFM1024, "Mushrooms512", "Nish1024", "Test4CS1024" and "WestConcord364". From left to right: reconstructed images; image spectra EC-zones (white dots) and borders of the corresponding chosen EC-zone approximating shapes (white solid line); plots of RMS of all (red solid line) and the smallest 90% of reconstruction errors (blue dash line) *vs.* the number of iterations.

6.3. SOME PRACTICAL ISSUES

In this section, four issues of the practical application of the ASBSR method of image sampling and reconstruction are addressed: (i) how robust is the method to the presence of noise in image sensors; (ii) practical considerations regarding choosing the EC-zone approximating shapes for bounding image spectra in image sampling and reconstruction, (iii) image anti-aliasing pre-filtering, and (iv) the computational complexity of the method.

Noise Robustness of the ASBSR-Method: In distinction from the compressed sensing methods, the ASBSR method is insensitive to noise in image signals. From the method description in Section 6.1, one can see that the ASBSR method, just as the conventional sampling and reconstruction methods, is linear, *i.e.*, it satisfies the superposition principle. No parameter of sampling and reconstruction algorithms depends on signal values and, in particular, on whether the noise is present in the signal. Therefore sampling and reconstruction of an image that contains additive noise will result in a reconstructed image that also contains additive noise with the power spectrum bounded by the spectrum EC-zone approximating shape used for image reconstruction. In particular, if the sensor's noise with variance σ^2 has a uniform power spectrum within the sampling baseband, noise in the reconstructed image will have variance $\kappa\sigma^2$, where $\kappa < 1$ is the relative area of the reconstruction EC-zone approximating shape, and its power spectrum will be uniform within this shape and zero outside it.

This conclusion is illustrated in Fig. (**6.7**) by the results of the sampling and reconstruction of the test image "Barbara" taken with and without additive noise. As one can see in the figure, the presence of noise in the image does not influence the work of the reconstruction algorithm.

Choosing Approximating Shapes of Image Spectra EC-zones for bounding image spectra for image sampling and reconstruction. As mentioned in Sect. 6.1, no fine-tuning is required for specifying the shape parameters. Therefore it is suggested that several standard shapes, such as those presented in Fig. (**6.1**), should be found for different classes of images such as landscape, portrait, micrographs, aerial, and space photographs of a different kind and alike. This can be based, for instance, on a machine learning algorithm trained on various image databases. For sampling images in a particular application, the user should only specify an image class. Note that specifying an image class is a standard option for setting parameters of modern digital photographic cameras.

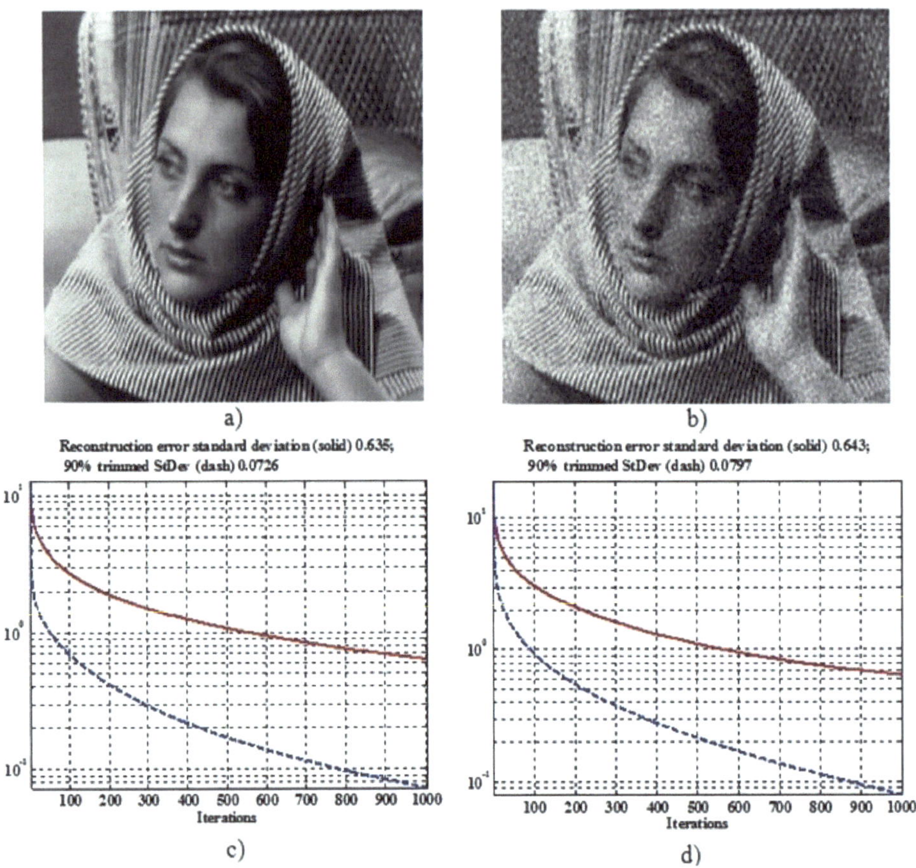

Fig. (6.7). Images reconstructed from sampled noiseless test image (**a**) and from samples of the same image contaminated with additive uncorrelated Gaussian noise with standard deviation 20 gray levels (**b**), and the corresponding plots (**c, d**) of RMS of all (red solid lines) and the smallest 90% of reconstruction errors (blue dash lines) *vs.* the number of iterations.

Image Anti-aliasing Pre-filtering: According to the sampling theorems, image pre-filtering is necessary before sampling in order to avoid aliasing errors and to secure convergence of the iterative reconstruction algorithm to an image with a bounded spectrum. In ordinary imaging devices, anti-aliasing pre-filtering is carried out by imaging optics together with apertures of image sensors. The ASBSR method envisages, generally, choosing an EC-zone approximating shape individually for every particular image. Ordinary image sensors are not capable of implementing this choice. As a solution to this problem, the usage of synthetic multiple aperture sensors can be proposed. In these sensors, several individual sub-sensors are allocated for each image sample as it is depicted in a schematic diagram in Fig. (**6.8**). With $K_x \times K_y$ sub-sensors per image sample, image samples are obtained by weighted summation of outputs of the sub-sensors:

$$\tilde{a}_{k,l} = \sum_{m=0}^{K_y-1} \sum_{n=0}^{K_x-1} \eta_{m,n} \iint_{X\,Y} a(x,y) PSF_{m,n}^{(s)}\left(x - k\Delta_x, y - l\Delta_y\right) dxdy, \tag{6.2}$$

where $\left\{\eta_{m,n}\right\}$ are sub-sensors' weight coefficients and $\left\{PSF_{m,n}^{(s)}(x,y)\right\}$ are the point spread functions of the sub-sensors.

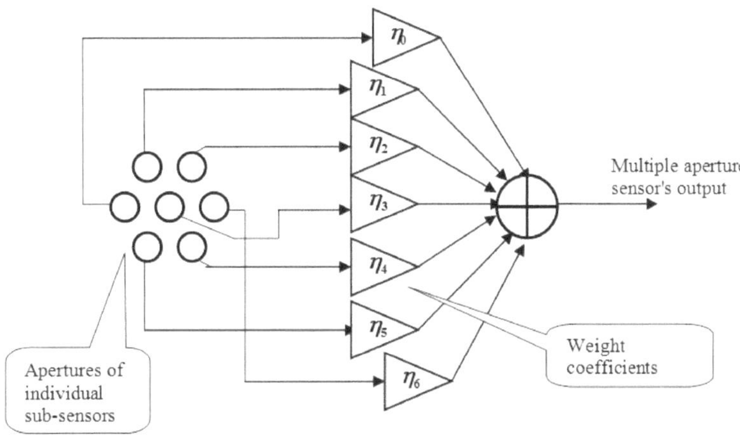

Fig. (6.8). Schematic diagram of multiple aperture sensors.

According to the definition of the frequency response of a digital filter (see Sect. 7.2), sub-sensor weight coefficients $\left\{\eta_{m,n}\right\}$ are coefficients of the inverse DFT of the shape $Sh_{r,s}$ chosen for approximating image spectrum EC-zone:

$$\eta_{m,n} = \frac{1}{\sqrt{N_x N_y}} \sum_{r=0}^{N_x-1} \sum_{s=0}^{N_y-1} Sh_{r,s} \exp\left[-i2\pi\left(\frac{mr}{N_x} + \frac{ns}{N_y}\right)\right]. \tag{6.3}$$

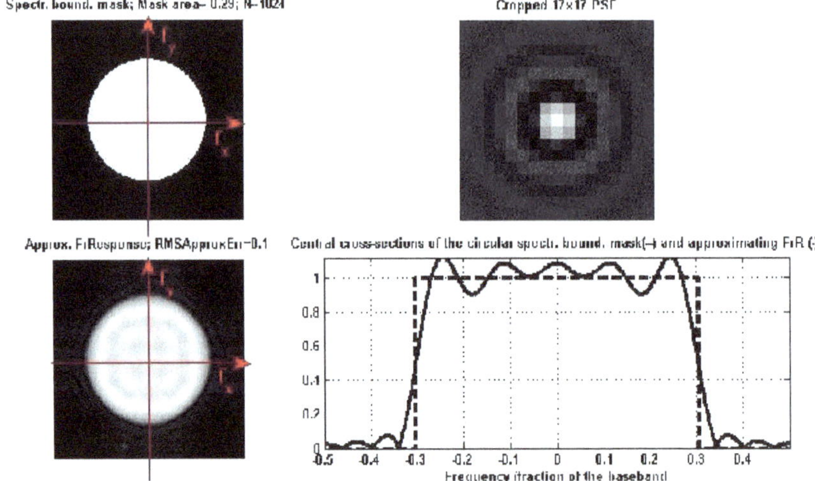

Fig. (6.9). An illustrative example of a synthetic multiple aperture sensor. Upper left: circular target Fourier spectrum bounding shape (dark - zero, bright - 1). Upper right: a map of weight coefficients of 17x17 sub-sensors coded in a grayscale. Bottom left: Fourier spectrum of the synthetic bounding shape approximating the target one. Bottom right: central cross-section of the approximating shape (solid line) and the target one (dash line).

The multiple aperture sensors are especially well suited for the so-called *single-pixel cameras*, where sampling is carried out using *digital micro-mirror devices*, which enable the possibility of arbitrary arrangement of sampling positions.

Choosing the anti-aliasing filters individually adjusted for each particular image is advisable but it is not very critical. As a practical alternative, the use of a universal "all-purpose" shape can be considered. As such a universal ("all-purpose") EC-zone approximating shape, a "pie-sector" shape can be suggested, which fits the majority of natural images quite well. It has only one adjustment parameter, its radius. As mentioned in Sect. 6.1, substantial variations of EC-zone shape parameters do not lead in practice to substantial variations of the image approximation RMSE. This is why the worsening the image approximation accuracy due to the use of an "all-purpose" shape instead of a "dedicated" one will be, as a rule, not dramatic. For instance, total RMS error 4.72 of reconstruction of test image "BloodVessels512" using an "all-purpose" pie-sector zone (Fig. **6.10**) is only 7.7% larger than the reconstruction RMSE 4.38 obtained, when a triangular EC-zone that fits image spectrum (Fig. **6.5**) was used. One should however admit that in this case a certain loss of image resolving power in the vertical direction is possible because the width of the "all-purpose" circular shape in the vertical direction is lower than the width of the image EC-zone in this direction.

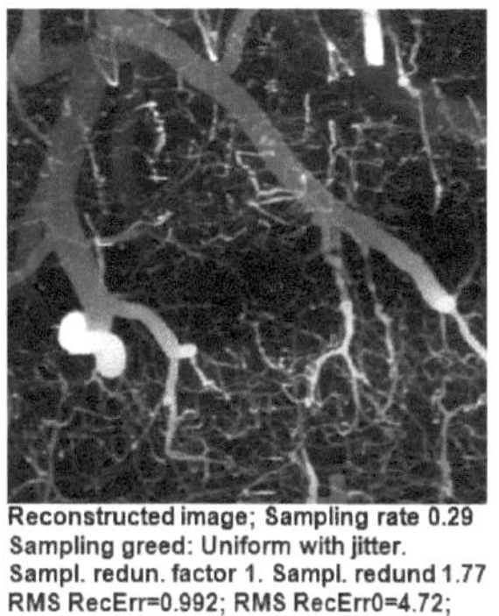

Reconstructed image; Sampling rate 0.29
Sampling greed: Uniform with jitter.
Sampl. redun. factor 1. Sampl. redund 1.77
RMS RecErr=0.992; RMS RecErr0=4.72;

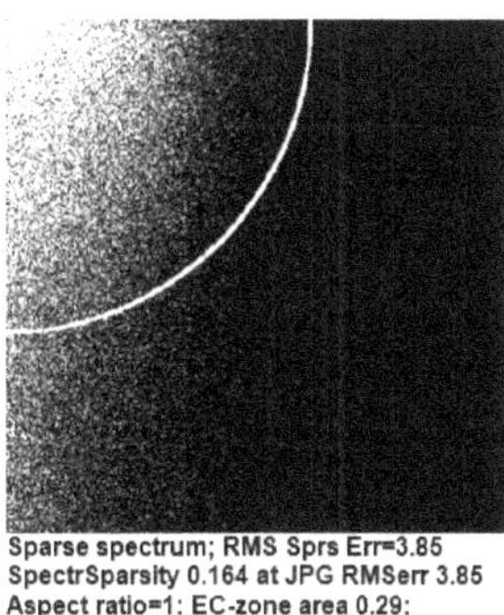

Sparse spectrum; RMS Sprs Err=3.85
SpectrSparsity 0.164 at JPG RMSerr 3.85
Aspect ratio=1; EC-zone area 0.29;
RMS BS Err 4.6

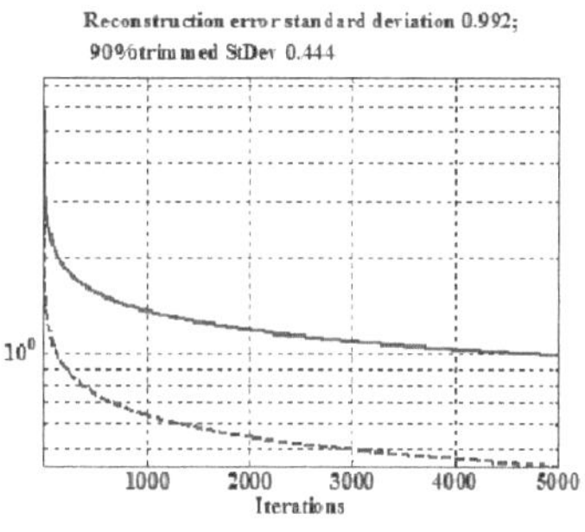

Fig. (6.10). Left image: an example of reconstruction of test image "BloodVessels512" using a pie-sector EC-zone approximating shape of the same area as that of the triangular shape (Fig. 6.5) that better fits the image spectrum EC zone. Middle image: image spectrum EC-zone (white dots) and the border of the EC-zone approximating shape (solid line). Right image: plot of RMS of the reconstruction errors (solid red line) and that of the smallest 90% of errors (dash blue line) *vs.* the number of iterations.

The Computational Complexity: The computational complexity of the iterative reconstruction algorithm per iteration step is determined by the complexity $O(2N\log N)$ of floating-point operations for the direct and inverse fast transforms plus $O(N)$ replacement operations of sample wise modifications of data in the image domain (M operations) and in its transform domain ($N - M$ operations). The order of magnitude of time required for one iteration can be estimated from these data: elapsed time for the MATLAB direct or inverse DCT of an array of $N = 512 \times 512$ numbers implemented on a PC "Lenovo ThinkPad X201" with processor Intel i7 and operating system Windows-7 is 52 msec.

6.4. OTHER POSSIBLE APPLICATIONS OF THE ASBSR METHOD OF IMAGE SAMPLING AND RECONSTRUCTION

As already mentioned, the above-discussed task of reconstruction of images of N samples from $M < N$ sampled data can be considered as a special case of the under-determined inverse imaging problems. One can expect that the found solution to this problem, the bounded spectrum (BS) image reconstruction, may find application for solving other under-determined inverse imaging problems as well. In what follows, this possibility is illustrated in five applications:

(i)   demosaicing color images;
(ii) image super-resolution from multiple chaotically sampled video frames;
(iii) image reconstruction from their sparsely sampled or decimated projections,
(iv) image reconstruction from their sparsely sampled Fourier spectra, and
(v) image reconstruction from the modulus of its Fourier spectrum.

6.4.1. Demosaicing Color Images

Individual cells of light-sensitive arrays of modern color photo cameras are split into three groups allocated for the corresponding Red, Green, and Blue components of color images. It is made through placing in front of the photo-sensitive cells arrays of red, green, and blue filters. Most frequently used is the Bayer's arrangement of the filters (Fig. **6.11a**). This arrangement will be called "Regular Bayer". There is also an alternative method illustrated in Fig. (**6.11b**). It assumes the regular Bayer arrangement of green pixels and pseudo-random arrangements of red and blue pixels. This arrangement will be called "Semi-random". In both arrangements, the density of green pixels is 0.5, and the densities of red and blue pixels are correspondingly 0.25 of the overall pixel density, *i.e.*, half of all cells of the sensor array are allocated for green pixels, one quarter is allocated for red and one quarter for blue pixels.

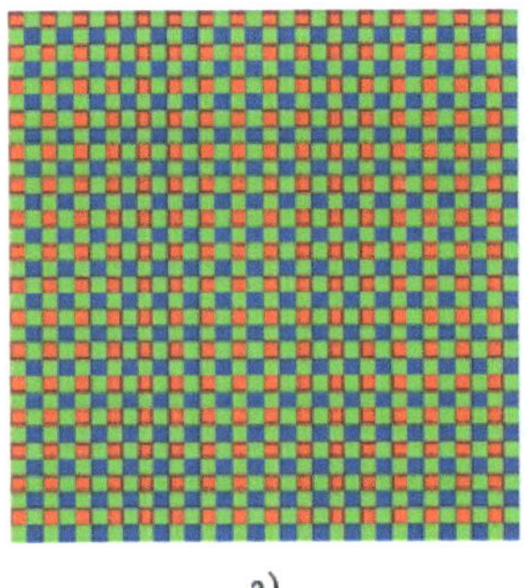

a)

b)

Fig. (6.11). Regular Bayer (**a**) and semi-random (**b**) arrangements of color separated pixels in photosensitive arrays of modern color cameras.

Images captured by color cameras are displayed in full resolution of the sensor, for which purpose half of pixels of the green image component and three-quarters of pixels of the red and blue image components should be reconstructed from their corresponding available pixels. This reconstruction of unavailable color-separated pixels is called *image demosaicing*. In practice, bilinear interpolation is ordinarily used as a demosaicing mechanism. This method of color image demosaicing will be called "Bilinear demosaicing".

Bilinear interpolation is one of the simplest 2D interpolation methods. Its performance is discussed in Chapter 7, where it is shown that bilinear interpolation is far from being perfect since it distorts images in their baseband and introduces spectrum aliasing errors. From the theory outlined in Chapters 2 through 4, it follows that, given the number of available pixels, optimal, in terms of the reconstruction RMSE, image reconstruction is Bounded Spectrum (BS) reconstruction, *i.e.*, reconstruction of images with spectra bounded by the chosen for them EC-zone approximating shapes. In application to image demosaicing, the most natural is using as the spectrum bounding shape the "All-purpose" shape "pie-sector" that allows implementing the image anti-aliasing pre-filtering before their sampling by camera optics and by apertures of the cells of the photosensitive arrays. This method of demosaicing will be called "BS-demosaicing".

Performance of the image BS-demosaicing in comparison with that of the Bilinear demosaicing is illustrated in Fig. (**6.12**) on a test image LightHouse512 for two cases: regular Bayer arrangement and Semi-random arrangement of pixels, correspondingly.

Images in the top row in Fig. (**6.12**) are (from left to right) the test color image of 512x512 pixels and EC-zones of spectra of the image red, green and blue components (white dots) that contain spectral coefficients, which reconstruct corresponding images with reconstruction RMSEs equal those of the JPEG image coding. Solid lines in the images of spectra indicate borders of EC-zone approximating the "pie sector" shapes used for image reconstruction by the BS-method. According to the rates of pixels in red, green, and blue image components, relative areas of the EC-zone approximating shapes are set to 0.25, 0.5, and 0.25, correspondingly. Images in the middle and bottom rows of the figure are bottom right 128x128 pixel fragments of the test and of the demosaiced images obtained by the BS- and Bilinear demosaicing methods for the regular Bayer (middle row) and semi-random (bottom row) color pixel arrangements. The fragments are magnified for better visibility of demosaicing distortions. One can easily see in these images that the Bilinear demosaicing produces much severe color distortions compared to those of the BS-demosaicing, for which the distortions are quite subtle.

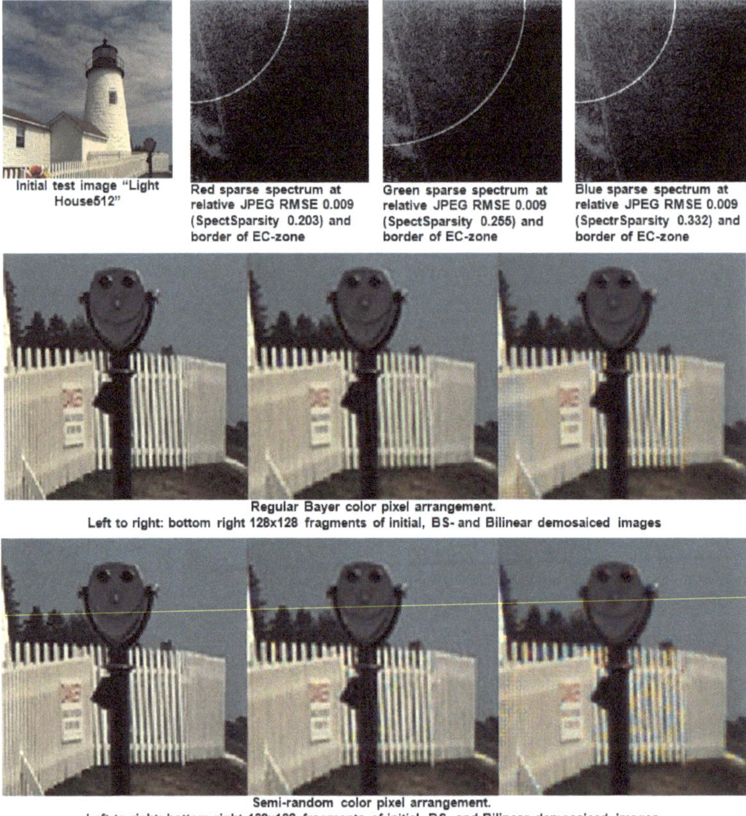

Fig. (6.12). Comparison of the BS-demosaicing and Bilinear demosaicing of a test color image with regular Bayer and semi-random pixel arrangements. Top row (left to right): the test image of 512x512 pixels and EC-zones of the spectra of its red, green, and blue components (white dots) along with borders of the corresponding chosen EC-zone approximating shapes (white solid line). Middle and bottom rows (left to right): 128x128 pixels bottom right fragments of the initial test image and of the BS- and Bilinear demosaiced images for the "Regular Bayer" and "Semi-random" color pixel arrangements, correspondingly.

Numerical data on the reconstruction RMSE for both demosaicing methods and the regular Bayes and Semi-random pixel arrangements are given in Table **6.2**. According to them, the BS-demosaicing outperforms the Bilinear Bayer demosaicing in terms of the reconstruction RMSE as well. In particular, the total reconstruction RMSE for the BS- and Bilinear methods are, correspondingly, 7.98 and 9.76 for the case of the "Regular Bayes" arrangement and 8.23 and 11.05 for "Semi-random" arrangement of color pixels. Relatively large values of image reconstruction errors can be attributed to the fact that, as one can see from the image spectra (first row in Fig. (**6.12**)), quite large portions of spectra of red, green and, especially, of blue components fall outside the EC-zone approximating shapes used for image reconstruction.

Table 6.2. RMS reconstruction errors for the Bilinear and BS-demosaicing.

"Regular Bayes" Color Pixel Arrangement			
BS-demosaicing, RMS of the reconstruction errors	Red compone nt 9.11	Green component 4.38	Blue component 9.43	Total average 7.98
Bilinear demosaicing RMS of the reconstruction errors	Red component 11	Green component 6.31	Blue component 11.2	Total average 9.76
"Semi-random" color pixel arrangement			
BS-demosaicing, RMS of the reconstruction errors	Red component 9.55	Green component 4.36	Blue component 9.64	Total average 8.23
Bilinear demosaicing RMS of the reconstruction errors	Red component 13	Green component 6.26	Blue component 12.6	Total average 11.05

6.4.2. Image Super-resolution from Multiple Chaotically Sampled Video Frames

In long-distance observation systems, images and videos are frequently damaged by atmospheric turbulence, which causes spatially and temporally chaotic fluctuations in the index of refraction of the atmosphere and results in chaotic spatial displacements of pixels from their regular positions in square sampling lattice. This causes substantial degradations of the quality of acquired images and videos. Fortunately, for still scenes, this damage can be converted into a profit because multiple chaotically sampled video frames of still scenes contain much more image samples in different sampling positions than do individual frames, which opens an opportunity for achieving image super-resolution with respect to the resolution of the video camera. Results of experiments reported in [12] that illustrate this opportunity are provided in what follows.

Through an *elastic registration* of neighborhoods of pixels in a sequence of frames of the same scene, one can determine, for each image frame and with sub-pixel accuracy, pixel displacements caused by the random acquisition factors. Elastic registration is measuring, with sub-pixel accuracy, positions of small neighborhoods of every pixel in a reference frame that can be formed by one or another method of averaging of available video frames. Using the results of these measurements, a synthetic fused image can be generated by placing pixels from all available video frames in their proper positions on the correspondingly denser sampling grid according to their found displacements. In this process, some pixel positions on the denser sampling grid will remain unoccupied, especially when a limited number of image frames are fused. These missing pixels can then be reconstructed using the above-described iterative bounded spectrum image reconstruction algorithm.

In the implementation of the algorithm, the denser sampling grid of the fused image is formed accordingly to the sub-pixel accuracy, with which pixels' positions are measured in the sequence of the turbulent frames. The bandwidth limitation of the super-resolved image depends on the scatter of image samples acquired in the process of fusion and on the number of frames used for fusion. In the experiment, the final size of the fused-image sampling lattice was set to be twice that of the original frames. The results of the experiment are represented by the images in Fig. (**6.13**): one of the low-resolution turbulent frames (a), image fused from 50 frames (b), and the result of the iterative reconstruction achieved after 50 iterations (c). These images demonstrate the substantial improvement of image resolution and quality. Some technical details concerning the implementation of the described super-resolution reconstruction algorithm as well as the results of experiments with real-life turbulent video can be found in Ref. [12].

6.4.3. Image Reconstruction from their Sparsely Sampled or Decimated Projections

In computed tomography, it quite frequently happens that body slice occupies only a fraction of the area of the entire acquired image. This means that slice projections are Radon transform "bounded spectrum" functions. Therefore, whatever number of projections or their samples is available, a certain number of additional projections or samples, commensurable, according to the discrete sampling theorem, with the size of the slice empty zone, can be obtained and the corresponding resolution increase in the reconstructed images can be achieved using the method of image BS-reconstruction. This option is illustrated in Figs. (**6.14** and **15**).

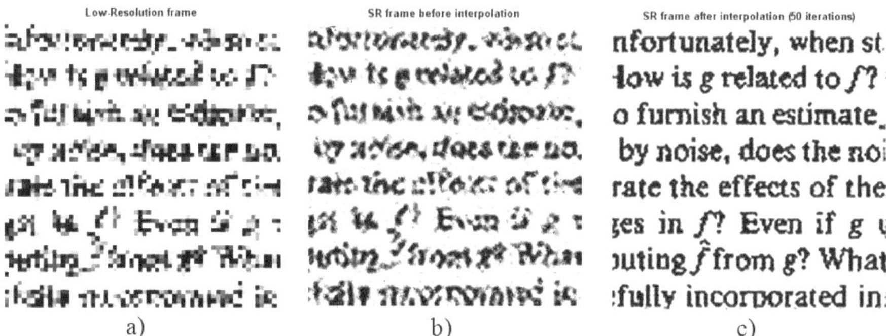

Fig. (6.13). Image reconstruction with super-resolution from multiple chaotically sampled frames: one of the low-resolution frames (**a**); image fused by the elastic image registration from 50 frames (**b**); a result of the image iterative reconstruction with enhanced resolution (**c**), obtained from after 50 iterations.

Fig. (**6.14**) presents results of a simulation experiment on the recovery of missing samples of an image slice projections sampled at random positions. For a test image (Fig. **6.14a**), it was found using its simple segmentation that the outer 55% of its area is empty. Then the same percentage of projection samples selected randomly using the MATLAB random number generator were zeroed (Fig. **6.14c**). The rest of the samples were used for recovering the zeroed samples and, correspondingly, for image reconstruction using the iterative reconstruction algorithm identical to the above-described image BS-reconstruction algorithm except that the direct and inverse Discrete Cosine Transforms were replaced by the direct and inverse discrete Radon Transforms.

At each iteration of the algorithm, the current set of projections is subjected to the inverse Radon transform for obtaining a current estimate of the reconstructed image. Then the outer empty area of the reconstructed image is zeroed and the modified in this way image is subjected to the direct Radon transform for obtaining the next estimate of slice projections. In the obtained projections, their available samples are restored and the process repeats. The plot of RMS of slice projections reconstruction error *vs.* the iteration number in Fig. (**6.14f**), and the result of recovering missing samples of the projection (Fig. **6.14e**) demonstrate that virtually perfect recovery of the missing 55% samples of slice projections is achieved with the iterative reconstruction algorithm after a few hundreds of iterations.

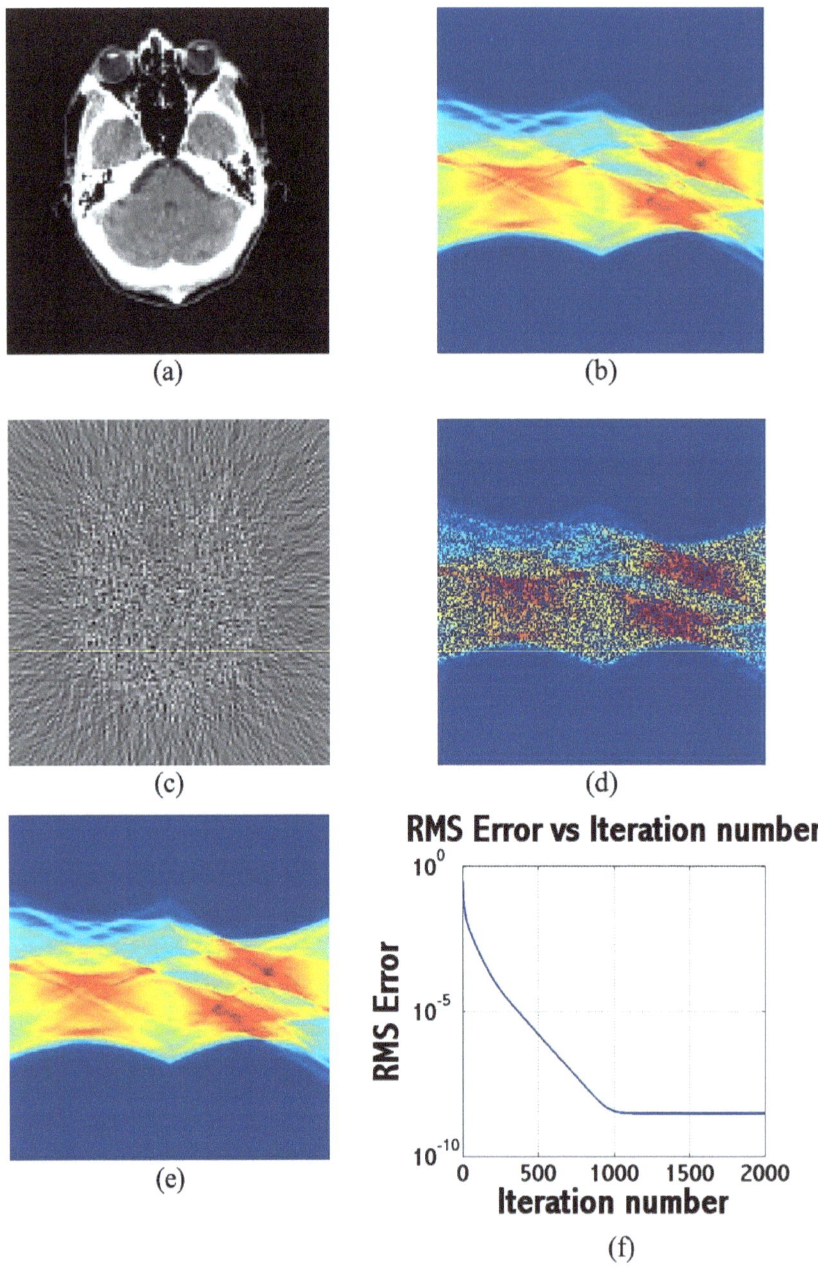

Fig. (6.14). Recovery of a randomly sampled slice projections: a test image (**a**); its slice projections displayed for better visibility in pseudo-colors using the MATLAB© color map "jet" (**b**); a result of the reconstruction of the test image (**c**) from slice projections randomly sub-sampled with the rate 0.45 (**d**); slice projections recovered by the iterative algorithm (**e**). and a plot of the slice projections reconstruction RMSE *vs.* the iteration number (**f**).

Fig. (**6.15**) demonstrates that the recovery of completely missing projections is also possible. In the experiment it represents, every second projection of the test image (Fig. **6.15a**) was removed (Fig. **6.15b**) and then all initial projections were recovered (Fig. **6.15c**) by the above described iterative algorithm that makes use of the fact that the outer 55% part of the image area is known to be empty. This result implies that for such cases when a part of the image area is known to be empty, one can use the BS image reconstruction method to achieve image reconstruction with a correspondingly larger number of image projections than are available.

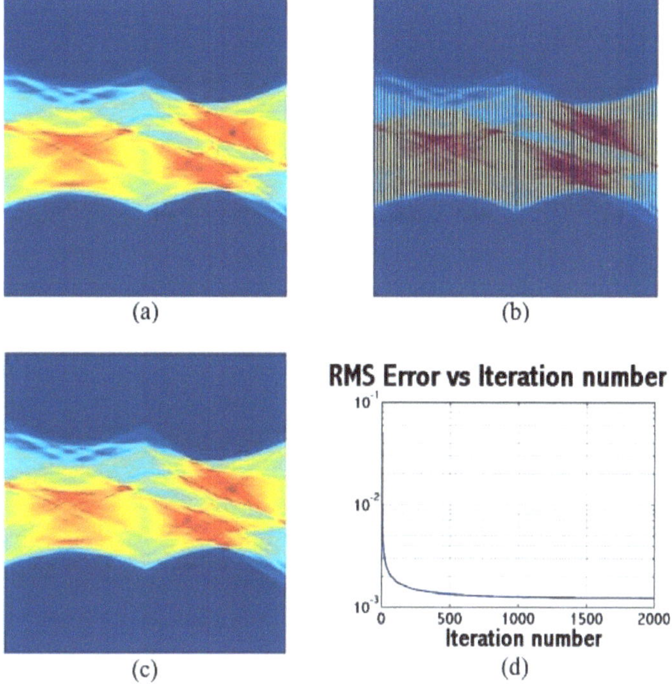

Fig. (6.15). Recovery of missing image projections: original projections of the test image (Fig. **6.14a**) (**a**); decimated projections with every second projection removed (**b**); slice projections recovered from the decimated slice projections using the iterative reconstruction algorithm (**c**); a plot of the reconstruction RMSE *vs*. the number of iterations.

6.4.4. Image Reconstruction from their Sparsely Sampled Fourier Spectra

There exist some imaging devices (*e.g.* some healthcare scanners), where sampling is done in a transform domain. The described ASBSR image reconstruction method can be used in such devices in the above-mentioned frequent cases when it is known that the object image is surrounded by some empty space. Fig. (**6.16**) obtained using the program SparseSampl_Recon_DFTspectrum_BNTM.m provided in the

Exercises illustrates this option as an example of image reconstruction from its sparsely sampled Fourier spectrum.

In this example, the Fourier spectrum of the test image bounded by a circular binary image mask was randomly sampled with a sampling rate equal to the ratio of the image bounding circular area to the area of the entire image frame. Additionally, the spectrum was bounded by a circular binary spectral mask with a radius equal to the highest spatial frequency of the baseband. This gives an additional $1-\pi/4$ reduction in the number of spectrum samples.

For image reconstruction, the iterative algorithm was used in the experiment. At each iteration, the iterated spectrum is inverse Fourier transformed for obtaining an iterated reconstructed image and then the latter is multiplied by the bounding circular image mask, which empties its outer space, and Fourier transformed. Samples of the obtained spectrum at positions of the available original ones are replaced by them, and the spectrum is bounded by a circular binary spectral mask to form an iterated spectrum for the next iteration. As a spectrum zero-order approximation, from which the iterative reconstruction starts, the initial sparsely sampled and bounded spectrum was used.

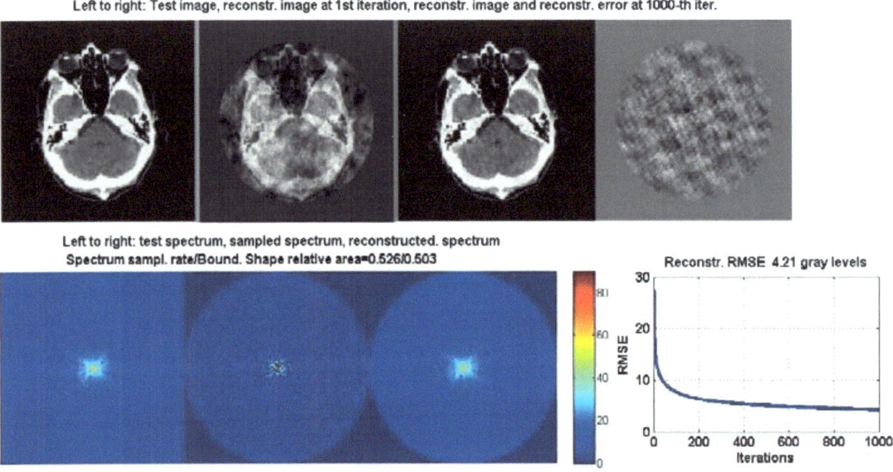

Fig. (6.16). Image reconstruction from its sparsely sampled spectrum. Upper row (left to right): a test image bounded by a binary circular mask with a radius equal to 0.4 of the image size; reconstructed image at the first iteration, in which the circular bounding mask can be seen; reconstructed image at 1000-th iteration; the pattern of the reconstruction errors after 1000 iterations. Bottom row (from left to right): Fourier spectrum of the test image, its spectrum randomly sampled with sampling rate $\pi \times 0.4^2 \times \pi/4 = 0.398$, and reconstructed spectrum (for display purposes, absolute values of spectral samples are raised to a power 0.3 and are displayed color-coded with MATLAB$^{\copyright}$ color map "jet"); the plot of the reconstruction RMSE *vs.* the number of iterations.

6.4.5. Image Reconstruction from the Modulus of its Fourier Spectrum

Modulus of image Fourier spectrum lacks the phase component of the spectrum. It bears only half of the spectral information, in fact, the less important half, and therefore is not sufficient for reconstructing the image. To enable image reconstruction from the modulus of its Fourier spectrum one should supplement the spectrum modulus with sufficient a priori information. The ideology of the ASBSR method of image sampling and reconstruction suggests the following way to solving this problem through a two-stage procedure.

At the first stage, the imaging one, the object should be imaged through a randomized binary (opaque-transparent) mask that produces occlusions in the object image. The fraction of the transparent area of the mask should be equal or larger than the required by the ASBSR-method sampling rate, *i.e.*, than the fraction of the area occupied in the spectrum baseband by the chosen for this image EC-zone approximating the shape of the image spectrum. Measured is the modulus of the Fourier spectrum of the object occluded by the mask. The occluded image and estimates of the phase component of its Fourier spectrum can then be reconstructed from the modulus of its Fourier spectrum using the iterative reconstruction algorithm. At each iteration, a current spectrum phase component estimate is combined with the measured modulus of the spectrum to form an estimate of the complete spectrum, which is inverse Fourier transformed to obtain a current estimate of the reconstructed image with occlusions. Then this image is multiplied by the binary occlusion mask, which restores the occlusions, and Fourier transformed. The phase component of the obtained spectrum is used as the next estimate of the image spectrum phase component, and iterations are repeated. As a zero-order estimate of the image spectrum phase component, the phase component of the Fourier spectrum of the binary occlusion mask can be used.

At the second stage of image reconstruction, the reconstructed image with occlusions is used for reconstruction of the entire image using one or another method of image in-painting, *i.e.*, of filling-in occlusions in images. An illustrative example of image reconstruction from the module of its Fourier spectrum is presented in Fig. (**6.17**) obtained using the program ReconstrModuleSpectrum_BNTM.m provided in the Exercises. In this example, a simple filtering algorithm was used for in-painting missing pixels, in which pixels marked as occluded were replaced by a weighted sum of their three the closest non occluded pixels taken with weights inversely proportional to their distances from the pixel to be corrected. In principle, for this purpose the ASBSR-method iterative algorithm can be utilized as well, however, the experimental experience tells that for occlusions that occupy several pixels the iterative algorithm stagnates and provides worse results than even the above-described simple filtering method.

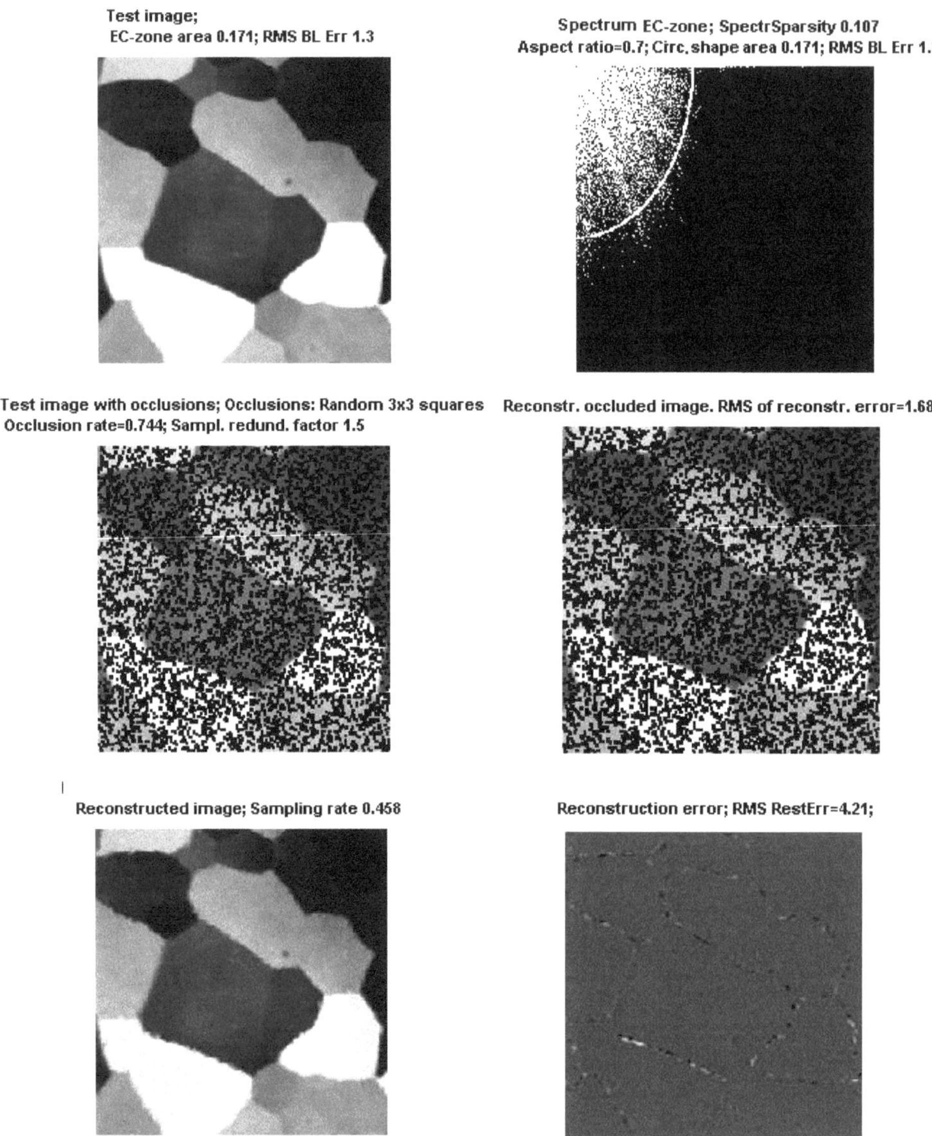

Fig. (6.17). Image BS-reconstruction from the modulus of its Fourier spectrum: a test image (upper left); image spectrum EC-zone (upper right, white dots) and the border of its approximating shape (white line); the test image occluded by randomly placed 3x3 pixel opaque squares (middle left); an occluded image BS-reconstructed from the modulus of its Fourier spectrum (middle right); image reconstructed by inpainting from the reconstructed occluded image (bottom left); the pattern of the reconstruction errors (bottom right).

6.5. EXERCISES

- **ArbitrSamplingAndBSReconstr_BNTM.m**;

Simulation on a discrete model of the ASBSR-method of image sampling and reconstruction.

Implemented is DCT bounded spectrum iterative reconstruction of images sampled with sampling Rate (SR) equal to the area (in a fraction of the sampling baseband in DCT domain) of user-defined spectrum bounding shape times user-defined sampling redundancy factor Rednd (slightly larger than one). The latter is recommended for accelerating iteration convergence.

The number of iterations is a user-defined parameter

Four types of spectrum bounding shapes can be chosen:

- Rectangular;
- Triangle;
- Oval;
- Super ellipse

Three types of sampling lattices can be used:

- "uniform": positions of image samples are rounded off to positions of the regular square sampling lattice that corresponds to the chosen numbers of samples NofSamplX, NofSamplY (square root of the product of image display size SzXxSzY and sampling rate)
- "uniform with random jitter": X and Y coordinates of image samples are randomly distributed between nodes of the square sampling lattice of NofSamplXxNofSamplY pixels
- "totally random": positions of image samples are randomly distributed over nodes of the image display sampling lattice.

Zero-order approximation of the reconstructed image, from which the iterative reconstruction starts, is obtained using replacing not available image pixels by a weighted sum of available samples over Nint available pixels, which are nearest to the sample being interpolated within a window of a pre-defined size Lxy, with interpolation weights that are inversely proportional to the distance of each nearest available sample from the position of the pixel to be interpolated (subprogram Interpolation_RandomGrid_BNTM.m);

Displayed are:

- test image;
- sampled test image;
- reconstructed image;
- test image EC-zone and the border of the chosen image spectrum bounding shape;
- plot of RMS of the reconstruction error *vs.* the number of iterations;
- pattern of the reconstruction error (the difference between test and reconstructed images).

Reconstructed image, reconstruction errors, and plots of RMS reconstruction error are displayed at each of the first 100 iterations and then at each hundredth iterations. Non-square images are cropped to a square shape.

- **SparseSampl_Recon_DFTspectrum_BNTM.m**

Image reconstruction from its sparsely sampled DFT spectrum.

The image is supposed to be bounded by a circle with a user-defined radius.

Image DFT spectrum is sampled at random positions with sampling rate equal to the relative area of the image bounding circle times a user-defined sampling redundancy coefficient. Slight redundancy (5-10%) is useful for the acceleration of the algorithm convergence.

- **ReconstrModuleSpectrum_BNTM.m**

The program is intended for illustration of the possibility of recovering images from the modulus of its Fourier spectrum. Implemented is DCT bounded spectrum reconstruction of images sampled with Sampling Rate (SR) equal to the fraction of spectrum area in DCT domain that limits image spectrum (in a fraction of image area).

Spectrum bounding shapes (rectangular, triangular, pie sector, oriented oval, or superellipse) are user-defined.

The number of image samples equals the number of samples of a regular sampling lattice used for image display times Sampling Rate and times Sampling redundancy factor. The latter is needed for accelerating the iteration convergence.

The reconstruction algorithm is iterative with applying, at each iteration step, the chosen bounding to the iterated DCT spectrum in the spectral domain and replacement of samples obtained after inverse DCT of the bounded iterated spectrum by the corresponding available image samples.

The number of iterations is a user-defined parameter

For acceleration of iteration convergence, restored image is subjected to non-linear filtering for the elimination of outliers in course of the first 50 iteration steps.

Reconstructed image and reconstruction errors are displayed at each of the first 100 iterations and then at each hundredth iteration.

Non-square images are cropped to have a square shape.

Part II

IMAGE RESAMPLING

CHAPTER 7

Image Resampling: Preliminaries and Problem Formulation

7.1. IMAGE RESAMPLING AS A DIGITAL FILTERING PROBLEM

Precise and fast image resampling is a key operation in many digital image processing applications, such as multi-modality data fusion, image reconstruction from projections, image super-resolution from video sequences, stabilization of video images distorted by atmosphere turbulence, target location and tracking with sub-pixel accuracy, *etc*.

Image resampling assumes building an approximation to the original analog (non-sampled) image, *i.e.*, building an analog image digital model that is subsequently resampled according to a required new sampling lattice. For solving this problem, one can consider the image coordinate shift as a general resampling operation. This is justified by the fact that samples of the resampled image for any arbitrary resampling lattice can be obtained one by one through the corresponding shifts of the analog image digital model to the given sample positions. The required image shifts can be achieved by interpolation of available image samples to obtain samples "in-between" the available ones.

The most feasible and amenable to optimization is image interpolation through digital convolution. For samples $\left\{ a_{k,l}; k = 0,1,..., N_x - 1; l = 0,1,..., N_y - 1 \right\}$ of an image to be shifted by $\left(\delta_x, \delta_y \right)$-th fractions of sampling intervals in x and y coordinates and resampled, the resampling digital convolution is defined as

$$\widetilde{a}_{k,l} = \sum_{m=0}^{N_x^{(h)}-1} \sum_{n=0}^{N_y^{(h)}-1} h_{m,n}^{\left(\delta_x,\delta_y\right)} a_{k-m,l-n}, \tag{7.1}$$

where $\left\{ \widetilde{a}_{k,l} \right\}$ are samples of the shifted and resampled image and $\left\{ h_{m,n}^{\left(\delta_x,\delta_y\right)} \right\}$ are $\left(N_x^{(h)} \times N_y^{(h)} \right)$ interpolation coefficients, *i.e.*, point spread function (PSF) of the shifting and resampling filter $\left(N_x^{(h)} \leq N_x; N_y^{(h)} \leq N_y \right)$.

Although digital filters operate with sampled images, they should be appropriately characterized in terms of corresponding to them analog filters that act on original analog (not sampled) images. To this goal, the concept of an analog filter equivalent to a given digital filter is introduced (Fig. **7.1**). Analog filter equivalent to a given digital filter is a filter, which, being applied to an analog (non-sampled) image produces the same image as the image reconstructed from samples generated by the digital filter from samples of the sampled image.

The design of the required shifting and resampling digital filters assumes introducing and defining the concepts of point spread functions and frequency responses of digital and their equivalent analog filters and determination on this

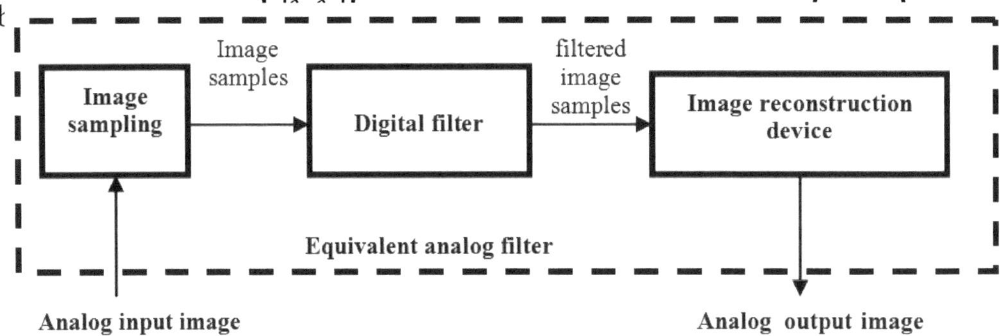

Fig. (7.1). The concept of an analog filter equivalent to a given digital filter.

7.2. POINT SPREAD FUNCTIONS AND FREQUENCY RESPONSES OF DIGITAL FILTERS AND THEIR EQUIVALENT ANALOG FILTERS

For the sake of simplicity, first consider filters. Let $\{a_k\}$ and $\{b_k\}$, $k = 0,1,..., N-1$ be samples of input and output signals of a digital filter defined as

$$b_k = \sum_{n=0}^{N^{(h)}-1} h_n a_{k-n}; \quad N^h \le N . \tag{7.2}$$

The set of N coefficients $\{h_n\}$, is called the *Digital Filter Discrete Point Spread Function* (DFDPSF). Let's establish a link between DFDPSF and PSF of its equivalent analog filter. Analog signal $b(x)$ reconstructed from a finite number N of output samples $\{b_k\}$ of a digital filter is defined as

$$b(x) = \sum_{k=0}^{N-1} b_k PSF^{(r)}(x - k\Delta_x) = \sum_{k=0}^{N-1}\left(\sum_{n=0}^{N-1} h_n a_{k-n}\right) PSF^{(r)}(x - k\Delta_x), \tag{7.3}$$

where $PSF^{(r)}(x)$ is the point spread function of the signal reconstruction filter and Δ_x is the signal sampling interval.

Consider samples $\{a_k\}$ as samples of an analog signal $a(x)$

$$a_k = \int_{-\infty}^{\infty} a(x) PSF^{(s)}\left[\left(k + u^{(s)}\right)\Delta_x - x\right]dx, \qquad (7.4)$$

where $PSF^{(s)}(.)$ is point spread function of the signal sampling device.

Eq. (7.4) is a 1D analog of Eq. (3.1). It contains an additional shift parameter $u^{(s)}$, which implies that the sampling lattice of signal $a(x)$ can be, generally, shifted with respect to the origin of the signal coordinates by an arbitrary fraction $u^{(s)}$ of the sampling interval Δ_x.

Insert now expression of Eq. (7.4) for samples $\{a_{k-n}\}$ of the input analog signal $a(x)$ into Eq. (7.3) and obtain:

$$b(x) = \sum_{k=0}^{N-1}\left(\sum_{n=0}^{N-1} h_n \int_{-\infty}^{\infty} a(\xi) PSF^{(s)}\left[\left(k - n + u^{(s)}\right)\Delta_x - \xi\right]d\xi\right) PSF^{(r)}(x - k\Delta_x) =$$

$$\int_{-\infty}^{\infty} a(x)dx \sum_{k=0}^{N-1}\sum_{n=0}^{N_h-1} h_n PSF^{(s)}\left[\left(k - n + u^{(s)}\right)\Delta_x - \xi\right] PSF^{(r)}(x - k\Delta_x). \qquad (7.5)$$

The double sum in this equation

$$h_{eq}(x,\xi) = \sum_{k=0}^{N-1}\sum_{n=0}^{N_h-1} h_n PSF^{(s)}\left[\left(k - n + u^{(s)}\right)\Delta_x - \xi\right] PSF^{(r)}(x - k\Delta_x) \qquad (7.6)$$

can be considered as a point spread function of an analog filter equivalent to a given digital filter:

$$b(x) = \int_{-\infty}^{\infty} a(\xi) h_{eq}(x,\xi)d\xi \qquad (7.7)$$

Characterization of digital filters in terms of their point spread functions is complemented by their characterization in terms of filter frequency responses. In order to derive them, consider Fourier spectrum of the filter output signal $b(x)$ defined by Eq. (7. 7):

$$\beta(f) = \int_{-\infty}^{\infty} b(x)\exp(i2\pi fx)dx = \int_{-\infty}^{\infty}\left[\int_{-\infty}^{\infty} a(\xi)h_{eq}(x,\xi)d\xi\right]\exp(i2\pi fx)dx =$$

$$\int_{-\infty}^{\infty}\int_{-\infty}^{\infty}\left[\int_{-\infty}^{\infty}[\alpha(p)\exp(-i2\pi p\xi)dp]h_{eq}(x,\xi)d\xi\right]\exp(i2\pi fx)dx$$

$$\int_{-\infty}^{\infty}\alpha(p)dp\int_{-\infty}^{\infty}\int_{-\infty}^{\infty}h_{eq}(x,\xi)d\xi\exp[i2\pi(fx-p\xi)]dx = \int_{-\infty}^{\infty}\alpha(p)H_{eq}(f,p)dp, \qquad (7.8)$$

Function

$$H_{eq}(f,p) = \int_{-\infty}^{\infty}\int_{-\infty}^{\infty} h_{eq}(x,\xi)\exp[i2\pi(fx-p\xi)]dxd\xi \qquad (7.9)$$

can be regarded as a frequency response of a general filter defined by Eq. (7. 7). Now frequency response of an analog filter equivalent to a given digital filter can be expressed through the filter discrete point spread function $\{h_n\}$, for which Eq. (7. 6) for $h_{eq}(x,\xi)$ is inserted into Eq. (7. 9):

$$H(f,p) = \int_{-\infty}^{\infty}\int_{-\infty}^{\infty}\left\{\sum_{k=0}^{N-1}\sum_{n=0}^{N_h-1} h_n PSF^{(s)}\left[\left(k-n+u^{(s)}\right)\Delta_x - \xi\right]PSF^{(r)}(x-k\Delta_x)\right\}\times$$

$$\exp[i2\pi(fx-p\xi)]dxd\xi =$$

$$\sum_{k=0}^{N-1}\sum_{n=0}^{N_h-1} h_n \int_{-\infty}^{\infty}\int_{-\infty}^{\infty} PSF^{(s)}(\xi)PSF^{(r)}(x)\exp\left\{i2\pi\left[f(x+k\Delta_x)+p\xi-\left(k-n+u^{(s)}\right)p\Delta_x\right]\right\}dxd\xi =$$

$$\sum_{k=0}^{N}\sum_{n=0}^{N_h-1} h_n \int_{-\infty}^{\infty} PSF^{(s)}(\xi)\exp(i2\pi p\xi)d\xi \int_{-\infty}^{\infty} PSF^{(r)}(x)\exp(i2\pi fx)dx\times$$

$$\exp\left\{i2\pi\left[(f-p)k\Delta_x + p\left(n-u^{(s)}\right)\Delta_x\right]\right\} =$$

$$\left[\int_{-\infty}^{\infty} PSF^{(r)}(x)\exp(i2\pi fx)dx\right]\times\left[\int_{-\infty}^{\infty} PSF^{(s)}(\xi)\exp(i2\pi p\xi)d\xi\right]\times$$

$$\left[\sum_{n=0}^{N_h-1} h_n \exp\left(i2\pi p\left(n-u^{(s)}\right)\Delta_x\right)\right]\times\left[\sum_{k=0}^{N-1}\exp[i2\pi(f-p)k\Delta_x]\right]$$

$$(7.10)$$

The first two multiplicands in the right part of Eq. (7. 10) are frequency responses of the signal reconstruction and sampling devices:

$$FR^{(r)}(f)=\int_{-\infty}^{\infty}PSF^{(r)}(x)\exp(i2\pi fx)dx \tag{7.11}$$

$$FR^{(s)}(p)=\int_{-\infty}^{\infty}PSF^{(r)}(\xi)\exp(i2\pi p\xi)d\xi \tag{7.12}$$

The third multiplicand

$$DFCFR(p)=\sum_{n=0}^{N_h-1}h_n\exp\left[i2\pi p\left(n-u^{(s)}\right)\Delta_x\right], \tag{7.13}$$

that depends solely on digital filter PSF $\{h_n\}$ can be treated as *Digital Filter Continuous Frequency Response* (DFCFR).

The fourth multiplicand

$$DFSVM_N(f-p)=\sum_{k=0}^{N-1}\exp\left[i2\pi(f-p)k\Delta_x\right] \tag{7.14}$$

is defined only by the number of digital filter output samples involved in the reconstruction of its analog output (Eq. (7. 3). It can be regarded as a Digital Filter Space Variance Measure (DFSVM) since it reflects the fact that analog equivalents of digital filters are according to Eq. (7. 7) space-variant.

The function $DFSVM_N(f-p)$ can be computed in a closed-form as

$$\begin{aligned}DFSVM_N(f-p)&=\sum_{k=0}^{N}\exp\left[i2\pi(f-p)k\Delta_x\right]=\frac{\exp\left[i2\pi(f-p)N\Delta_x\right]-1}{\exp\left[i2\pi(f-p)\Delta_x\right]-1}=\\&\frac{\exp\left[i\pi(f-p)N\Delta_x\right]-\exp\left[-i\pi(f-p)N\Delta_x\right]}{\exp\left[i\pi(f-p)\Delta_x\right]-\exp\left[-i\pi(f-p)\Delta_x\right]}\exp\left[i\pi(f-p)(N-1)\Delta_x\right]=\\&\frac{\sin\left[\pi(f-p)N\Delta_x\right]}{\sin\left[\pi(f-p)\Delta_x\right]}\exp\left[i\pi(f-p)(N-1)\Delta_x\right]=\\&N\,\text{sincd}\left[N;\pi(f-p)N\Delta_x\right]\exp\left[i\pi(f-p)(N-1)\Delta_x\right],\end{aligned} \tag{7.15}$$

where

$$\mathrm{sincd}(N;x) = \frac{\sin(x)}{N\sin(x/N)} \qquad (7.16)$$

is called the *discrete sinc-function*.

The second multiplicand $\exp[i\pi(f-p)(N-1)\Delta_x]$ in the right part of Eq. (7. 16) is only a phase-shift function that is defined solely by the order, in which signal samples $\{b_k\}$ are counted. It carries no important information and can be disregarded, and the *Digital Filter Shift Variance Measure* is defined as:

$$DFSVM(f-p) = N\,\mathrm{sincd}[\pi(f-p)N\Delta_x] \qquad (7.17)$$

Finally obtain that frequency response of an analog filter equivalent to a digital filter defined by its discrete point spread function $\{h_n\}$ is

$$DFOFR_N(f,p) = FR^{(r)}(f)FR^{(s)}(p)DFCFR(p)N\,\mathrm{sincd}[N;\pi(f-p)N\Delta_x] \qquad (7.18)$$

This function links the Fourier spectra of filter input and output analog signals and can, therefore, be called *Digital Filter Overall Frequency Response*.

When N tends to infinity, the function $\mathrm{sincd}[N;\pi(f-p)N\Delta_x]$ converts to the sinc-function $\mathrm{sinc}[\pi(f-p)N\Delta_x]$, which, in its turn, tends to the delta-function

$$\lim_{N\to\infty} N\,\mathrm{sincd}[N;\pi(f-p)N\Delta_x] = \delta(f-p). \qquad (7.19)$$

Therefore, in the limit, when the number of signal samples involved in its analog reconstruction tends to infinity, digital filter overall frequency response converts to

$$\lim_{N\to\infty}\{OFRDF_N(f,p)\} = FR^{(r)}(f)FR^{(s)}(p)CFRDF^{(h)}(p)\delta(f-p), \qquad (7.20)$$

and Eq. (7. 8) converts to

$$\beta(f) = \int_{-\infty}^{\infty} \alpha(p)OFRDF(f,p)dp = \int_{-\infty}^{\infty} \alpha(p)FR^{(r)}(f)FR^{(s)}(p)CFRDF^{(h)}(p)\delta(f-p)dp =$$

$$FR^{(r)}(f)FR^{(s)}(f)DFCFR(f)\alpha(f), \qquad (7.21)$$

which is the expression that, according to the convolution theorem for Fourier transform, links spectra $\alpha(f)$ and $\beta(f)$ of input and output of shift-invariant analog filters. Therefore, for the sufficiently large number N of signal samples an analog filter equivalent to a given digital filter can be considered as shift-invariant. Shift invariant approximation to digital filter overall frequency response

$$DFOFR_{SpInv}(f) = FR^{(r)}(f)FR^{(s)}(f)DFCFR(f) \tag{7.22}$$

has a clear physical interpretation: it equals a product of frequency responses of all stages of digital filtering analog signals. In particular, it implies that through an appropriate design of digital filters (term $DFCFR(f)$) one can compensate signal distortions in its sampling baseband caused by sampling and reconstruction devices (terms $FR^{(r)}(f)$ and $FR^{(s)}(f)$).

Note also that continuous frequency response of a digital filter $DFCFR(f)$ is, according to Eq. (7. 13), a periodic function with a period $1/\Delta_x$. Periodical replicas of this function outside the signal sampling baseband affect periodical replicas of the signal spectrum, which, ideally, are supposed to be cut off by frequency responses of signal sampling and reconstruction devices. Otherwise, they contribute to signal sampling distortions.

The extension of the above relationships for 1D signals to 2D signals is straightforward. In particular, 2D digital filter is defined as

$$b_{k,l} = \sum_{n=0}^{N_h-1}\sum_{m=0}^{M_h-1} h_{m,n} a_{k-m,l-n} , \tag{7.23}$$

where $\{h_{n,m}\}$ is the filter discrete point spread function. The overall frequency response of 2D digital filter is

$$DFOFR_{N_x,N_y}(f_x,p_x;f_y,p_y) = FR^{(r)}(f_x,f_y)FR^{(s)}(-p_x,-p_y)DFCFR(p_x,p_y) \times$$
$$N_x N_y \, \text{sincd}[\pi(f_x - p_y)N_x\Delta_x]\text{sincd}[\pi(f_y - p_y)N_y\Delta_y], \tag{7.24}$$

where $FR^{(s)}(p_x,p_y)$ and $FR^{(r)}(f_x,f_y)$ are frequency responses of signal sampling and reconstruction devices, (f_x,f_y) and (p_x,p_y) are spatial frequencies,

$$\text{and } DFCFR(p) = \sum_{n=0}^{N_h-1}\sum_{m=0}^{M_h-1} h_{m,n}\exp\left[i2\pi\left(p_x m\Delta_x + p_y y\Delta_y\right)\right] \qquad (7.25)$$

is continuous frequency response of a 2D digital filter with a discrete point spread function $\{h_{m,n}\}$.

The continuous frequency response of digital filter (Eq. (7.13)) can be expressed through discrete Fourier transform coefficients of its discrete PSF. Consider continuous frequency response of a digital filter defined by its discrete point spread function $\{h_n\}$ (Eq. (7.13)):

$$DFCFR(f) = \sum_{n=0}^{N-1} h_n \exp\left[i2\pi f\Delta_x\left(n - u^{(s)}\right)\right], \qquad (7.26)$$

and introduce a spectrum sampling interval Δ_f in the frequency domain as

$$\Delta_f = 1/N\Delta_x . \qquad (7.27)$$

so that

$$DFCFR(f) = \sum_{n=0}^{N-1} h_n \exp\left(i2\pi \frac{f}{\Delta_f}\frac{n - u^{(s)}}{N}\right) . \qquad (7.28)$$

Let $\{\eta_r^{(u)}\}$ be a set of coefficients of a u-Shifted DFT of the filter DPSF $\{h_n\}$ such that:

$$\eta_r^{(u)} = \frac{1}{\sqrt{N}}\sum_{n=0}^{N-1} h_n \exp\left(i2\pi \frac{n+u}{N}r\right), \qquad (7.29)$$

$$h_n = \frac{1}{\sqrt{N}}\sum_{r=0}^{N-1} \eta_r^{(u)} \exp\left(-i2\pi \frac{n+u}{N}r\right). \qquad (7.30)$$

The set of coefficients $\{\eta_r^{(u)}\}$ can be called the *Digital Filter Discrete Frequency Response* (DFDFR). Substitute now Eq.   (7.30) into Eq. (7.28) and obtain:

$$DFCFR(f) = \frac{1}{\sqrt{N}} \sum_{n=0}^{N-1} \left\{ \sum_{r=0}^{N-1} \eta_r^{(u)} \exp\left(-i2\pi \frac{n+u}{N} r \right) \right\} \exp\left(i2\pi \frac{f}{\Delta_f} \frac{n-u^{(s)}}{N} \right) =$$

$$\frac{1}{\sqrt{N}} \sum_{r=0}^{N-1} \eta_r^{(u)} \exp\left[-i2\pi \left(\frac{f}{\Delta_f} \frac{u^{(s)}}{N} + \frac{ur}{N} \right) \right] \left\{ \sum_{n=0}^{N-1} \exp\left[i2\pi \left(\frac{f}{\Delta_f} - r \right) \frac{n}{N} \right] \right\} =$$

$$\frac{1}{\sqrt{N}} \sum_{r=0}^{N-1} \eta_r^{(u)} \exp\left[-i2\pi \left(\frac{f}{\Delta_f} \frac{u^{(s)}}{N} + \frac{ur}{N} \right) \right] \frac{\exp\left[i2\pi \left(f/\Delta_f - r \right) \right] - 1}{\exp\left(i2\pi \frac{f/\Delta_f - r}{N} \right) - 1} =$$

$$\frac{1}{\sqrt{N}} \sum_{r=0}^{N-1} \eta_r^{(u)} \exp\left[-i2\pi \left(\frac{f}{\Delta_f} \frac{u^{(s)}}{N} + \frac{ur}{N} \right) \right] \frac{\exp\left[i\pi \left(f/\Delta_f - r \right) \right] - \exp\left[-i\pi \left(f/\Delta_f - r \right) \right]}{\exp\left(i\pi \frac{f/\Delta_f - r}{N} \right) - \exp\left(-i\pi \frac{f/\Delta_f - r}{N} \right)} =$$

$$\frac{1}{\sqrt{N}} \sum_{r=0}^{N-1} \eta_r^{(u)} \exp\left[-i2\pi \left(\frac{f}{\Delta_f} \frac{u^{(s)}}{N} + \frac{ur}{N} \right) \right] \frac{\sin\left[\pi \left(f/\Delta_r - r \right) \right]}{\sin\left(\pi \frac{f/\Delta_f - r}{N} \right)} \exp\left[i\pi \left(\frac{f}{\Delta_f} - r \right) \frac{N-1}{N} \right] =$$

$$\sum_{r=0}^{N-1} \eta_r^{(u)} \exp\left[-i\pi \left(\frac{f}{\Delta_f} \frac{2u^{(s)} - (N-1)}{N} + \frac{2u + N - 1}{N} r \right) \right] \sqrt{N} \frac{\sin\left[\pi \left(f/\Delta_f - r \right) \right]}{N \sin\left(\pi \frac{f/\Delta_f - r}{N} \right)} \qquad (7.31)$$

Finally, with the natural choice of the shift parameters $u^{(s)} = -u = (N-1)/2$, obtain that continuous frequency response of a digital filter with discrete frequency response $\left\{ \eta_r^{((N-1)/2,0)} \right\}$ is

$$DFCFR(f) = \sqrt{N} \sum_{r=0}^{N-1} \eta_r^{((N-1)/2)} \operatorname{sincd}\left[N, \pi \left(f/\Delta_f - r \right) \right]. \qquad (7.32)$$

Eq. (7.32) implies that, at points $f = r\Delta f$, $r = 0,..., N-1$ within the sampling baseband $\left[-1/2\Delta_x, 1/2\Delta_x \right]$ values of continuous frequency response of a digital filter are proportional to coefficients $\left\{ \eta_r^{((N-1)/2)} \right\}$ of the filter discrete frequency response. Between these sampling points, $DFCFR(f)$ is interpolated from coefficients $\left\{ \eta_r^{((N-1)/2)} \right\}$ of the filter discrete frequency response with discrete sinc-function as an interpolation kernel. This type of interpolation is called *discrete sinc interpolation*. It will be discussed in details in the next two sections.

Fig. (**7.2**) illustrates discrete and continuous frequency responses of a digital filter with $\mathrm{PSF}[-1,1]$, which is the simplest numerical differentiator. Solid line in the figure presents absolute value of the filter continuous frequency response in the sampling baseband $[-1/2\Delta_x \div 1/2\Delta_x]$; stems indicate samples $\left\{\eta_r^{((N-1)/2,0)}\right\}$ of the continuous frequency response, *i.e.*, the filter discrete frequency response.

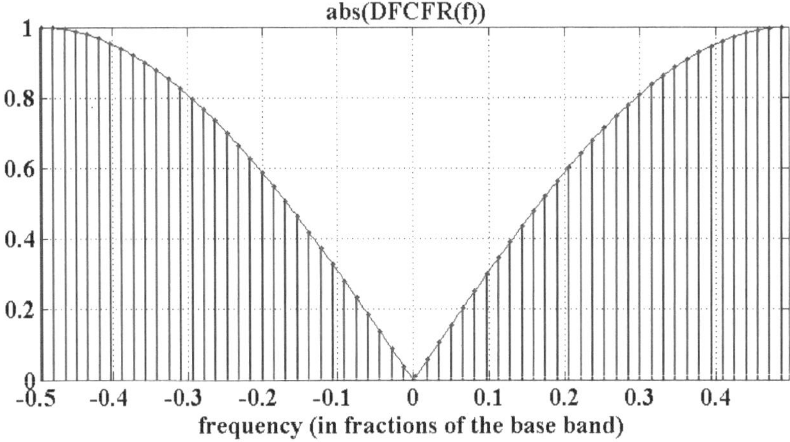

Fig. (7.2). Discrete frequency response (stems) and continuous frequency response (solid line) of a digital filter with PSF [-1, 1].

7.3. THE PERFECT FRACTIONAL SHIFT FILTER-INTERPOLATOR

This section addresses the problem of the design of a digital filter that generates a δ_x-shifted copy of its input sampled signal equivalent to a shifted copy of its corresponding not sampled signal that would be produced by an analog δ_x-shifting filter. This filter will be called the *perfect shifting filter*. This definition implies the requirement that the overall frequency response of the perfect digital δ_x-shifting filter should equal the frequency response of an analog δ_x-shifting filter. In the filter design, the following simplifying assumptions will be assumed:

- the number of signal samples is sufficiently large to allow neglecting spatial variance of the analog filter equivalent to our shifting digital filter;
- frequency responses of signal sampling and reconstruction devices are sufficiently flat within the sampling baseband to allow disregarding signal distortions by these devices.

With these assumptions, the continuous frequency response of the perfect shifting digital filter $DFCFR(f)$ should equals the frequency response $H_{\delta x}^{(Shift)}(f)$ of an analog δ_x-shifting filter, which, by virtue of the Fourier transform shift theorem, is $\exp(i2\pi f\delta_x)$:

$$DFCFR(f) = \sqrt{N}\sum_{r=0}^{N-1}\eta_r^{(\delta_x)}\operatorname{sincd}\left[N,\pi\left(f/\Delta_f - r\right)\right] = H_{\delta x}^{(Shift)}(f) = \exp(i2\pi f\delta_x). \quad (7.33)$$

This relationship enables determining coefficients $\left\{\eta_r^{(\delta_x)}\right\}$ of the sought filter discrete frequency response. In doing so, one should take into account complex conjugated symmetry of continuous and discrete frequency responses for real-valued signals:

$$H_{\delta x}^{(Shift)}(f) = \left(H_{\delta x}^{(Shift)}(-f)\right)^*;$$

$$\eta_r^{(\delta_x)} = \left(\eta_{N-r}^{(\delta_x)}\right)^* \qquad\qquad (7.34)$$

and the following rule of the mutual correspondence between analog signal frequencies f in the baseband and indices $\{r\}$ of the filter discrete frequency response $\left\{\eta_r^{(r)}\right\}$:

- indices $\{r = 0,1,... N/2\}$ for even N and $\{r = 0,1,...(N-1)/2\}$ for odd N correspond to positive analog frequencies $0 < f < 1/2\Delta x$ of the signal baseband;
- indices $\{r = N/2+1,..., N-1\}$ for even N and $\{r = (N+1)/2,..., N-1\}$ for odd N correspond to negative analog frequencies $-1/2\Delta x < f < 0$.

In this way, one can conclude from Eq. (7.32) that coefficients $\left\{\eta_r^{(\delta_x)}\right\}$ of discrete frequency response of the perfect δ_x-shifting filter, for indices from $r = 0$ to $r = (N-1)/2$ for odd N and from $r = 0$ to $r = N/2$ for even N, must be samples, at sampling points $\left\{r\Delta_f = r/N\Delta_x\right\}$, of its continuous frequency response $\exp(i2\pi f\delta_x)/\sqrt{N}$. The rest of coefficients should be set according to the complex conjugate symmetry property given by Eq. (7.34). Thus, for odd number of signal samples N, coefficients $\left\{\eta_r^{(\delta_x)}\right\}$ must be set to

$$\eta_r^{(\bar{\delta}_x)} = \begin{cases} \dfrac{1}{\sqrt{N}} \exp\left(i2\pi \dfrac{r\bar{\delta}_x}{N} \right), & r = 0,1,...,(N-1)/2 \\ \left(\eta_{N-r}^{(\bar{\delta}_x)} \right)^*, & r = (N+1)/2,..., N-1 \end{cases}$$

(7. 35)

where the shift $\bar{\delta}_x$ is expressed in fractions of signal sampling interval:

$$\bar{\delta}_x = \delta_x / \Delta_x ,$$

(7. 36)

For even number of signal samples N, from the same requirement $\eta_r^{(\delta_x)} = \eta_{N-r}^{*(\delta_x)}$, it follows that coefficient $\eta_{N/2}^{(\delta_x)}$, which corresponds to the signal highest frequency in its baseband, must be a real number. Because of that, for even N this coefficient cannot be taken just as a sample of $\exp\left(i2\pi r\, \bar{\delta}_x / N\Delta_x \right)$ for $r = N/2$ and it requires a special treatment. The most natural setting is:

$$\eta_{r,opt}^{(\delta_x)} = \begin{cases} \dfrac{1}{\sqrt{N}} \exp\left(i2\pi\, r\bar{\delta}_x / N \right), & r = 0,1,..., N/2 - 1 \\ \dfrac{C}{\sqrt{N}} \cos\left(\pi\bar{\delta}_x \right), & r = N/2 , \\ \eta_{r,opt}^{(\delta_x)} = \left(\eta_{N-r,opt}^{(\delta_x)} \right)^*, & r = N/2 + 1,..., N-1 \end{cases}$$

(7. 37)

where C is a weight coefficient that defines signal spectrum shaping at its the highest frequency component $r = N/2$. In what follows, the following three options for C for even N will be considered

Case-0: $C = 0$;
Case-1: $C = 1$;
Case-2: $C = 2$.

(7. 38)

Find now point spread function $\left\{ h_n^{(\delta_x)} \right\}$ of the perfect δ_x-shifting filter by inverse DFT of its discrete frequency response. For odd N, it follows from Eq. (7. 37) that:

$$h_n^{(\delta_x)} = \frac{1}{\sqrt{N}} \sum_{r=0}^{N-1} \eta_r^{(\delta_x)} \exp\left(-i2\pi\frac{nr}{N}\right) =$$

$$\frac{1}{\sqrt{N}}\left\{ \sum_{r=0}^{(N-1)/2} \eta_r^{(\delta_x)} \exp\left(-i2\pi\frac{nr}{N}\right) + \sum_{r=(N+1)/2}^{N-1} \eta_r^{(\delta_x)} \exp\left(-i2\pi\frac{nr}{N}\right) \right\} =$$

$$\frac{1}{\sqrt{N}}\left\{ \sum_{r=0}^{(N-1)/2} \eta_r^{(\delta_x)} \exp\left(-i2\pi\frac{nr}{N}\right) + \sum_{r=1}^{(N-1)/2} \eta_{N-r}^{(\delta_x)} \exp\left[-i2\pi\frac{n}{N}(N-r)\right] \right\} =$$

$$\frac{1}{\sqrt{N}}\left\{ \sum_{r=0}^{(N-1)/2} \eta_r^{(\delta_x)} \exp\left(-i2\pi\frac{nr}{N}\right) + \sum_{r=1}^{(N-1)/2} \left(\eta_r^{(\delta_x)}\right)^* \exp\left(i2\pi\frac{nr}{N}\right) \right\} =$$

$$\frac{1}{N}\left\{ \sum_{r=0}^{(N-1)/2} \exp\left(i2\pi\frac{\overline{\delta}_x}{N}r\right)\exp\left(-i2\pi\frac{nr}{N}\right) + \sum_{r=1}^{(N-1)/2} \exp\left(-i2\pi\frac{\overline{\delta}_x}{N\Delta x}\right)\exp\left(i2\pi\frac{nr}{N}\right) \right\} =$$

$$\frac{1}{N}\left\{ \sum_{r=0}^{(N-1)/2} \exp\left(-i2\pi\frac{n-\overline{\delta}_x}{N}r\right) + \sum_{r=1}^{(N-1)/2} \exp\left(i2\pi\frac{n-\overline{\delta}_x}{N}r\right) \right\} =$$

$$\frac{1}{N}\left\{ \frac{\exp\left(-i\pi\frac{N+1}{N}(n-\overline{\delta}_x)\right)-1}{\exp\left(-i2\pi\frac{n-\overline{\delta}_x}{N}\right)-1} + \frac{\exp\left(i\pi\frac{N+1}{N}(n-\overline{\delta}_x)\right)-\exp\left(i2\pi\frac{n-\overline{\delta}_x}{N}\right)}{\exp\left(i2\pi\frac{n-\overline{\delta}_x}{N}\right)-1} \right\} =$$

$$\frac{1}{N}\left\{ \frac{\exp\left(-i\pi\frac{N+1}{N}(n-\overline{\delta}_x)\right)-1}{\exp\left(-i2\pi\frac{n-\overline{\delta}_x}{N}\right)-1} - \frac{\exp\left(i\pi\frac{N-1}{N}(n-\overline{\delta}_x)\right)-1}{\exp\left(-i2\pi\frac{n-\overline{\delta}_x}{N}\right)-1} \right\} =$$

$$\frac{1}{N}\left\{\frac{\exp\left(-i\pi\frac{N+1}{N}\left(n-\bar{\delta}_x\right)\right)-1-\exp\left(i\pi\frac{N-1}{N}\left(n-\bar{\delta}_x\right)\right)+1}{\exp\left(-i2\pi\frac{n-\bar{\delta}_x}{N}\right)-1}\right\}=$$

$$\frac{1}{N}\frac{\exp\left[-i\pi\left(n-\bar{\delta}_x\right)\right]-\exp\left[i\pi\left(n-\bar{\delta}_x\right)\right]}{\exp\left(-i\pi\frac{n-\bar{\delta}_x}{N}\right)-\exp\left(i\pi\frac{n-\bar{\delta}_x}{N}\right)}=\frac{\sin\left[\pi\left(n-\bar{\delta}_x\right)\right]}{N\sin\left(\pi\frac{n-\bar{\delta}_x}{N}\right)}, \tag{7.39}$$

i.e.,

$$h_n^{(\delta_x)}=\mathbf{sincd}\left[N,\pi\left(n-\bar{\delta}_x\right)\right], \tag{7.40}$$

where $\mathbf{sincd}(N;x)$ is the discrete sinc-function defined by Eq. (7. 16).

Similarly one can obtain that for even N, Case 0 and Case 2, the perfect shifting filter point spread functions are

$$h_n^{(\delta_x,0)}=\mathbf{sincdd}\left[N-1;N;\pi\left(n-\bar{\delta}_x\right)\right] \tag{7.41}$$

and

$$h_n^{(\delta_x,2)}=\mathbf{sincdd}\left[N+1;N;\pi\left(n-\bar{\delta}x\right)\right], \tag{7.42}$$

correspondingly, where $\mathbf{sincdd}(\cdot;\cdot;\cdot)$ is the *sincdd-function* defined as

$$\mathbf{sincdd}(M,N,x)=\frac{\sin\left[Mx/N\right]}{N\sin\left(x/N\right)}. \tag{7.43}$$

Case-1 is obviously a combination of Case-0 and Case-2:

$$
h_n^{(\delta_x,1)}(\bar{\delta}_x) = \left[h_n^{(\delta_x,0)}(\bar{\delta}_x) + h_n^{(\delta_x,2)}(\bar{\delta}_x) \right]/2 =
$$

$$
\frac{\sin\left[\pi \dfrac{(N-1)(n-\bar{\delta}_x)}{N}\right] + \sin\left[\pi \dfrac{(N+1)(n-\bar{\delta}_x)}{N}\right]}{N \sin\left[\pi \dfrac{(n-\bar{\delta}_x)}{N}\right]} =
$$

$$
\frac{\sin[\pi(n-\bar{\delta}_x)]}{N \sin\left(\pi \dfrac{n-\bar{\delta}_x}{N}\right)} \cos\left(\pi \dfrac{n-\bar{\delta}_x}{N}\right), \tag{7.44}
$$

that is

$$
h_n^{(\delta_x,1)}(\bar{\delta}_x) = \cos\left(\pi \frac{n-\bar{\delta}_x}{N}\right) \operatorname{sincd}[\pi(n-\bar{\delta}_x)]. \tag{7.45}
$$

These three versions of discrete sinc-functions for Cases 0-2 are presented for comparison in Fig. (**7.3**). As one can see from this figure, discrete sinc-function being apodized by a cosine window for the Case-1 (Eq. (7. 45) converges to zero substantially faster than the sincdd-functions for Case-0 and Case-2. This makes the Case-1 preferable in practical applications.

As was already mentioned in the previous section, numerical interpolation given by Eqs. (7.40 – 7.45) with discrete sinc-functions as an interpolation kernel is called the *discrete sinc interpolation (sincd-interpolation)*.

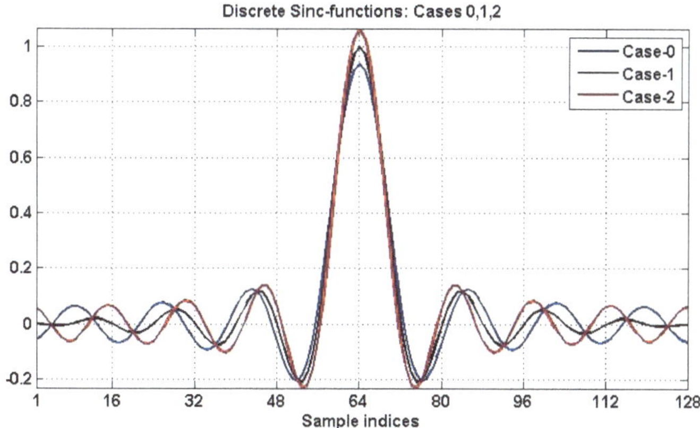

Fig. (7.3). Three versions of the discrete sinc-functions given by Eqs.(7. 16), (7. 41), and (7. 42).

Fig. (**7.4**) presents continuous and discrete frequency responses of the perfect shifting digital filter, which implements signal resampling by discrete sinc interpolation.

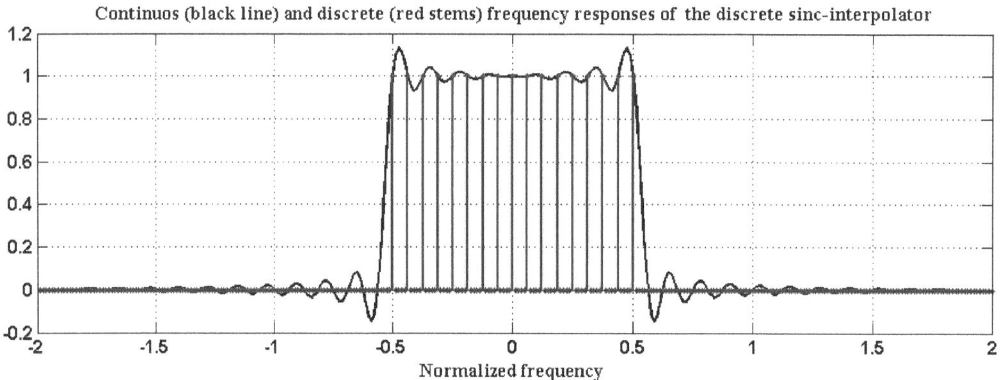

Fig. (7.4). Module of continuous (black line) and discrete (red stems) frequency responses of the perfect shifting digital filter.

By definition (Eqs.(7. 35) and (7. 37)), discrete frequency response of the perfect digital shifting filter (Fig. **7.4**) that acts as a discrete sinc interpolator is a flat function within the signal baseband except that for even number N of signal samples the signal spectrum highest frequency coefficient with index $N/2$-th is by the necessity modified: depending on the version (Case-0, Case-1 and Case-2) chosen for the filter implementation it is zeroed, halved or doubled, correspondingly. This implies that discrete sinc interpolation does not distort the module of signal discrete spectrum within the baseband and, therefore, it secures perfect, for a given number of signal samples, resampling of discrete signals with preservation of energy of the corresponding continuous signal spectra in their sampling points. All resampling filters with point spread functions other than the discrete sinc-function will distort samples of signal spectrum in the signal baseband and, therefore, will introduce interpolation error. This justifies considering discrete sinc interpolation as the "gold standard" of sampled signal interpolation.

Discrete sinc-function $\mathbf{sincd}(N, x) = \dfrac{\sin x}{N \sin(x/N)}$ is a discrete analog of the

continuous sinc-function $\mathbf{sinc}(x) = \dfrac{\sin x}{x}$, which is a point spread function of the

ideal low-pass filter required, as it is stated by the general sampling theorem (Sect.

4.3), for reconstruction of signals from their samples with minimal MSE. Discrete sinc-function tends to the continuous one when $N \to \infty$:

$$\lim_{N \to \infty}\left(\mathbf{sincd}(N,x) = \frac{\sin x}{N \sin(x/N)} \right) = \frac{\sin x}{x}. \tag{7.46}$$

Both functions are plotted for comparison in Fig. (**7.5**).

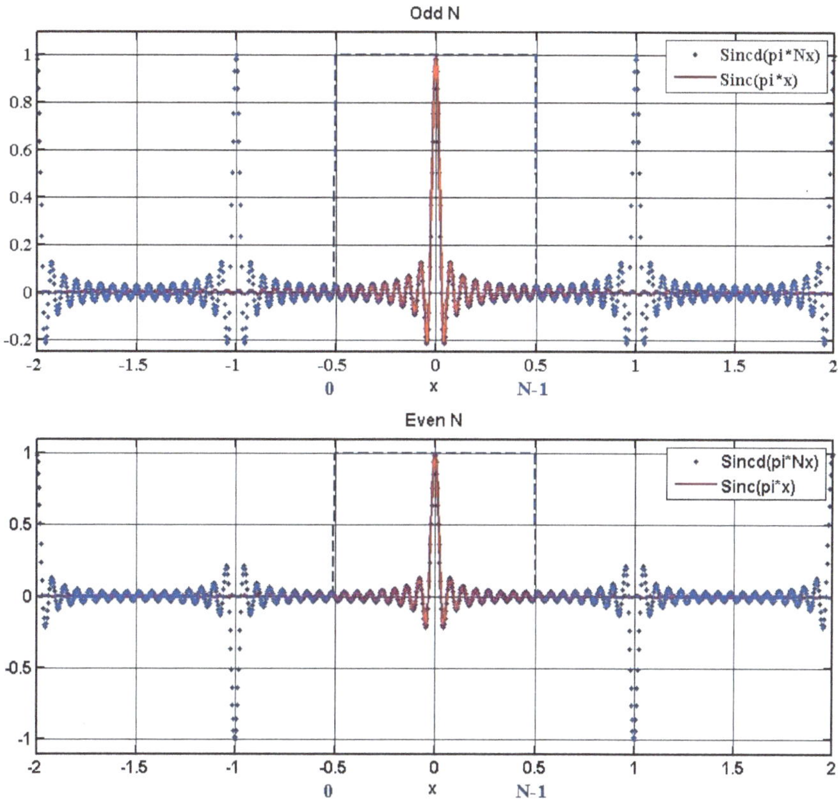

Fig. (7.5). Continuous (red) and discrete (blue) sinc-functions. The latter is plotted for odd (upper plot) and even (bottom plot) number of signal samples N .

One can see from the figure that continuous sinc-function and discrete sinc-function are almost identical within the basic interval of N samples for the discrete sinc function and its corresponding interval $N\Delta_x$ for the continuous sinc-function: within this interval, their relative difference does not exceed 10^{-2}. Outside this interval, they differ dramatically. While sinc-function continues decaying, discrete sinc-function $\mathbf{sincd}(N;\pi x)$ is a periodical function with a period N. The type of its periodicity depends on whether N is odd or even number:

$$\mathbf{sincd}(N;\pi(k+gN)) = (-1)^{g(N-1)}\,\mathbf{sincd}(N;\pi k).$$

$$(7.47)$$

for any integer number g.

CHAPTER 8

Image Resampling: Fast Computational Algorithms

8.1. FAST FRACTIONAL SHIFT ALGORITHMS AND BUILDING ANALOG IMAGE MODELS

8.1.1. FFT Based Algorithm

The perfect shifting filter introduced in Sect. 7.3 is the base for computationally efficient signal resampling algorithms. Consider algorithms implemented through DFT domain filtering using Fast Fourier Transform. An algorithm for generating a $\bar{\delta}_x$-shifted copy of the signal   is defined by the equation:

$$a_k^{(\delta_x)} = \mathbf{IFFT}_N\left\{\left[\eta_r^{(\bar{\delta}_x)}\right]\bullet\left[\mathbf{FFT}_N\left(a_k\right)\right]\right\}, \quad k = 0,1,...,N-1 \tag{8.1}$$

where $\mathbf{FFT}_N(\cdot)$ and $\mathbf{IFFT}_N(\cdot)$ $\{a_k\}$ are direct and inverse N-point Fast Fourier transforms, "$\bullet$" symbolizes component-wise (Hadamard) matrix product of elements of two arrays and $\left\{\eta_r^{(\bar{\delta}_x)}\right\}$ is a set of coefficients defined, for odd and even N by Eqs. (7.35), (7.37) and (7.38), correspondingly.

One of the immediate applications of this algorithm is signal/image sub-sampling (zooming-in) with an arbitrary integer zoom-factor, *i.e.*, building digital models of analog images for their arbitrary resampling. For zoom factor L, 1D signal zooming-in can be implemented through generating subsequently computed signal copies shifted by the corresponding multiples of $1/L$ shifts:

$$a_{kL+l}^{(l\delta x)} = \mathbf{IFFT}_N\left\{\left[\eta_r^{(l/L)}\right]\bullet\left[\mathbf{FFT}_N\left(a_k\right)\right]\right\}, \quad l = 0,...,L-1, \quad k = 0,...,N-1 \tag{8.2}$$

$$L-1$$

The work of this algorithm is illustrated by plots in Fig. (**8.1**) obtained using the program Sincd_interpol_2D_BNTM.m provided in Exercises. The upper plot in this figure is a test signal in a form of a delta-function and its subsequent 7 times shifted copies that all-together make up the eight times sub-sampled signal. For this particular test signal, the sub-sampled signal represents discrete sinc-function, the point spread function of the sub-sampling filter. The bottom plot is the DFT spectrum of the sub-sampled signal, which, for this particular test signal, is the sub-sampling filter discrete frequency response. As one can see, it is the discrete frequency response of the ideal low-pass filter that halves the highest frequency component of the signal spectrum as it is dictated by the version C-1 of the perfect shifting filter (Eqs. (7. 37) and (7. 38)).

For 2D image sub-sampling (zooming-in), the described 1D algorithm should be applied in two passes, say, row-wise and then column-wise as it is illustrated in Fig. (**8.2**) using the program Sincd_interpol_2D_BNTM.m provided in Exercises.

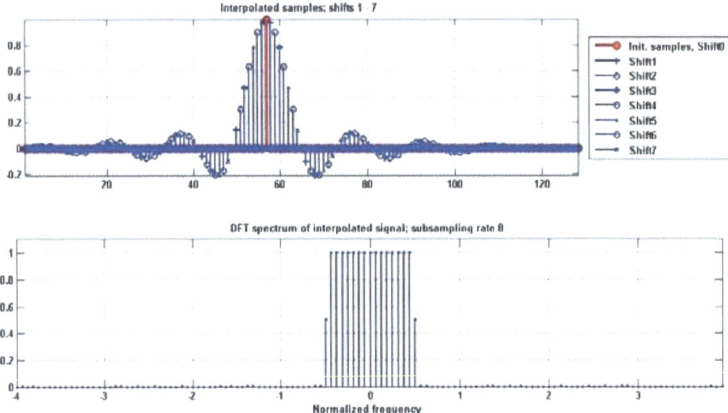

Fig. (8.1). Upper plot: a test signal (red bold) and its seven sub-samples shifted subsequently 7 times by 1/8 of the sampling interval by the prefect shifting filter. Bottom plot: DFT spectrum of the sub-sampled test signal, which, for this particular test signal, represents the resampling filter discrete frequency response.

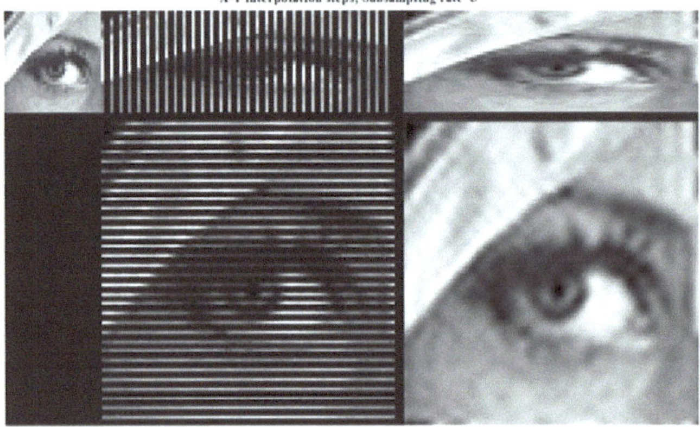

Fig. (8.2). Upper row: a test image (left), an image, in which rows two zero pixels are inserted after each of its pixel (middle), and a row-wise interpolated image (right). Bottom row: the row-wise interpolated image, in which two zero pixels are inserted after each pixel in image columns (left), and a column-wise interpolated image (right).

Obtained in this way, sub-sampled images represent the most perfect models of analog images that can be generated from given samples for a given sub-sampling rate. Such models can be used for performing subsequent image resampling over an arbitrary sampling lattice. In this process, the required image samples, whose positions do not coincide with one of the sampling nodes of the denser sampling lattice of the zoomed-in image, can be approximated by the nearest available sample of the sub-sampled image as it is illustrated in Fig. (**8.3**).

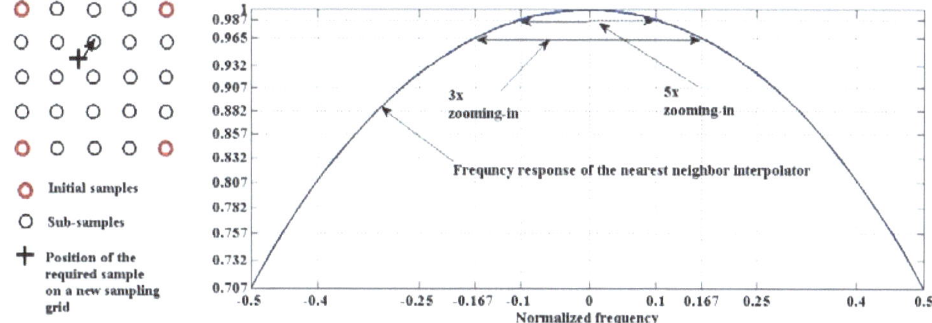

Fig. (8.3). Nearest neighbor interpolation in resampling of zoomed-in images (left) and its frequency response (right) within the sub-sampled image baseband ($[-0.5 \div 0.5]$). Double arrows indicate basebands of initial images before their 5x and 3x sub-sampling.

Provided appropriately chosen sub-sampling factor, the nearest neighbor interpolation in combination with the discrete sinc interpolated sub-sampling will not compromise the interpolation accuracy substantially. For instance, as one can see from the plot of the frequency response of the nearest neighbor interpolator (Fig. **8.3**, right plot), for sub-sampling factor 5, the decay of the frequency response on the highest spatial frequency of the initial image is only 1.3% and for sub-sampling -factor 3, it is 3.5% (point spread function and frequency response of the nearest neighbor interpolators are discussed in Sect. 9.2.2).

One of the important applications, in which perfect models of analog images are required, is the fast location and tracking of moving targets in video sequences. In this case, template images of the target with arbitrary orientation and scale can be very rapidly computed through the corresponding resampling of the sub-sampled template image of the target obtained with a sufficiently large sub-sampling factor. Other application examples will be discussed in detail below in Chapter 9.

8.1.2. Fast DCT Based Algorithm

Being a cyclic convolution, the above described "DFT-based" signal fractional shift algorithm suffers from boundary effects. In cyclic convolution, samples at opposite borders of signals, which are distant from one another by the signal length, are treated as immediate neighbors, and any signal discontinuity between them causes signal oscillations of the discrete sinc-function at signal borders. This phenomenon is illustrated in Fig. (**8.4**), which shows an example of sub-sampling a ramp test signal using the DFT based fractional shift algorithm.

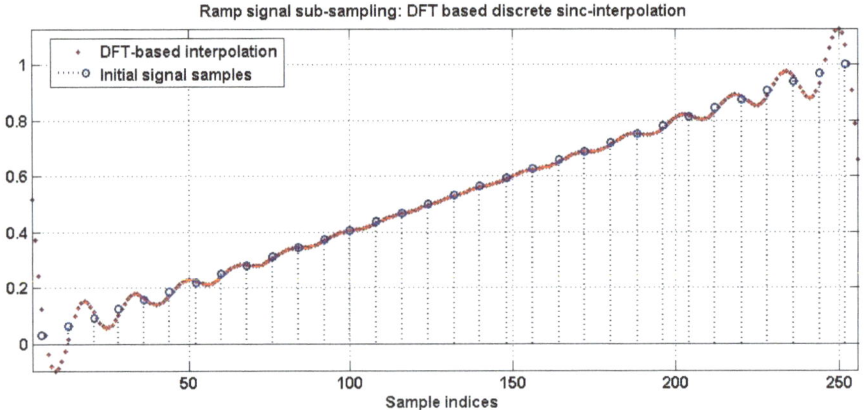

Fig. (8.4). The phenomenon of oscillations induced at signal borders by signal DFT based discrete sinc interpolation: a result (red dots) of 8 times sub-sampling of a test ramp signal (dash stems).

An efficient practical solution of the problem is applying this algorithm to an artificially symmetrized signal formed by an extension of signals to be sub-sampled by their copies mirror reflected from signal borders. Such a signal's even extension to double length eliminates possible discontinuities at extended signal borders when the signal is periodically replicated in the cyclic convolution.

Show that applying the DFT based convolution to such evenly extended signals translates to a convolution in the DCT domain. Let signal $\{\tilde{a}_k\}$ be a signal of $2N$ samples obtained from signal $\{a_k\}$ of N samples by its mirror reflection extension:

$$\tilde{a}_{(k)\bmod 2N} = \begin{cases} a_k, & k = 0,1,...,N-1; \\ a_{2N-k-1}, & k = N, N+1,...,2N-1 \end{cases}. \tag{8.3}$$

and let $\{\widetilde{h}_n\}$ be a desired convolution kernel $\{h_n\}$ of N samples ($n = 0,1,..., N-1$) zero-padded to the length $2N$.

$$\widetilde{h}_n = \begin{cases} 0, & n = 0,...,\lfloor N/2 \rfloor - 1 \\ h_{n-\lfloor N/2 \rfloor}, & n = \lfloor N/2 \rfloor,...,\lfloor N/2 \rfloor + N - 1., \\ 0, & \lfloor N/2 \rfloor + N,...,2N-1 \end{cases} \quad (8.4)$$

where $\lfloor N/2 \rfloor$ is an integer part of $N/2$. Such an extension of the convolution kernel is necessary to keep it unchanged in its cyclic convolution with the extended signal. Then the first N samples of cyclic convolution

$$c_{(k)\bmod 2N} = \sum_{n=0}^{N-1} \widetilde{h}_n \widetilde{a}_{(k-n+\lfloor N/2 \rfloor)\bmod 2N} \quad (8.5)$$

are the sought-for convolution result, in which involvement of distant signal samples from signal's opposite sites associated with the cyclicity of the DFT based convolution is eliminated thanks to the signal mirrored extension.

Consider computing convolution of such signals by means of inverse DFT of the product of signal and convolution kernel DFT spectra. DFT spectrum of the extended signal $\{\widetilde{a}_k\}$ is:

$$\widetilde{\alpha}_r = \frac{1}{\sqrt{2N}} \sum_{k=0}^{2N-1} \widetilde{a}_k \exp\left(i2\pi \frac{kr}{2N} \right) =$$

$$\left\{ \frac{2}{\sqrt{2N}} \sum_{k=0}^{N-1} a_k \cos\left(\pi \frac{k+1/2}{N} r \right) \right\} \exp\left(-i\pi \frac{r}{2N} \right) = \alpha_r^{(DCT)} \exp\left(-i\pi \frac{r}{2N} \right), \quad (8.6)$$

where $\{\alpha_r^{(DCT)}\}$ are discrete cosine transform (DCT) coefficients of signal $\{a_k\}$. For computing convolution, signal spectrum defined by Eq. (8.6) should be multiplied by DFT coefficients $\{\widetilde{\eta}_r\}$ of the zero-padded convolution kernel $\{\widetilde{h}_n\}$:

$$\widetilde{\eta}_r = \frac{1}{\sqrt{2N}} \sum_{n=0}^{2N-1} \widetilde{h}_n \exp\left(i2\pi \frac{nr}{2N} \right). \quad (8.7)$$

and then inverse DFT of the product $\tilde{\alpha}_r\tilde{\eta}_r$ should be computed for the first N samples:

$$b_k = \frac{1}{\sqrt{2N}} \sum_{r=0}^{2N-1} \alpha_r^{(DCT)} \exp\left(-i\pi\frac{r}{2N}\right)\tilde{\eta}_r \exp\left(-i2\pi\frac{kr}{2N}\right) =$$

$$\frac{1}{\sqrt{2N}} \sum_{r=0}^{2N-1} \alpha_r^{(DCT)}\tilde{\eta}_r \exp\left(-i2\pi\frac{k+1/2}{2N}r\right), \tag{8.8}$$

Split the sum in this equation into two terms and change index r of summation in the second term to $2N - r$. Then obtain:

$$b_k = \frac{1}{\sqrt{2N}} \sum_{r=0}^{2N-1} \alpha_r^{(DCT)}\tilde{\eta}_r \exp\left(-i2\pi\frac{k+1/2}{2N}r\right) =$$

$$\frac{1}{\sqrt{2N}}\left\{ \sum_{r=0}^{N-1} \alpha_r^{(DCT)}\tilde{\eta}_r \exp\left(-i2\pi\frac{k+1/2}{2N}r\right) + \sum_{r=N}^{2N-1} \alpha_r^{(DCT)}\tilde{\eta}_r \exp\left(-i2\pi\frac{k+1/2}{2N}r\right) \right\} =$$

$$\frac{1}{\sqrt{2N}}\left\{ \sum_{r=0}^{N-1} \alpha_r^{(DCT)}\tilde{\eta}_r \exp\left(-i2\pi\frac{k+1/2}{2N}r\right) + \right.$$

$$\left. \sum_{r=1}^{N} \alpha_{2N-r}^{(DCT)}\tilde{\eta}_{2N-r} \exp\left[-i2\pi\frac{(k+1/2)(2N-r)}{2N}\right] \right\} =$$

$$\frac{1}{\sqrt{2N}}\left\{ \sum_{r=0}^{N-1} \alpha_r^{(DCT)}\tilde{\eta}_r \exp\left(-i2\pi\frac{k+1/2}{2N}r\right) + \right.$$

$$\left. \sum_{r=1}^{N} \alpha_{2N-r}^{(DCT)}\tilde{\eta}_{2N-r} \exp\left[-i2\pi(k+1/2)\right]\exp\left(i2\pi\frac{k+1/2}{2N}r\right) \right\} =$$

$$\frac{1}{\sqrt{2N}}\left\{ \sum_{r=0}^{N-1} \alpha_r^{(DCT)}\tilde{\eta}_r \exp\left(-i2\pi\frac{k+1/2}{2N}r\right) - \sum_{r=1}^{N} \alpha_{2N-r}^{(DCT)}\tilde{\eta}_{2N-r} \exp\left(i2\pi\frac{k+1/2}{2N}r\right) \right\} \tag{8.9}$$

As one can see from the definition of DCT (Eq. (4.14)), DCT signal spectrum is an odd (anti-symmetric) sequence if regarded outside its base interval $[0, N-1]$:

$$\alpha_r^{DCT} = -\alpha_{2N-r}^{DCT}; \alpha_N = 0. \tag{8.10}$$

By virtue of the conjugate symmetry property of DFT of real valued signals

$$\left\{ \widetilde{\eta}_r = \widetilde{\eta}^{*}_{2N-r} \right\}.$$ (8. 11)

Using these relationships in Eq. (8. 9), obtain:

$$b_k = \frac{1}{\sqrt{2N}} \left\{ \sum_{r=0}^{N-1} \alpha_r^{(DCT)} \widetilde{\eta}_r \exp\left(-i2\pi \frac{k+1/2}{2N} r \right) + \sum_{r=1}^{N-1} \alpha_r^{(DCT)} \widetilde{\eta}_r^{*} \exp\left(i2\pi \frac{k+1/2}{2N} r \right) \right\} =$$

$$\frac{1}{\sqrt{2N}} \left\{ \alpha_0^{(DCT)} \widetilde{\eta}_0 + 2\sum_{r=1}^{N-1} \alpha_r^{(DCT)} \widetilde{\eta}_r^{re} \cos\left(\pi \frac{k+1/2}{N} r \right) - \right.$$

$$\left. 2\sum_{r=1}^{N-1} \alpha_r^{(DCT)} \widetilde{\eta}_r^{im} \sin\left(\pi \frac{k+1/2}{N} r \right) \right\},$$ (8. 12)

where $\widetilde{\eta}_r^{re}$ and $\widetilde{\eta}_r^{im}$ are real and imaginary parts of $\widetilde{\eta}_r$. First two terms of this expression represent inverse DCT of the product $\left\{ \alpha_r^{(DCT)} \widetilde{\eta}_r^{re} \right\}$. The third term can be converted into DCT by changing the summation index r in it to $N-r$:

$$\sum_{r=1}^{N-1} \alpha_{N-r}^{(DCT)} \widetilde{\eta}_{N-r}^{im} \sin\left[\pi \frac{(k+1/2)(N-r)}{N} \right] = (-1)^k \sum_{r=1}^{N-1} \alpha_{N-r}^{(DCT)} \widetilde{\eta}_{N-r}^{im} \cos\left(\pi \frac{k+1/2}{N} r \right)$$ (8. 13)

Substitute this expression into Eq. (8. 12) and obtain the final formula for computing, through DCT, digital convolution with virtually no boundary effects:

$$b_k = \frac{1}{\sqrt{2N}} \left\{ \alpha_0^{(DCT)} \widetilde{\eta}_0 + 2\sum_{r=1}^{N-1} \alpha_r^{(DCT)} \widetilde{\eta}_r^{re} \cos\left(\pi \frac{k+1/2}{N} r \right) - \right.$$

$$\left. 2(-1)^k \sum_{r=1}^{N-1} \alpha_{N-r}^{(DCT)} \widetilde{\eta}_{N-r}^{im} \cos\left(\pi \frac{k+1/2}{N} r \right) \right\}.$$ (8. 14)

This implies the following DCT-based signal $\bar{\delta}_x$-shifting algorithm

$$\widetilde{a}_k^{(\bar{\delta}_x)} = \frac{1}{\sqrt{2N}} \left\{ \alpha_0^{(DCT)} \widetilde{\eta}_0^{(\bar{\delta}_x)} + 2\sum_{r=1}^{N-1} \alpha_r^{(DCT)} \left(\widetilde{\eta}_r^{(\bar{\delta}_x)} \right)^{re} \cos\left(\pi \frac{k+1/2}{N} r \right) - \right.$$

$$\left. 2(-1)^k \sum_{r=1}^{N-1} \alpha_{N-r}^{(DCT)} \left(\widetilde{\eta}_{N-r}^{(\bar{\delta}_x)} \right)^{im} \cos\left(\pi \frac{k+1/2}{N} r \right) \right\}.$$ (8. 15)

The filter coefficients $\left\{\tilde{\eta}_r^{(\bar{\delta}_x)}\right\}$ in this equation are defined by Eqs. (8. 4) and (8. 7), in which one of the discrete sinc-functions defined by Eqs. (7. 41), (7. 42) and (7. 45) should be used as a convolution kernel $\{h_n\}$. Because of this, the DCT-based algorithm is equivalent, in terms of the interpolation accuracy, to the above DFT-based versions of the perfect fractional shift algorithm.

For signal L times sub-sampling, the algorithm has to be applied repeatedly $(L-1)$ times with shifts $\bar{\delta}_x = l/L$, $l = 1,2,..., L-1$ similarly to the DFT-based algorithm (Eq. (8. 2)).

The high efficiency of the DCT based algorithm in terms of reducing boundary effects characteristic for the DFT-based algorithm is demonstrated in Fig. (8.5) in an example of sub-sampling of the same test ramp-signal as shown in Fig. (8.4). Fig. (8.5) presents the ramp test signal (stems) along with the result of its 8 times sub-sampling using the above described DCT-based fractional shift algorithm. As one can see, severe oscillations that propagate from signal borders in the case of the DFT-based discrete sinc interpolation (Fig. **8.4**) completely disappear, when the DCT based discrete sinc interpolation algorithm is used (Fig. **8.5**).

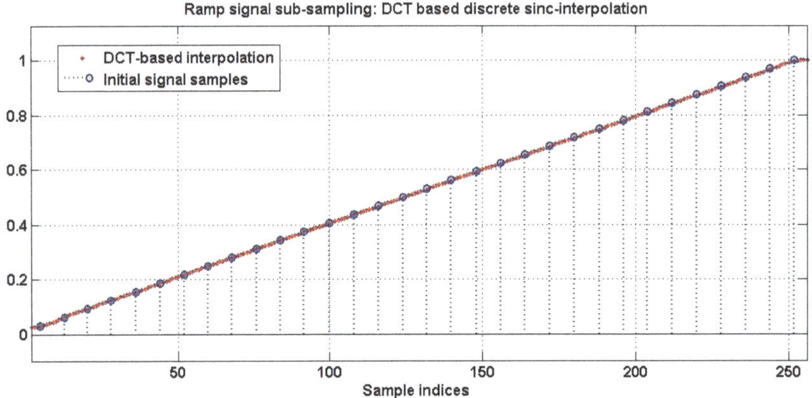

Fig. (8.5). The result (solid red) of DCT-based 8 times sub-sampling of the test ramp signal (dotted stems).

8.2. DISCRETE SINC INTERPOLATED SUB-SAMPLING SIGNALS BY ZERO PADDING THEIR DFT AND DCT SPECTRA

8.2.1. Zero Padding DFT Spectra of Signals

An alternative method of signal sub-sampling with discrete sinc interpolation is signal DFT and DCT spectrum zero padding. Begin with a version of this method capable of an arbitrary integer times signal sub-sampling, which is an alternative of the above-described signal sub-sampling using the perfect fractional shift algorithm.

Let a discrete signal $\{a_k\}$ of N_0 samples ($k = 0,1,...N_0 - 1$) be a signal to be sub-sampled and $\{\ddot{a}_{\tilde{n}}\}$ be an auxiliary signal of LN_0 samples ($\tilde{n} = 0,1,..., LN_0 - 1$) obtained from the signal $\{a_k\}$ by placing between its samples ($L-1$) zero samples:

$$\ddot{a}_{\tilde{n}} = a_k \overline{\delta}(l), \quad \tilde{n} = kL + l, \qquad\qquad , l = 0,1,...,L-1 \qquad\qquad (8.16)$$

where $\delta(\cdot)$ is the Kronecker delta ($\delta(l) = 0^l$). Compute DFT of this signal:

$$\ddot{\alpha}_{\tilde{r}} = \frac{1}{\sqrt{LN_0}} \sum_{\tilde{n}=0}^{LN-1} \ddot{a}_{\tilde{n}} \exp\left(i2\pi \frac{\tilde{n}\tilde{r}}{LN_0} \right) = \frac{1}{\sqrt{LN_0}} \sum_{l=0}^{L-1} \sum_{k=0}^{N-1} a_k \delta(l) \exp\left(i2\pi \frac{kL+l}{LN_0} \tilde{r} \right) =$$

$$\frac{1}{\sqrt{LN_0}} \sum_{k=0}^{N-1} a_k \exp\left(i2\pi \frac{k\tilde{r}}{N_0} \right) = \frac{1}{\sqrt{L}} \alpha_{(\tilde{r}) \bmod N_0}, \tilde{r} = 0,1,..., LN_0 - 1, \qquad (8.17)$$

where $\{\alpha_{(r) \bmod N_0}\}$, is DFT of the signal $\{a_k\}$. This equation implies that placing zeros between signal samples results in a periodical replication of its DFT spectrum with the number of replicas equals the number of zeros plus one. This property of DFT spectra is illustrated in Fig. (**8.6**). As one can see, it is an analog of the virtual signal spectrum replication in sampling continuous signals discussed in connection with the sampling theorem in Chapt. 2 (Eq. (2.18)).

Let's now set to zero all periods in the spectrum $\{\ddot{\alpha}_{\tilde{r}}\}$ but the initial one (Fig. **8.7**, upper row). This operation is called *spectrum zero padding*. In the spectrum zero padding, one should maintain the spectrum complex conjugated symmetry $\{\alpha_{\tilde{r}} = \alpha^*_{LN_0 - \tilde{r}}\}$ for real-valued signals. Thus, the way, in which spectrum zero-padding should be done depends on whether N_0 is an odd or an even number.

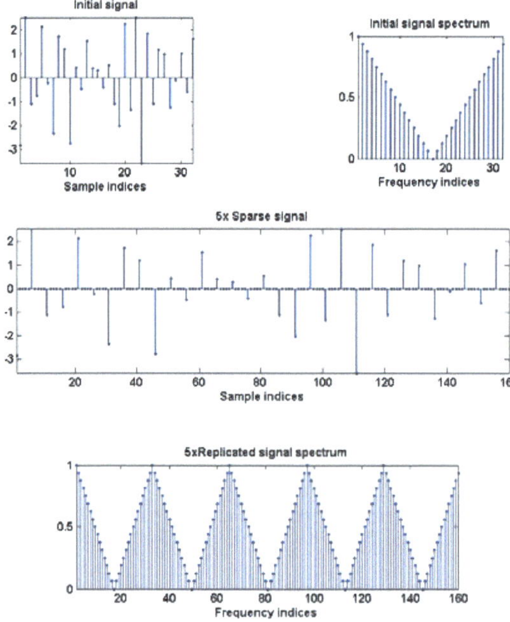

Fig. (8.6). A test signal (upper row, left); its DFT spectrum (upper row, right); a sparse signal obtained from the test signal by placing 4 zeros between its samples (middle row); DFT spectrum of the obtained sparse signal (bottom row).

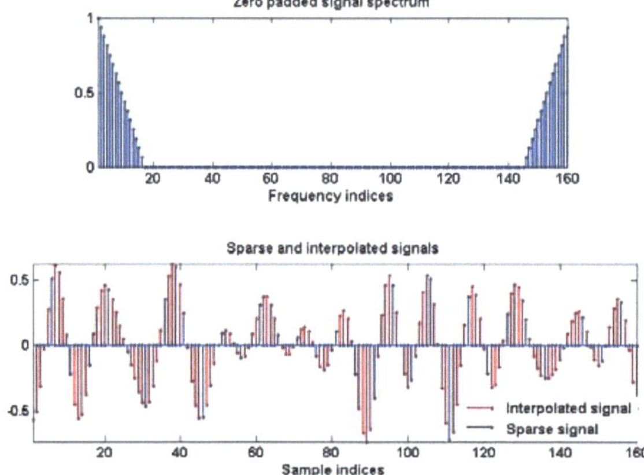

Fig. (8.7). Zero padded spectrum of the sparse signal after removing all of its periodical components but one (upper) and discrete sinc interpolated signal reconstructed from the zero-padded spectrum (bottom).

For odd N_0, zeroed should be spectral coefficients with indices from $\widetilde{r} = (N_0 + 1)/2$ to $\widetilde{r} = LN_0 - (N_0 + 1)/2$. In this case, inverse DFT of the zero-padded spectrum of samples produces the signal

$$\widetilde{a}_{\widetilde{k}} = \frac{1}{\sqrt{LN_0}}\left[\sum_{\widetilde{r}=0}^{(N_0-1)/2} \alpha_{(\widetilde{r})\bmod N} \exp\left(-i2\pi\frac{\widetilde{k}\widetilde{r}}{LN_0}\right) + \right.$$

$$\left. \sum_{\widetilde{r}=LN_0-(N_0-1)/2}^{LN_0-1} \alpha_{(\widetilde{r})\bmod N} \exp\left(-i2\pi\frac{\widetilde{k}\widetilde{r}}{LN_0}\right)\right] =$$

$$\frac{1}{\sqrt{LN_0}}\left\{\sum_{\widetilde{r}=0}^{(N_0-1)/2}\left[\frac{1}{\sqrt{N_0}}\sum_{n=0}^{N_0-1}a_n \exp\left(i2\pi\frac{n\widetilde{r}}{N_0}\right)\right]\exp\left(-i2\pi\frac{\widetilde{k}\widetilde{r}}{LN_0}\right) + \right.$$

$$\left. \sum_{\widetilde{r}=LN_0-(N_0-1)/2}^{LN_0-1}\left[\frac{1}{\sqrt{N_0}}\sum_{n=0}^{N_0-1}a_n \exp\left(i2\pi\frac{n\widetilde{r}}{N_0}\right)\right]\exp\left(-i2\pi\frac{\widetilde{k}\widetilde{r}}{LN_0}\right)\right\} =$$

$$\frac{1}{N_0\sqrt{L}}\left\{\sum_{n=0}^{N_0-1}a_n\left[\sum_{\widetilde{r}=0}^{(N_0-1)/2}\exp\left(-i2\pi\frac{\widetilde{k}-Ln}{LN_0}\widetilde{r}\right) + \sum_{\widetilde{r}=LN_0-(N_0-1)/2}^{LN_0-1}\exp\left(-i2\pi\frac{\widetilde{k}-Ln}{LN_0}\widetilde{r}\right)\right]\right\} =$$

$$\frac{1}{N_0\sqrt{L}}\left(\sum_{n=0}^{N_0-1}a_n\left\{\frac{\exp\left[-i2\pi\frac{(\widetilde{k}-Ln)(N_0+1)}{2LN_0}\right]-1}{\exp\left(-i2\pi\frac{\widetilde{k}-Ln}{LN_0}\right)-1} + \right.\right.$$

$$\left.\left.\frac{\exp\left[-i2\pi\frac{LN_0(\widetilde{k}-Ln)}{LN_0}\right]-\exp\left[-i2\pi\frac{(\widetilde{k}-Ln)(LN_0-(N_0-1)/2)}{LN_0}\right]}{\exp\left(-i2\pi\frac{\widetilde{k}-Ln}{LN_0}\right)-1}\right\}\right) =$$

$$\frac{1}{N_0\sqrt{L}}\sum_{n=0}^{N_0-1}a_n\frac{\exp\left[-i2\pi\frac{\left(\tilde{k}-Ln\right)\left(N_0+1\right)}{2LN_0}\right]-\exp\left[-i2\pi\frac{\left(\tilde{k}-Ln\right)\left(N_0-1\right)}{2LN}\right]}{\exp\left(-i2\pi\frac{\tilde{k}-Ln}{LN_0}\right)-1}=$$

$$\frac{1}{\sqrt{L}}\sum_{n=0}^{N_0-1}a_n\frac{\sin\left(\pi N_0\frac{\tilde{k}-Ln}{LN_0}\right)}{N\sin\left(\pi\frac{\tilde{k}-Ln}{LN_0}\right)}=\frac{1}{\sqrt{L}}\sum_{n=0}^{N_0-1}a_n\,\mathrm{sincd}\left[N_0;\pi\left(\tilde{k}-nL\right)/L\right]. \qquad (8.18)$$

Thus, for an odd number   of signal samples, its spectrum padding with $(L-1)N_0$ zeros results in the signal

$$\tilde{a}_{Lk+l}=\frac{1}{\sqrt{L}}\sum_{n=0}^{N_0-1}a_n\mathrm{sincd}\left[N_0;\pi\left(k-n+\frac{l}{L}\right)\right],\ k=0,1,...,N_0-1\,,l=0,1,...,L-1 \qquad (8.19)$$

in which each Lk-th sample equals $1/\sqrt{L}$ of the k-th sample of the initial signal and the rest of other samples are discrete sinc interpolated from those initial samples.

For even N_0, $N_0/2$-th spectrum sample has no its symmetrical counterpart in the spectrum complex conjugated symmetry $\left\{\alpha_{\tilde{r}}=\alpha^{*}_{LN_0-\tilde{r}}\right\}$. Therefore it needs a special treatment. The following three options of spectrum zero padding, identical to those introduced for the perfect shifting algorithm (Eq. (7.38)) can be considered:

- Case-0: replace $N_0/2$-th spectral component by $N-N_0+1$ zeros, which means zeroing the signal highest frequency component;
- Case-1: halve $N_0/2$-th component, repeat it twice and insert between them $N-N_0-1$ zeros;
- Case-2: repeat $N_0/2$-th component twice and insert between them $N-N_0-1$ zeros, which means duplication of the signal highest frequency component.

These options are visualized in Fig. (**8.8**).

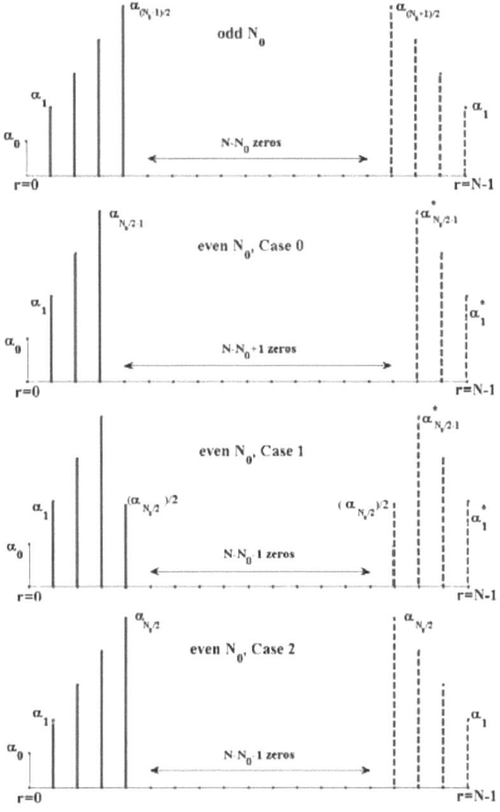

Fig. (8.8). Versions of signal DFT spectrum zero paddings for odd and even number of samples N_0.

One can, using derivations similar to that of Eq. (8. 18), obtain that in the Case-0 and in the Case-2 of spectrum zero-padding signals reconstructed by inverse DFT of the zero-padded spectrum of the signal $\{a_k\}$ are defined by the equations

$$\tilde{a}^{(0)}_{kL+l} = \frac{1}{\sqrt{L}} \sum_{n=0}^{N_0-1} a_n \mathbf{sincdd}\left[N_0 - 1; N_0; \pi\left(k - n + \frac{l}{L} \right) \right] \tag{8. 20}$$

and

$$\tilde{a}^{(2)}_{kL+l} = \frac{1}{\sqrt{L}} \sum_{n=0}^{N_0-1} a_n \mathbf{sincdd}\left[N_0 + 1; N_0; \pi\left(k - n + \frac{l}{L} \right) \right], \tag{8. 21}$$

correspondingly, where $\mathbf{sincdd}(M; N; x)$ is *sincdd-function* defined by Eq. (7.43). In the case Case-1 of zero padding reconstructed signal is

$$\tilde{a}^{(1)}_{kL+l} = \frac{\tilde{a}^{(0)}_{kL+l} + \tilde{a}^{(2)}_{kL+l}}{2} = \frac{1}{\sqrt{L}} \sum_{n=0}^{N-1} a_n \cos(x/N)\,\mathrm{sincd}\left[N;\pi\left(k-n+\frac{l}{L}\right)\right], \qquad (8.22)$$

Eqs. (8. 20), (8. 21) and (8. 22) are identical to Eqs. (7. 41), (7. 42) and (7. 45) for signal sub-sampling using the perfect fractional shift filter. Therefore, these two methods of signal sub-sampling are mathematically identical. However, the zero-padding method is computationally less efficient that the perfect fractional shift method. Signal sub-sampling by spectrum zero-padding implemented using Fast Fourier Transform requires $O(\log LN_0)$ operations per output signal sample, whereas the perfect fractional shift method requires only $O(\log N_0)$ operations.

Despite that, the zero-padding method has its application niche. In distinction from the fractional shift method, the zero-padding method is capable of sub-sampling signals with sub-sampling factors, which are arbitrary non-integer rational numbers of the form N/N_0 , where N is the sub-sampled signal length.

Consider, for instance, a signal $\{a_n\}$ with an odd number N_0 of samples and its DFT spectrum

$$\alpha_r = \frac{1}{\sqrt{N_0}} \sum_{n=0}^{N_0-1} a_n \exp\left(i2\pi\frac{nr}{N_0}\right) \qquad (8.23)$$

Pad this spectrum to the length N with $N - N_0$ zeros in the following way

$$\tilde{\alpha}_r = \begin{cases} \alpha_r, & r = 0 : (N_0 - 1)/2 \\ 0, & r = (N_0 + 1)/2 : N - (N_0 + 1)/2) \\ \alpha_{r-N+N_0}, & r = N - (N_0 - 1)/2 : N - 1) \end{cases} \qquad (8.24)$$

and compute inverse Fourier transform of this zero-padded spectrum:

$$\tilde{a}_k = \frac{1}{\sqrt{N}} \sum_{r=0}^{N-1} \tilde{\alpha}_r \exp\left(-i2\pi\frac{kr}{N}\right) =$$
$$\frac{1}{\sqrt{N}} \sum_{r=0}^{(N_0-1)/2} \tilde{\alpha}_r \exp\left(-i2\pi\frac{kr}{N}\right) + \frac{1}{\sqrt{N}} \sum_{r=N-(N_0-1)/2}^{N-1} \tilde{\alpha}_r \exp\left(-i2\pi\frac{kr}{N}\right) =$$

$$\frac{1}{\sqrt{N}} \sum_{r=0}^{(N_0-1)/2} \tilde{\alpha}_r \exp\left(-i2\pi \frac{kr}{N}\right) + \frac{1}{\sqrt{N}} \sum_{r=N-(N_0-1)/2}^{N-1} \tilde{\alpha}_{r-N+N_0} \exp\left(-i2\pi \frac{kr}{N}\right) =$$

$$\frac{1}{\sqrt{N}} \sum_{r=0}^{(N_0-1)/2} \alpha_r \exp\left(-i2\pi \frac{kr}{N}\right) + \frac{1}{\sqrt{N}} \sum_{r=(N_0+1)/2}^{N_0-1} \alpha_r \exp\left(-i2\pi \frac{k(r+N-N_0)}{N}\right). \qquad (8.\,25)$$

Now replace in this equation spectral coefficients $\{\alpha_r\}$ by their expression (Eq. (8.23)) through signal samples $\{a_n\}$ and change the order of summation:

$$\tilde{a}_k = \frac{1}{\sqrt{NN_0}} \sum_{r=0}^{(N_0-1)/2} \sum_{n=0}^{N_0-1} a_n \exp\left(i2\pi \frac{nr}{N_0}\right) \exp\left(-i2\pi \frac{kr}{N}\right) +$$

$$\frac{1}{\sqrt{NN_0}} \sum_{r=(N_0+1)/2}^{N_0-1} \sum_{n=0}^{N_0-1} a_n \exp\left(i2\pi \frac{nr}{N_0}\right) \exp\left(-i2\pi \frac{k(r-N_0)}{N}\right) =$$

$$\frac{1}{\sqrt{NN_0}} \sum_{n=0}^{N_0-1} a_n \sum_{r=0}^{(N_0-1)/2} \exp\left(i2\pi \frac{nr}{N_0}\right) \exp\left(-i2\pi \frac{kr}{N}\right) +$$

$$\frac{1}{\sqrt{NN_0}} \sum_{n=0}^{N_0-1} a_n \sum_{r=(N_0+1)/2}^{N_0-1} \exp\left(i2\pi \frac{nr}{N_0}\right) \exp\left(-i2\pi \frac{k(r-N_0)}{N}\right) =$$

$$\frac{1}{\sqrt{NN_0}} \sum_{n=0}^{N_0-1} a_n \left\{ \sum_{r=0}^{(N_0-1)/2} \exp\left[i2\pi \left(\frac{n}{N_0} - \frac{k}{N}\right)r\right] + \right.$$

$$\left. \exp\left(i2\pi \frac{kN_0}{N}\right) \sum_{r=(N_0+1)/2}^{N_0-1} \exp\left[i2\pi \left(\frac{n}{N_0} - \frac{k}{N}\right)r\right] \right\} =$$

$$\frac{1}{\sqrt{NN_0}} \left\{ (\Sigma)_1 + \exp\left(i2\pi \frac{kN_0}{N}\right)(\Sigma)_2 \right\}. \qquad (8.\,26)$$

Compute the sums in the figure brackets:

$$(\Sigma)_1 = \sum_{r=0}^{(N_0-1)/2} \exp\left[i2\pi \left(\frac{n}{N_0} - \frac{k}{N}\right)r\right] = \frac{\exp\left[i\pi \left(\frac{n}{N_0} - \frac{k}{N}\right)(N_0+1)\right] - 1}{\exp\left[i2\pi \left(\frac{n}{N_0} - \frac{k}{N}\right)\right] - 1}. \qquad (8.\,27)$$

$$\exp\left(i2\pi\frac{kN_0}{N}\right)(\Sigma)_2 = \exp\left(i2\pi\frac{kN_0}{N}\right)\sum_{r=.(N_0+1)/2}^{N_0-1}\exp\left[i2\pi\left(\frac{n}{N_0}-\frac{k}{N}\right)r\right]\Big\} =$$

$$\exp\left(i2\pi\frac{kN_0}{N}\right)\frac{\exp\left[i2\pi\left(\frac{n}{N_0}-\frac{k}{N}\right)N_0\right]-\exp\left[i\pi\left(\frac{n}{N_0}-\frac{k}{N}\right)(N_0+1)\right]}{\exp\left[i2\pi\left(\frac{n}{N_0}-\frac{k}{N}\right)\right]-1} =$$

$$\frac{1-\exp\left(i2\pi\frac{kN_0}{N}\right)\exp\left[i\pi\left(\frac{n}{N_0}-\frac{k}{N}\right)(N_0+1)\right]}{\exp\left[i2\pi\left(\frac{n}{N_0}-\frac{k}{N}\right)\right]-1}. \tag{8.28}$$

After some identical transformations obtain for the product of two exponential terms in Eq. (8. 28):

$$\exp\left(i2\pi\frac{kN_0}{N}\right)\exp\left[i\pi\left(\frac{n}{N_0}-\frac{k}{N}\right)(N_0+1)\right] = \exp\left[i\pi\left(\frac{kN_0}{N}+n+\left(\frac{n}{N_0}-\frac{k}{N}\right)\right)\right] =$$

$$\exp\left[i\pi\left(\frac{kN_0}{N}+n-2n+\left(\frac{n}{N_0}-\frac{k}{N}\right)\right)\right] = \exp\left[-i\pi\left(\left(\frac{n}{N_0}-\frac{k}{N}\right)(N_0-1)\right)\right]. \tag{8.29}$$

Therefore

$$\exp\left(i2\pi\frac{kN_0}{N}\right)(\Sigma)_2 = \frac{1-\exp\left(-i\pi\left[\left(\frac{n}{N_0}-\frac{k}{N}\right)(N_0-1)\right]\right)}{\exp\left[i2\pi\left(\frac{n}{N_0}-\frac{k}{N}\right)\right]-1}. \tag{8.30}$$

and

$$\tilde{a}_k = \frac{1}{\sqrt{NN_0}}\left\{(\Sigma)_1 + \exp\left(i2\pi\frac{kN_0}{N}\right)(\Sigma)_2\right\} =$$

$$\frac{1}{\sqrt{NN_0}}\frac{\left(\exp\left[i\pi\left(\frac{n}{N_0}-\frac{k}{N}\right)(N_0+1)\right]-1+1-\exp\left(-i\pi\left[\left(\frac{n}{N_0}-\frac{k}{N}\right)(N_0+1)\right]\right)\right)}{\exp\left[i2\pi\left(\frac{n}{N_0}-\frac{k}{N}\right)\right]-1} =$$

$$\frac{1}{\sqrt{NN_0}}\frac{\left(\exp\left[i\pi\left(\frac{n}{N_0}-\frac{k}{N}\right)N_0\right]-\exp\left(-i\pi\left[\left(\frac{n}{N_0}-\frac{k}{N}\right)N_0\right]\right)\right)}{\exp\left[\pi\left(\frac{n}{N_0}-\frac{k}{N}\right)\right]-\exp\left[-\pi\left(\frac{n}{N_0}-\frac{k}{N}\right)\right]} =$$

$$\frac{1}{\sqrt{NN_0}}\frac{\sin\left[\pi N_0\left(\frac{n}{N_0}-\frac{kN_0}{N}\right)\right]}{\sin\left[\pi\left(\frac{n}{N_0}-\frac{kN_0}{N}\right)\right]}. \qquad (8.31)$$

Hence, finally

$$\tilde{a}_k = \sqrt{\frac{N_0}{N}}\sum_{n=0}^{N_0-1}a_n\,\mathrm{sincd}\left\{N_0;\left[\pi\left(n-\frac{kN_0}{N}\right)\right]\right\},\quad k=0,...,N-1, \qquad (8.32)$$

which means that the signal spectrum zero-padding results in N/N_0 times sub-sampled and discrete sinc interpolated signal.

For signals with an even number N_0 of signal samples the same above-mentioned options of spectrum zero padding (Fig. **8.8**) are possible: zeroing the highest frequency component (Case-0), halving the highest frequency component and duplicating it (Case-1), and duplicating the highest frequency component (Case-2). Similarly to the above derivation, one can obtain for these cases the following equations, complete analogs of Eqs. (8.20), (8.21), and (8.22):

$$\tilde{a}_k^{(0)} = \frac{1}{\sqrt{L}}\sum_{n=0}^{N_0-1}a_n\,\mathrm{sincdd}\left[N_0-1;N_0;\pi\left(n-\frac{kN_0}{N}\right)\right],$$

$$(8.33) \quad \widetilde{a}_k^{(2)} = \frac{1}{\sqrt{L}} \sum_{n=0}^{N_0-1} a_n \mathbf{sincd}\left[N_0 + 1; N_0; \left(n - \frac{kN_0}{N} \right) \right],$$

(8.34)

$$\widetilde{a}_k^{(1)} = \frac{1}{\sqrt{L}} \sum_{n=0}^{N-1} a_n \cos(x/N)\mathbf{sincd}\left[N; \pi\left(n - \frac{kN_0}{N} \right) \right], \qquad (8.35)$$

To summarize the said in this Section, one can define the algorithm of signal sub-sampling by its SDFT spectrum zero padding by the equation:

$$\widetilde{a}_k = IFFT_N\left\{ DFTZP_{N/N_0}\left\{ FFT_{N_0}\left\{ a_k \right\} \right\} \right\}, \qquad (8.36)$$

where $\{\widetilde{a}_k\}$, $k = 0,1,..., N-1$ are samples of the N/N_0 times sub-sampled signal $\{a_n\}$, $n = 0,1,..., N_0 - 1$, $IFFT_N\{\ \}$ is N point inverse Fast Fourier Transform, $FFT_{N_0}\{a_k\}$ is points direct Fast Fourier Transform, and $DFTZP_{N/N_0}$ is a DFT spectrum zero-padding operator. For sub-sampling images the algorithm has to be applied separably in both coordinates, say, row-wise and column-wise.

8.2.2 Zero Padding Signal DCT Spectra

Signal DFT spectrum zero padding method of signal sub-sampling has the same drawback as the DFT based perfect fractional shift algorithm: it suffers from the boundary effects associated with the cyclicity of DFT.

A simple and very practical solution to this problem is zero padding in the domain of the Discrete Cosine Transform. For 1D signals, the DCT zero-padding algorithm for the sub-sampling signal $\{a_k\}$ of samples ($k = 0,1,..., N_0 - 1$) to obtain $N > N_0$ samples of a sub-sampled signal $\{\widetilde{a}_{\widetilde{k}}\}$, $\widetilde{k} = 0,1,..., N-1$ is defined by the equation:

$$\widetilde{a}_{\widetilde{k}} = \mathbf{IDCT}_N\left\{ \mathbf{DCT\_ZP}_{N/N_0}\left[\mathbf{DCT}_{N_0}\left\{ a_k \right\} \right] \right\}, \qquad (8.37)$$

where $\mathbf{DCT}_{N_0}(\cdot)$ and $\mathbf{IDCT}_N(\cdot)$ are N_0-points direct and N-points inverse fast Discrete Cosine Transforms and $\mathbf{DCT\_ZP}_L[\cdot]$ is a DCT spectrum zero-padding operator that places $N - N_0$ zeros after the last $(N_0 - 1)$-th DCT spectrum sample.

For faster decay of the interpolation kernel, it is also advisable to halve this last sample that, for DCT, represents the signal highest frequency component. For 2D signals and images, this algorithm has to be applied separably over both coordinate indices.

Point spread function and frequency response of the DCT spectrum zero padding with and without halving its the highest frequency component do not exactly coincide with those of DFT, but they are very close to them. Fig. (**8.9**) presents for comparison point spread functions and frequency responses of DFT and DCT zero-padding on an example of signal 5 times sub-sampling.

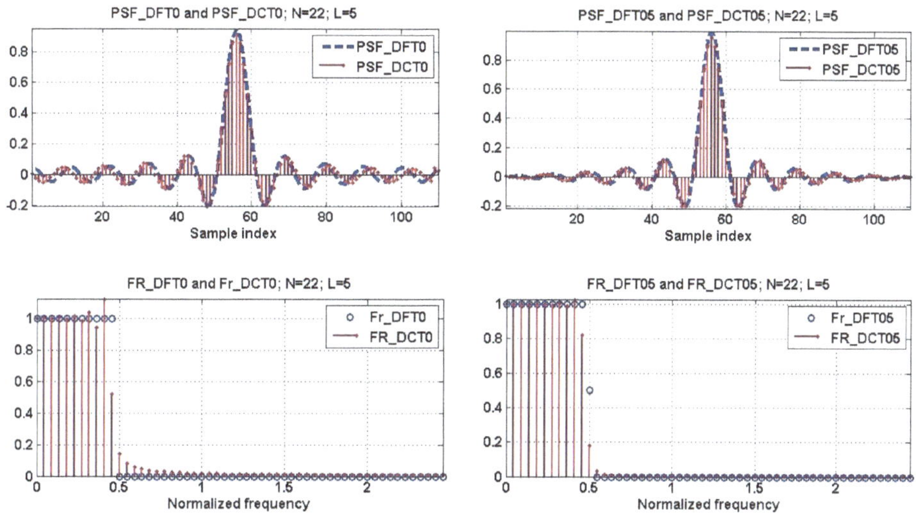

Fig. (8.9). Discrete point spread functions (PSFs, supper row) and frequency responses (FRs, bottom row) of DFT and DCT zero-padding for signal 5x-subsampling (N0=22, L=5) with preserving (left column) and halving (right column) the highest signal frequency component.

One can see from this figure that halving the signal's highest frequency component fastens the decay of the oscillations of the interpolation point spread functions very substantially.

In distinction from point spread function of the DFT zero padding, which is a cyclic discrete sinc-function with a period equals the number N of sub-sampled signal samples, point spread function of the DCT zero padding is cyclic with a double period. Thanks to this signal resampling through the DCT spectrum zero padding does not involve at signal borders signal samples from the signal opposite borders, whereas DFT zero-padding does. One can see this in Fig. (**8.10**) on plots of point spread functions of DFT and DCT zero padding at the left and the right borders of the signal interval. This property of the DCT zero-padding prevents the appearance of severe oscillations in the vicinity of image boards, which are characteristic for image sub-sampling by the DFT spectrum zero padding.

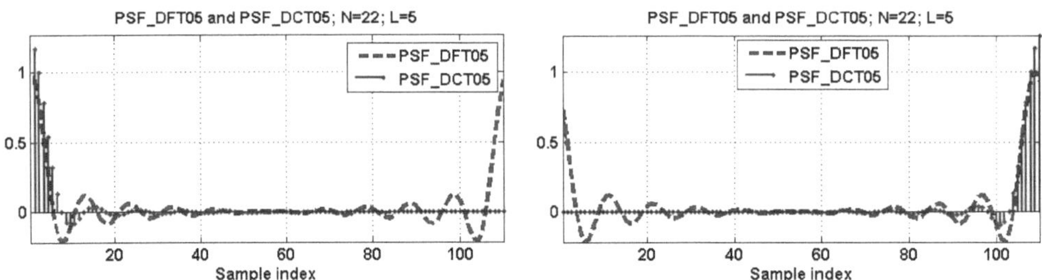

Fig. (8.10). Point spread functions of signal 5x-subsampling using DFT and DCT zero padding on left (left plot) and right (right plot) signal borders.

Image sub-sampling by DFT and DCT spectra zero-padding are compared also in Fig. **(8.11)** on an example of zooming-in an image fragment. Severe oscillations seen in the vicinity of the borders of the image fragment (white box in Fig. **(8.11a)**) zoomed-in by the DFT-based image sub-sampling algorithm (Fig. **8.11b**) are completely absent in the same fragment zoomed-in by the DCT-based algorithm (Fig. **8.11c**).

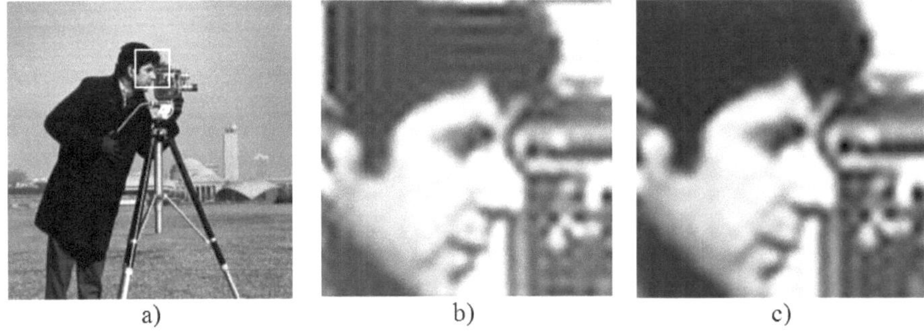

Fig. (8.11). Zooming-in an image fragment outlined by a white box (**a**) through DFT (**b**) and DCT- (**c**) spectra zero padding.

Computation wise, signal N/N_0 times zooming-in using zero-padding its DFT or DCT spectra requires, with the use of Fast Fourier Transform or Fast DCT algorithms, $O(N_0 \log N_0)$ operations for the direct transform and $O(N \log N)$ operation for the inverse transform of the zero-padded spectra.

Spectrum zero padding method is a good practical solution for image sub-sampling with rational sub-sampling factors. This is especially useful when the required sub-sampling factors are numbers only slightly larger or slightly less than integer numbers, such as, for instance, 1.1 or 1.15 or alike. This is required, for instance, in the target location, when target images might be slightly re-scaled with respect to available templates and, therefore templates should be appropriately re-scaled to better match the target image. Note that, when image de-magnification is needed with factors less that one, *i.e.*, when $N < N_0$, this de-magnification can be achieved by simple dropping $N_0 - N$ image high-frequency coefficients, which exactly corresponds to the image ideal low-pass filtering, the operation dictated by the sampling theorem.

Note also that image zooming-in using DCT spectra zero padding can be naturally used when images are JPEG compressed. In this case, sub-sampling can be carried out directly by zero-padding DCT spectra of image blocks without the need to decompress images.

8.3. EXERCISES

- **Sincd_interpol_2D_BNTM.m**;

Demonstration of the process of 1D and 2D signal discrete sinc interpolated fast sub-sampling using signal fractional shifts.

User defined parameter:

- type of test signals
- signal sub-sampling rate

CHAPTER 9

Examples of Applications of Signal   and Image Resampling Using Discrete Sinc Interpolation

9.1. QUASI-CONTINUOUS SPECTRAL AND CORRELATION ANALYSIS

Two the most immediate applications of sincd-interpolated signal sub-sampling algorithms are *"quasi-continuous" Fourier spectrum analysis* for detection and localization, with a sub-sample resolution of image periodical components and signal/image correlation analysis of position of the correlation peaks.

Signal spectrum analysis, with a sub-sample resolution, can be performed by applying the perfect fractional shift algorithm for computing DFT spectra of signals.

Let $\{a_k\}$ be a signal of N samples, $\{\alpha_r\}$ be samples of its DFT spectrum:

$$a_k = \frac{1}{\sqrt{N}} \sum_{r=0}^{N-1} \alpha_r \exp\left(-i2\pi\frac{kr}{N}\right), \qquad (9.1)$$

N be an odd number, and

$$\lambda_k^{(\omega_f)} = \begin{cases} \exp\left(i2\pi\dfrac{\omega_f k}{N}\right), & k = 0,1,...,\dfrac{N-1}{2} \\[2mm] \left(\lambda_{N-k}^{(\delta_f)}\right)^*, & k = \dfrac{N+1}{2},...,N-1 \end{cases} \qquad (9.2)$$

be a signal modulating function of an arbitrary (not necessarily integer) frequency ω_f with asterisk $*$ denoting the complex conjugacy. Let's compute DFT of the modulated signal $\{a_k\lambda_k\}$ and establish its link with signal DFT spectrum $\{\alpha_r\}$:

$$\tilde{\alpha}_s = \frac{1}{\sqrt{N}} \sum_{k=0}^{N-1} a_k \lambda_k^{(\omega_f)} \exp\left(i2\pi\frac{ks}{N}\right) =$$

$$\frac{1}{\sqrt{N}}\sum_{k=0}^{N-1}\lambda_k^{(\omega_f)}\left[\frac{1}{\sqrt{N}}\sum_{r=0}^{N-1`}\alpha_r\exp\left(-i2\pi\frac{kr}{N}\right)\right]\exp\left(i2\pi\frac{ks}{N}\right)=$$

$$\frac{1}{N}\sum_{r=0}^{N-1}\alpha_r\sum_{k=0}^{N-1`}\lambda_k^{(\omega_f)}\exp\left(i2\pi\frac{s-r}{N}k\right). \tag{9.3}$$

The internal sum over $\{\alpha_r\}$ in Eq. (9.3) is:

$$\sum_{k=0}^{N-1/2`}\lambda_k^{(\omega_f)}\exp\left(i2\pi\frac{s-r}{N}k\right)+\sum_{k=N+1/2}^{N-1`}\lambda_k^{(\omega_f)}\exp\left(i2\pi\frac{s-r}{N}k\right)=$$

$$\sum_{k=0}^{(N-1)/2`}\lambda_k^{(\omega_f)}\exp\left(i2\pi\frac{s-r}{N}k\right)+\sum_{k=1}^{(N-1)/2`}\lambda_{N-k}^{(\omega_f)}\exp\left[i2\pi\frac{(s-r)(N-k)}{N}\right]=$$

$$\sum_{k=0}^{(N-1)/2`}\exp\left(i2\pi\frac{s-r+\omega_f}{N}k\right)+\sum_{k=1}^{(N-1)/2`}\exp\left(-i2\pi\frac{s-r+\omega_f}{N}k\right)=$$

$$\frac{\exp\left[i\pi\dfrac{(s-r+\omega_f)(N+1)}{N}\right]-1}{\exp\left(i2\pi\dfrac{s-r+\omega_f}{N}\right)-1}+$$

$$\frac{\exp\left[-i\pi\dfrac{(s-r+\omega_f)(N+1)}{N}\right]-\exp\left(-i2\pi\dfrac{s-r+\omega_f}{N}\right)}{\exp\left(-i2\pi\dfrac{s-r+\omega_f}{N}\right)-1}=$$

$$\frac{\exp\left[i\pi(s-r+\omega_f)\dfrac{(N+1)}{N}\right]-1}{\exp\left(i2\pi\dfrac{s-r+\omega_f}{N}\right)-1}-\frac{\exp\left[-i\pi(s-r+\omega_f)\dfrac{(N-1)}{N}\right]-1}{\exp\left(i2\pi\dfrac{s-r+\omega_f}{N}\right)-1}=$$

$$\frac{\exp\left[i\pi(s-r+\omega_f)\frac{(N+1)}{N}\right]-\exp\left[-i\pi(s-r+\omega_f)\frac{(N-1)}{N}\right]}{\exp\left(i2\pi\frac{s-r+\omega_f}{N}\right)-1}=$$

$$\frac{\exp[i\pi(s-r+\omega_f)]-\exp[-i\pi(s-r+\omega_f)]}{\exp\left(i\pi\frac{s-r+\omega_f}{N}\right)-\exp\left(-i\pi\frac{s-r+\omega_f}{N}\right)}=\frac{\sin[\pi(s-r+\omega_f)]}{\sin\left(\pi\frac{s-r+\omega_f}{N}\right)} \tag{9.4}$$

Insert now this expression into Eq. (9. 3) and obtain finally that DFT spectrum of a signal $\left\{a_k \lambda_k^{(\omega_f)}\right\}$ modulated by function $\left\{\lambda_k^{(\omega_f)}\right\}$ with frequency ω_f is ω_f-shifted sincd-interpolated spectrum of the initial signal $\{a_k\}$

$$\tilde{\alpha}_r = \sum_{r=0}^{N-1} \alpha_r \, \mathrm{sincd}[N;\pi(s-r+\omega_f)]. \tag{9.5}$$

For even number N of signal samples and modulation function

$$\lambda_k^{(\omega_f)} = \begin{cases} \exp\left(i2\pi\dfrac{k\omega_f}{N}\right), & k=0,1,...,N/2-1 \\ C\cos(\pi\omega_f), & k=N/2 \\ \lambda_k^{(\omega_f)} = \left(\lambda_{N-k}^{(\omega_f)}\right)^*, & k=N/2+1,...,N-1 \end{cases} \tag{9.6}$$

there are the same three options as those for the signal fractional shift (Eq. (7.38):

- Case-0: $C=0$;
- Case-1: $C=1$;
- Case-2, $C=2$.

In Case-0, ω_f-shifted discrete sinc interpolated spectrum is

$$\tilde{\alpha}_r^{(\omega_f)} = \sum_{s=0}^{N-1} \alpha_s \, \mathrm{sincdd}[(N-1);N;\pi(r-s+\omega_f)]. \tag{9.7}$$

In Case-1, ω_f-shifted discrete sinc interpolated spectrum is

$$\tilde{\alpha}_r^{(\omega_f)} = \sum_{s=0}^{N-1} \alpha_s \cos\left[\pi\left(r - s + \omega_f\right)/N\right] \mathbf{sincd}\left[\pi\left(r - s + \omega_f\right)\right]. \tag{9.8}$$

In Case-2, ω_f -shifted discrete sinc interpolated spectrum is

$$\tilde{\alpha}_r^{(\omega_f)} = \sum_{s=0}^{N-1} \alpha_s \mathbf{sincdd}\left[(N+1); N; \pi\left(r - s + \omega_f\right)\right], \tag{9.9}$$

where $\mathbf{sincdd}[M; N; x]$ is the sincdd-function (Eq. (7.43)).

This method of signal spectral analysis with a sub-sample resolution can be algorithmically defined as:

$$\left\{\tilde{\alpha}_r^{(\omega_f)}\right\} = \mathbf{FFT}_N\left\{a_k \lambda_k^{(\omega_f)}\right\}, \tag{9.10}$$

Where, $\mathbf{FFT}_N$ is a N points Fast Fourier Transform operator. It is illustrated in Fig. (**9.1**) obtained using program ContinuousSpectralAnalysis_BNTM provided in Exercises.

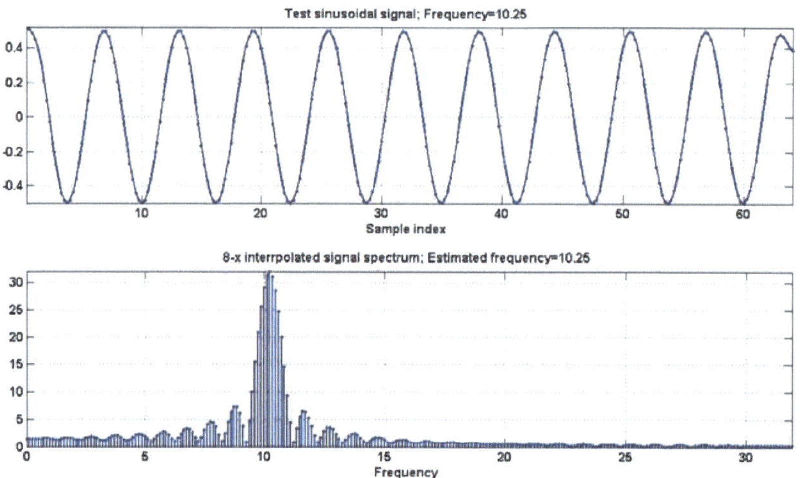

Fig. (9.1). Spectral analysis with a sub-sample resolution: a test sinusoidal signal (upper plot) and its sub-sampled DFT spectrum. The signal frequency is determined by the position of the spectrum maximum.

In the signal correlation analysis, localization of correlation peaks directly in sampled signals is possible to the accuracy of the signal sampling interval Δ_x, although in applications more accurate localization is frequently required. Such a "quasi-continuous" correlation analysis can be implemented using the perfect fractional shift algorithm. An algorithm of computing signal $\bar{\delta}_x$-shifted correlations is defined by the equation

$$c_k^{(\bar{\delta}_x)} = \mathbf{IFFT}_N\left\{\left[\eta_r^{(\bar{\delta}_x)}\right]\bullet\left[\mathbf{FFT}_N(a_k)\right]\bullet\left[\mathbf{FFT}_N(b_k)\right]^*\right\}, \tag{9.11}$$

where, $\mathbf{FFT}_N(\cdot)$ and $\mathbf{IFFT}_N(\cdot)$ are N-points direct and inverse Fast Fourier Transform operators, dot $\bullet$ symbolizes element-wise product of arrays, asterisk $*$ symbolizes the complex conjugacy, and the phase modulation coefficients $\left\{\eta_r^{(\bar{\delta}_x)}\right\}$ are coefficients of the frequency response of the perfect $\bar{\delta}_x$-shifting determined for odd and even N by Eqs. (7.35) and (7.37), correspondingly. This algorithm computes the correlation between signals:

$$c_k = \sum_{n=0}^{N-1} a_n b_{n-k}^{(\delta_x)},$$

one of which ($b_{n-k}^{(\delta_x)}$) is $\bar{\delta}_x$-shifted and discrete sinc interpolated. For odd N

$$b_{n-k}^{(\delta_x)} = \sum_{m=0}^{N-1} b_m \; \mathbf{sincd}\left[N; \pi\left(m + n + \bar{\delta}_x - k\right)\right]. \tag{9.12}$$

For even N, $\bar{\delta}_x$-shifted and discrete sinc interpolated signals are, respectively: for Case 0:

$$b_{n-k}^{(\delta_x)} = \sum_{m=0}^{N-1} b_m \; \mathbf{sincdd}\left[N-1; N; \pi\left(m + n + \bar{\delta}_x - k\right)\right] ; \tag{9.13}$$

for Case 1:

$$b_{n-k}^{(\delta_x)} = \sum_{r=0}^{N-1} b_m \; \cos\left[\pi\left(n - \bar{\delta}_x\right)/N\right]\mathbf{sincd}\left[m + n + \bar{\delta}_x - k\right]; \tag{9.14}$$

and for Case 2:

$$b_{n-k}^{(\bar\delta_x)} = \sum_{m=0}^{N-1} b_m \, \mathrm{sincdd}\left[N+1; N; \pi\left(m+n+\bar\delta_x - k\right)\right].$$

(9. 15)

Eqs. (9. 12), (9. 13), (9. 14), (9. 15) imply that one can perform quasi-continuous correlation analysis of two signals through varying the analog shift parameter $\bar\delta_x$.

9.2. IMAGE ROTATION

9.2.1. Fast Image Rotation Using the Fractional Shift Algorithms

Rotation of a 2D coordinate system (x,y) by an angle θ can be described as a multiplication of signal coordinate vector $[x, y]$ by rotation matrix $\mathbf{ROT}_\theta$:

$$\begin{bmatrix} \tilde{x} \\ \tilde{y} \end{bmatrix} = \mathbf{ROT}_\theta \begin{bmatrix} x \\ y \end{bmatrix} = \begin{bmatrix} \cos\theta & -\sin\theta \\ \sin\theta & \cos\theta \end{bmatrix}\begin{bmatrix} x \\ y \end{bmatrix}$$

(9. 16)

In digital images, physical co-ordinates (x, y) are represented, given sampling intervals (Δ_x, Δ_y), by integer indices $\{k, l\}$ of pixels:

$$\begin{vmatrix} x \\ y \end{vmatrix} = \begin{vmatrix} k\Delta_x \\ l\Delta_y \end{vmatrix},$$

(9. 17)

and the rotation matrix is applied to vectors of indices:

$$\mathbf{ROT}_\theta \begin{vmatrix} k \\ l \end{vmatrix} = \begin{vmatrix} \cos\theta & -\sin\theta \\ \sin\theta & \cos\theta \end{vmatrix}\begin{vmatrix} k \\ l \end{vmatrix}.$$

(9. 18)

In order to reduce the computational complexity of this geometrical transformation, it is advisable to factorize the rotation matrix into a product of three matrices, each of which modifies only one co-ordinate:

$$\mathbf{ROT}_\theta = \begin{bmatrix} \cos\theta & -\sin\theta \\ \sin\theta & \cos\theta \end{bmatrix} = \begin{bmatrix} 1 & -\tan(\theta/2) \\ 0 & 1 \end{bmatrix}\begin{bmatrix} 1 & 0 \\ \sin\theta & 1 \end{bmatrix}\begin{bmatrix} 1 & -\tan(\theta/2) \\ 0 & 1 \end{bmatrix}.$$

(9. 19)

This implementation of image rotation is known as the *three-pass rotation algorithm*. It performs, at each of three passes, only image shearing along one of two coordinates, say, along rows at the first pass, along with columns at the second pass and again along rows at the third pass, as it is illustrated in Fig. (**9.2a**). Specifically, in rotation of an image of $N_x \times N_y$ pixels ($k = 0,1,..., N_x - 1$, $l = 0,1,..., N_y - 1$) around point (k_0, l_0) ($0 \leq k_0 \leq N_x - 1$; $0 \leq l_0 \leq N_y - 1$), k-th image row is shifted by $\delta_x^{(k)}/\Delta_x = -\tan(\theta/2)(k - k_0)$ at the first pass, l-th column is shifted by $\delta_y^{(l)}/\Delta_y = \sin\theta(l - l_0)$ at the second pass, and then again k-th row is shifted by $\delta_x^{(k)}/\Delta_x = -\tan(\theta/2)(k - k_0)$ at the third pass.

Above described DFT- and DCT-based perfect fractional shift algorithms are ideally suited for performing these shifts. As far as these algorithms implement a cyclic convolution, image rotation, by this method, entails characteristic aliasing effects at image borders. They are illustrated in Fig. (**9.2b,d**). One can avoid them by inscribing images into an array of a correspondingly larger size (Fig. **9.2b**) or by using only the aliasing free image part inside the circle of the diameter equals the image linear size (Fig. **9.2d**).

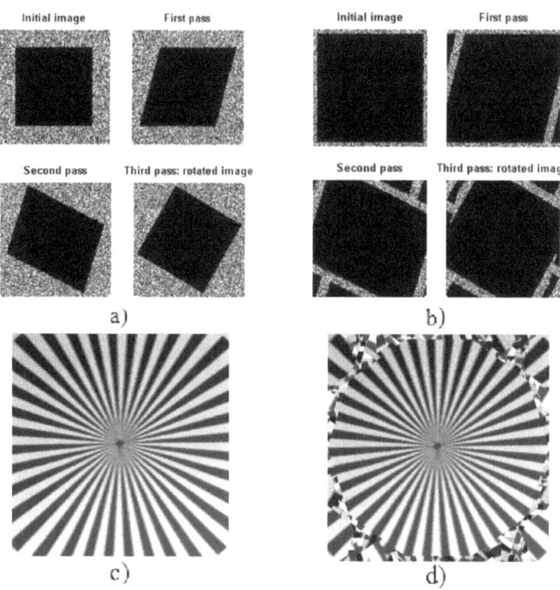

Fig. (9.2). The principle of the three pass image rotation algorithm and aliasing effects associated with the implementation of the interpolation as a cyclic convolution: three passes of rotation without aliasing (**a**); three passes of image rotation with aliasing effects owing to the cyclicity of the DFT based convolution (**b**); a test image (**c**) and its copy rotated ten times by 36° (**d**), which demonstrates image aliasing outside the circle of the diameter equals the image linear size.

9.2.2. Image Rotation: Discrete Sinc Interpolation *vs.* Other Interpolation Methods

Image rotation is an appropriate method for testing quality and comparison of interpolation methods used for image resampling. For this purpose, one should rotate test images by a multiple of 360 degrees and evaluate the difference between test and rotated images. This section provides experimental data of comparison of discrete sinc interpolation with other more traditional numerical interpolation methods in terms of the interpolation accuracy and signal preservation. Compared with discrete sinc interpolation are methods offered by the MATLAB© image processing toolbox: nearest-neighbor interpolation, linear (bilinear) interpolation, and cubic (bicubic) *spline interpolation.*

All of these interpolation methods are convolutional methods characterized by their point spread functions and frequency responses. Point spread functions and discrete frequency responses of the compared interpolation methods are presented in Fig. (**9.3**).

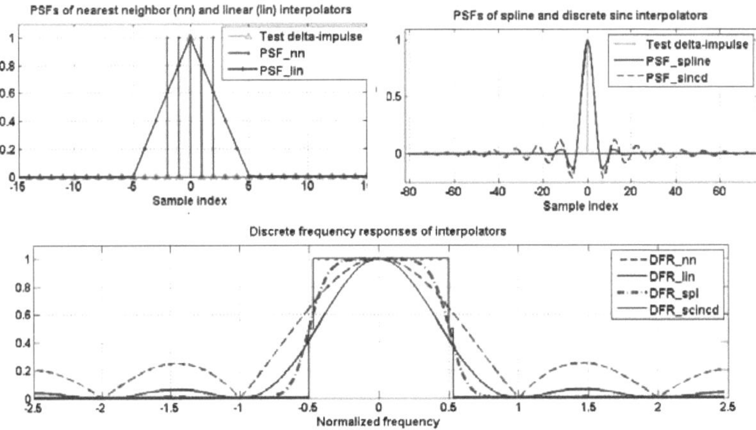

Fig. (9.3). Point spread functions (PSF, upper plots) and discrete frequency responses (DFR, bottom plots) of nearest neighbor (nn), linear (lin), bicubic spline (spl), and discrete sinc interpolators.

Plots of discrete frequency responses of the methods (Fig. **9.3**, bottom plots) reveal the major drawback of the traditional interpolation methods: they substantially attenuate high-frequency signal components within the signal baseband (frequency interval $[-0.5 \div 0.5]$) and pass substantial aliasing frequency components outside this interval. This tendency results in image blurring that can severely worsen visual image quality and image applicability for further analysis, for instance, for object recognition, target location, and alike. In distinction from the traditional methods, frequency response of the discrete sinc interpolation (curve "DFR_sincd" in the figure) is flat within the signal baseband and zero outside, which implies that the discrete sinc interpolation does not cause any distortions of interpolated signals, *i.e.*, it implements the perfect interpolation. These conclusions are supported by the results of experiments with image rotation using different interpolation methods presented in Figs. (**9.4-9.6**). obtained using program RotateComparis_demo_BNTM.m provided in Exercises.

a)   b)

Fig. (9.4). Test images for comparison of interpolation methods: "Text" image (**a**) and a realization of a pseudo-random image with a uniform spectrum within 0.7 of the baseband ("Prus" image).

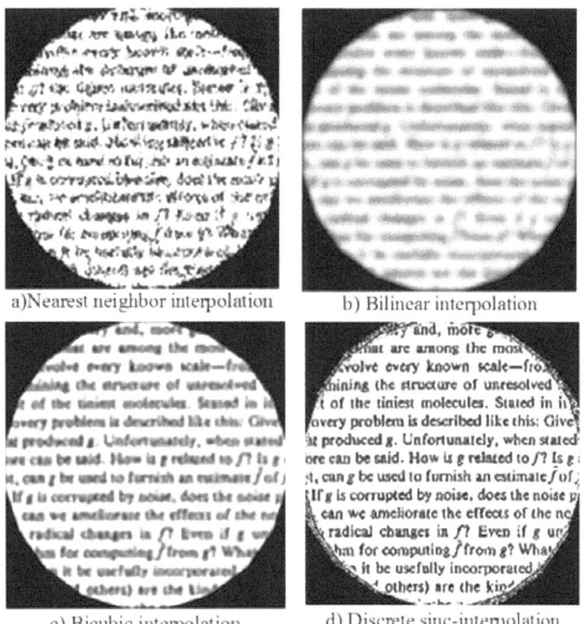

a) Nearest neighbor interpolation   b) Bilinear interpolation

c) Bicubic interpolation   d) Discrete sinc-interpolation

Fig. (9.5). Discrete sinc interpolation *versus* conventional numerical interpolation methods used for 60x18° rotations of test image "Text": nearest neighbor interpolation (**a**); bilinear interpolation (**b**); bicubic interpolation (**c**); discrete sinc interpolation (**d**).

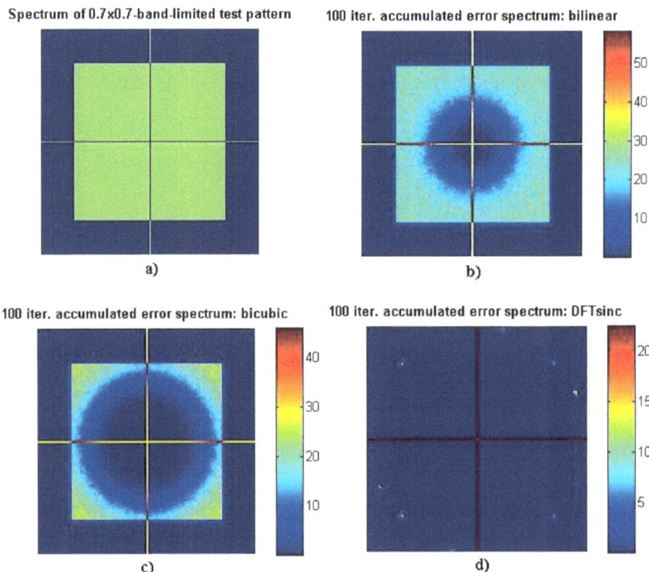

Fig. (9.6). The spectrum of test image "Prus" (**a**) and spectra of rotation errors after 60x18° rotations of the test image using bilinear (**b**), bicubic (**c**), and discrete sinc interpolation (**d**). All spectra are displayed in frequency coordinates centered at the spectrum zero frequency (dc-component), with image luminosity proportional to error spectra intensity (displayed in pseudo colors of MATLAB© colormap "jet"); bright points in figure (**d**) are spectral aliasing components intentionally left at the borders of the test image baseband to secure, for display purposes, the same image dynamic range as that of figures (**b**) and (**c**).

For nearest neighbor, bilinear, and bicubic interpolation methods, rotations were performed using the standard MATLAB program **imrotate.m** from the image processing tool box. For discrete sinc interpolated rotation, a program was used that implements the 3-step rotation algorithm through the DFT-based fractional shift algorithm described in Section 8.1.

Fig. (**9.4**) presents two test images used in the comparison experiments: an image of printed text "Text" (a) for checking text readability after multiple rotations, and a realization of a pseudo-random image, with uniform power spectrum within the central 0.7x0.7 fragment of the total spectral area (b). Fig. (**9.5**) demonstrates what has happened with the test image "Text" after 60 times rotations by 18 degrees. One can see that images rotated using bilinear and bicubic interpolation have completely lost their readability, whereas the image rotated using discrete sinc interpolation by the above described three-step rotation algorithm does not differ from the initial test image.

In the analysis of interpolation errors, it is very instructive to compare their power spectra to see which spectral components suffered from interpolation more. For this purpose, the image "Prus" is a very appropriate test image. Fig. (**9.6**) presents modules of spectrum of this image and spectra of the rotation errors computed as differences between the test image "Prus" and the results of its rotation by 1080° carried out in 60 steps using bilinear, bicubic and discrete sinc interpolations. It can be seen in the figure that in the case of discrete sinc interpolation, the error spectrum is practically zero within the base-band circle, whereas for bicubic and bilinear interpolation error spectra are low only for low spatial frequencies and grow quite substantially to high frequencies. Note that errors for bicubic interpolation are less severe than those for bilinear interpolation, which one can easily explain by comparing frequency responses of both methods in Fig. (**9.3**) (bottom plot).

9.3. IMAGE DATA RESAMPLING FOR IMAGE RECONSTRUCTION FROM PROJECTIONS

9.3.1. Discrete Radon Transform and the Filtered Back-projection Algorithm for Image Reconstruction from Parallel Beam Projections

Precise data resampling is a crucial issue in image reconstruction from projections. As known, image reconstruction from projections is based on properties of the integral Radon transform. The main problem in the discrete representation of the integral Radon Transform is definition, for computing image projections, of a line integral under an arbitrary angle over the image sampling lattice.

Any definition of the discrete line integral should assume one or another method of image interpolation for finding image values along the projection line in its points that do not coincide with positions of the available image samples. For commonly used regular square sampling lattices, only column-wise, row-wise, and 45° diagonal-wise integrations do not require any interpolation. One possible solution to this problem is line integration over a "continuous" image model, obtained using the above-described method of image sub-sampling with discrete sinc interpolation. An alternative and a more computationally efficient solution is the following algorithmic implementation of the Discrete Radon Transform through image rotation:

$$Pr(\theta_r, s) = \mathrm{SUM}_l \left[\mathrm{ROT}_{\theta_r} \left(\{ a_{k,l} \} \right) \right], \qquad\qquad (9.\,20)$$

where $\{k,l\}$ are sample indices of the image $\{a_{k,l}\}$ on a square sampling lattice, $Pr(\theta_r,s)$ are samples of the image r-th projection taken under angle θ_r, $\text{ROT}_{\theta_r}(\bullet)$ is an operator of image rotation by angle θ_r around the center of the sampling lattice and $\text{SUM}_l[\bullet]$ is an operator of the summation of samples of the rotated image over index l. The summation implements image projecting, *i.e.*, computing the line integral along the direction of projections.

According to this algorithm, the required image interpolation is carried out in the process of image rotation. To secure the least possible interpolation error, image rotation should be performed with discrete sinc interpolation. For the implementation of the rotation operator, the above-described fast three-step rotation algorithm can be used.

The most frequently used algorithm of image reconstruction from projections is the *filtered back-projection algorithm* (see, for instance, Ref. [4]). This algorithm reconstructs images using accumulation of derivatives of image projections projected backward (*i.e.*, repeated) in the directions, in which they were obtained. This image reconstruction algorithm can be implemented using image rotation as following:

$$a_{k,l} = \text{SUM}_r\left\{\text{ROT}_{-\theta_r}\left\{\text{BckP}_l\left\{\text{RAMPF}\left\{Pr(\theta_r,r)\right\}\right\}\right\}\right\}, \tag{9.21}$$

where $\{Pr(\theta_r,r)\}$ are samples of the image r-th projection, taken under angle θ_r, $\text{RAMPF}\{\bullet\}$ is an operator of ramp-filtering, which performs perfect differentiation described in Sect. 9.4.1., $\text{BckP}_l\{\bullet\}$ is a "back projection" operator implemented as replication of the operand over index r, and $\text{SUM}_r\{\bullet\}$ is a summation operator that sums up replicated (projected backward) ramp-filtered projections over the entire set of projection angles $\{\theta_r\}$.

Fig. (**9.7**) generated using program **radon_invradon_demo_SPIE.m** provided in Exercises illustrates discrete Radon Transform and image reconstruction using the filtered back-projection algorithm.

Test image; 256x256

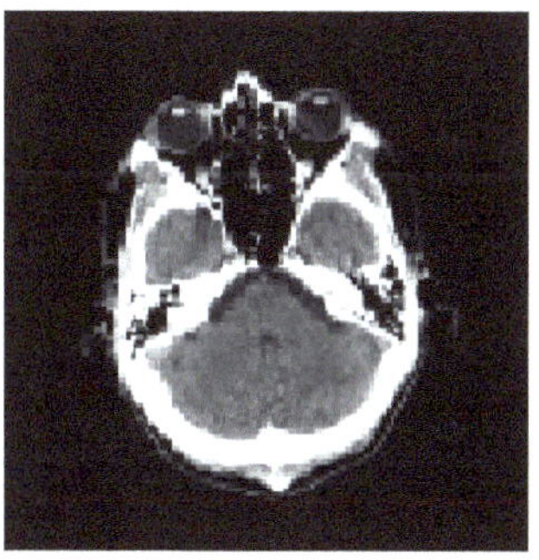

Radon Transform: 256 projections

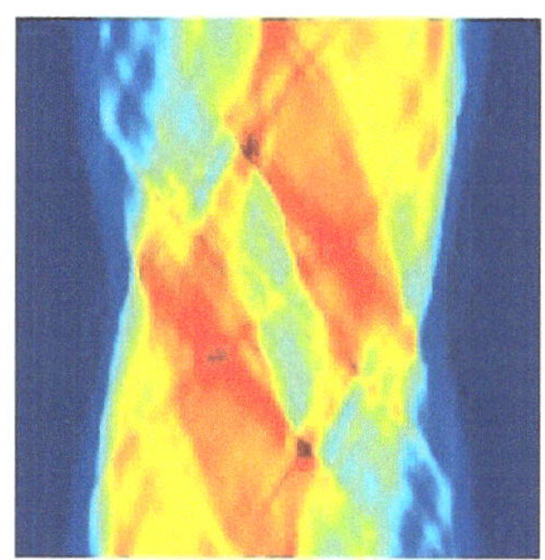

Rotated filtered back progection at angle 89.3⁰

Reconstructed image; 256-th projection

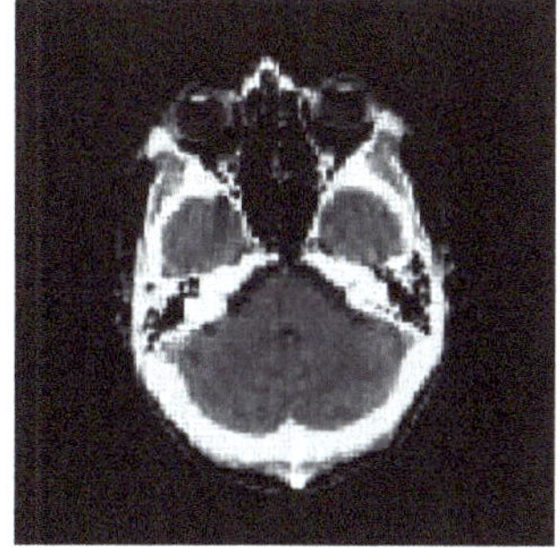

Fig. (9.7). A test image (upper left), set of its projections with projection angle as the vertical coordinate (upper right, shown in pseudo-colors, MATLAB© colormap "jet"), an example of filtered projection projected backward along at angle 89.3° (bottom left) and a reconstructed image (bottom right).

9.3.2. The Direct Fourier Method of Image Reconstruction

According to the projection theorem for Radon transform, the Fourier spectra of image projections are cross-sections of image 2D spectrum under the corresponding angles. Therefore, if one computes spectra of projections of an image and appropriately arranges them in a polar coordinate system in the Fourier domain to form a 2D image spectrum, one can reconstruct the image by inverse 2D Fourier transform of this spectrum. This method, called the *direct Fourier method of image reconstruction from projections,* is illustrated in Fig. (**9.8**).

The problem of implementation of this method is that Fast Fourier Transform algorithms used for computing DFTs assume that signals and their spectra are sampled in square sampling lattices in Cartesian coordinates whereas spectra of image projections define 2D image spectrum in polar coordinates.

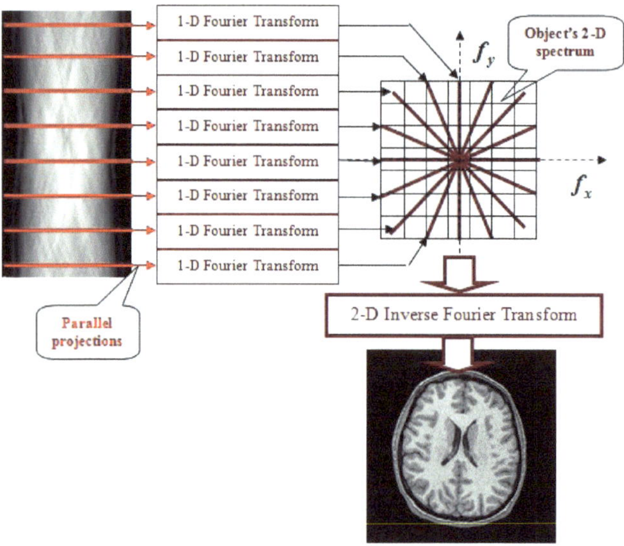

Fig. (9.8). The principle of the direct Fourier method of image reconstruction from parallel projections.

Fig. **(9.9)** illustrates mutual arrangements of spectral samples in polar and Cartesian coordinates. As one can see, spectral samples given in the polar coordinate system are non-uniformly spaced in the Cartesian coordinates and are very sparse especially high-frequency ones. Available 2D inverse FFT algorithms assume uniform sampling lattices in Cartesian coordinates. There are two options for using spectral samples given in polar coordinates for forming image 2D spectrum in Cartesian coordinates: (i) resampling spectra of projections sub-sampled for this purpose with a sufficiently large sub-sampling factor using algorithms presented in Chapter 8, and (ii) applying the algorithm for image recovery from sparse and non-uniform spectral samples presented in Section 6.4.4. However, the latter option does not seem feasible. Spectral samples given in polar coordinates are very non-uniform in Cartesian coordinates: low-frequency spectral components are very substantially oversampled, whereas high-frequency spectral samples are very sparse. This causes, as the author's experience shows, stagnation of the iterative reconstruction algorithm.

Fig. **(9.10)** presents an illustrative example of image reconstruction from projections achieved through inverse DFT of image 2D spectrum obtained by resampling of the sub-sampled spectrum of projections.

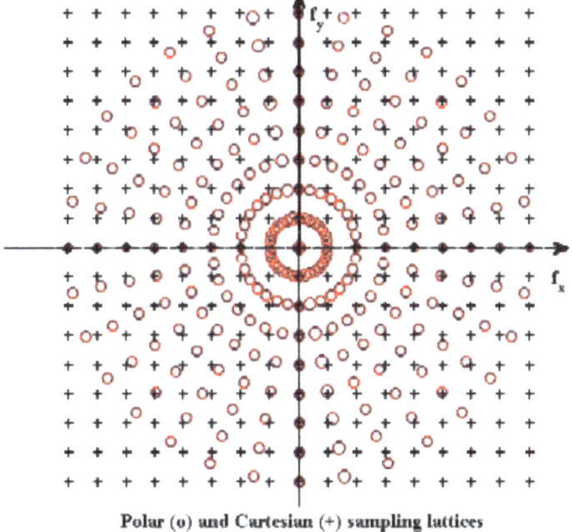

Fig. (9.9). Spectral samples in polar (small circles) and in Cartesian sampling lattices (crosses).

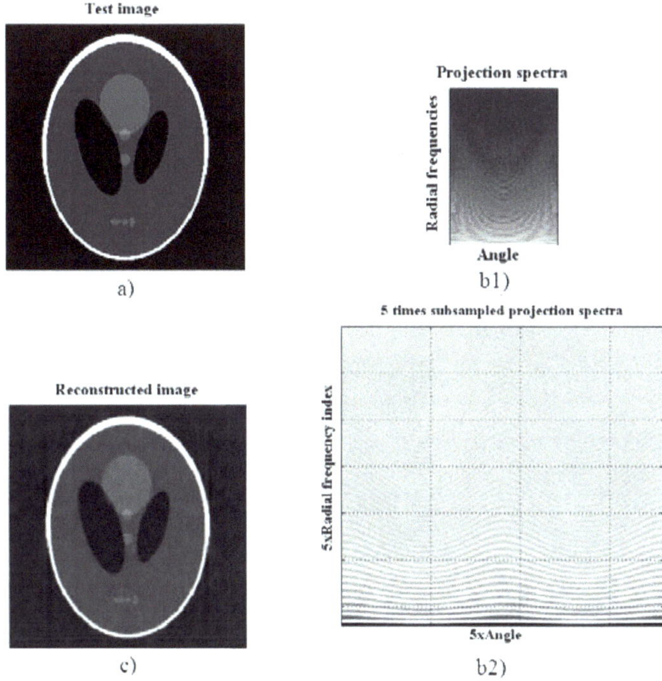

Fig. (9.10). An illustrative example of image reconstruction from projections by the direct Fourier reconstruction method through polar-to Cartesian coordinates resampling of sub-sampled spectra of projection: a) a test image; b1) spectra of projection; b2)- projection spectra 5 times sub-sampled in both coordinates (only half of the spectral coefficients from zero to the highest frequency ones are displayed; the others that are complex conjugate to them are not shown); c) image reconstructed by inverse DFT of the 2D spectrum obtained by resampling sub-sampled spectrum of projections.

9.3.3. Image Reconstruction from Fan-beam Projections

Above described methods of image reconstruction from projections assume image projection in parallel X-ray beams. This is the classic computed tomography method, for which well-developed reconstruction algorithms are available. In practice, in commercial CT scanners, fan-beam projections rather than parallel-beam ones are used because fan-beam projections can be obtained with a point source of X-ray, which is much easier for fabrication than collimated parallel beam sources.

The geometry of the fan beam projection is sketched in Fig. (**9.11**). The point source of radiation makes a full $360°$ revolution around the object and integrals of absorption of radiation by the object over projection lines form, for each position angle α of the point source, projections $\mathbf{Pr}(\alpha, \beta)$ as a function of the ray angles β. All set of projections $-\pi \leq \alpha \leq \pi$ is then used for image reconstruction.

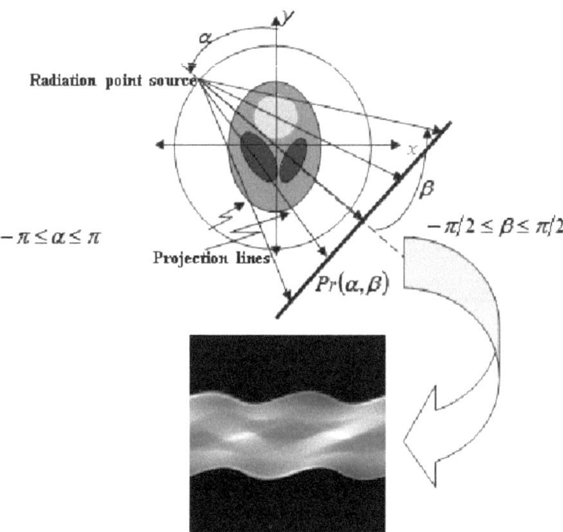

Fig. (9.11). Geometry of image fan projections.

In principle, for inverting Radon Transform in the fan-beam projection geometry corresponding dedicated reconstruction algorithms are required. There is, however, an alternative and attractive option of conversion, by an appropriate resampling, of the set of fan beam projections into a set of parallel projections to enable, in this way, image reconstruction using the regular image reconstruction algorithms from parallel projections. For the resampling, one can use the algorithms presented in

Chapter 8. This process of converting one type of projections into another type is called *data rebinning*. Fig. (**9.12**) illustrates this method of image reconstruction.

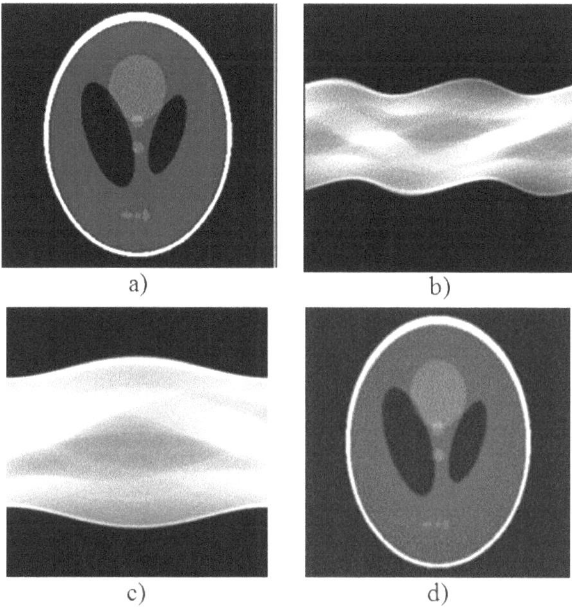

Fig. (9.12). Image reconstruction from fan-beam projections: initial test image (**a**); its fan-beam projections (**b**); parallel projections converted from the fan beam projections by their appropriate resampling (**c**); image reconstructed from the converted parallel projections (**d**).

9.4. PRECISE NUMERICAL DIFFERENTIATION AND INTEGRATION OF SAMPLED SIGNALS

9.4.1. The Perfect Digital Differentiator and Integrator

Signal numerical differentiation and integration are operations that require measuring infinitesimal increments of signals and their arguments. Therefore, numerical computing signal derivatives and integrals assume one of another method of building "continuous" models of sampled signals through explicit or implicit interpolation between available signal samples.

Because differentiation and integration are shift invariant linear operations, methods of computing derivatives and integrals of the sampled signal can be conveniently designed and compared in Fourier transform domain. Let $\alpha(f)$ be Fourier transform spectrum of an analog signal $a(x)$:

$$a(x) = \int_{-\infty}^{\infty} \alpha(f) \exp(-i2\pi f x) df \qquad (9.22)$$

Then Fourier spectrum of its derivative

$$\frac{d}{dx} a(x) = \int_{-\infty}^{\infty} [(-i2\pi f)\alpha(f)] \exp(-i2\pi f x) df \qquad (9.23)$$

will be $(-i2\pi f)\alpha(f)$ and Fourier spectrum of its integral

$$\bar{a}(x) = \int a(x) dx = \int_{-\infty}^{\infty} \left[\left(-\frac{1}{i2\pi f} \right) \alpha(f) \right] \exp(-i2\pi f x) df \qquad (9.24)$$

will be $\alpha(f)/(-i2\pi f)$. Therefore, signal differentiation and integration can be regarded as signal linear filtering with filter frequency responses, correspondingly

$$H^{(diff)}(f) = -i2\pi f \qquad (9.25)$$

and

$$H^{(intg)}(f) = i/2\pi f \qquad (9.26)$$

Let now signal $a(x)$ be represented by its samples $\{a_k\}$, $k = 0,1,..., N-1$ and $\{\alpha_r\}$ be its DFT coefficients:

$$a_k = \frac{1}{\sqrt{N}} \sum_{r=0}^{N-1} \alpha_r \exp\left(-i2\pi \frac{kr}{N} \right). \qquad (9.27)$$

Then, following the argumentation of Sect. 7.3 for the perfect resampling filter and using the relationship $f = r\Delta_f$ that links continuous signal frequency f, its sampling interval Δ_f and index r of DFT coefficients, one can conclude that samples $\{\eta_{r,opt}^{(diff)}\}$ and $\{\eta_{r,opt}^{(intg)}\}$ of continuous frequency responses of the perfect numerical differentiation and integration filters are defined for even N as:

$$\eta_r^{(diff)} = \begin{cases} -i2\pi r / N, & r = 0,1,..., N/2-1 \\ -\pi/2, & r = N/2 \\ i2\pi(N-r)/N, & r = N/2+1,..., N-1 \end{cases} ;$$

(9. 28)

$$\eta_r^{(intg)} = \begin{cases} 0, & r = 0 \\ iN/2\pi r, & r = 1,..., N/2-1 \\ -\pi/2, & r = N/2 \\ iN/2\pi(N-r), & r = N/2+1,..., N-1 \end{cases}$$

(9. 29)

and for odd N as

$$\eta_r^{diff} = \begin{cases} -i2\pi r / N, & r = 0,1,...,(N-1)/2-1 \\ i2\pi(N-r)/N, & r = (N+1)/2,..., N-1 \end{cases} ;$$

(9. 30)

$$\eta_r^{(intg)} = \begin{cases} iN/2\pi r, & r = 0,1,...,(N-1)/2-1 \\ iN/2\pi(N-r), & r = (N+1)/2,..., N-1 \end{cases} .$$

(9. 31)

Note that the coefficients $\eta_{N/2}^{(diff)}$ and $\eta_{N/2}^{(intg)}$ in Eqs. (9. 28) and (9. **29**) are halved, which corresponds to the above-described Case-1 of discrete sinc interpolation (Eq. 7.45).

Eqs. (9. **28**), (9.29), (9. **30**), and (9. **31**) imply the following algorithmic implementation for computing derivatives and integrals of analog signals specified by their samples:

$$\{\dot{a}_k\} = \mathbf{IFFT}\left(\{\eta_r^{(diff)}\} \bullet \mathbf{FFT}(\{a_k\})\right);$$

(9. 32)

$$\{\bar{a}_k\} = \mathbf{IFFT}\left(\{\eta_r^{(intg)}\} \bullet \mathbf{FFT}(\{a_k\})\right).$$

(9. 33)

Here, $\mathbf{FFT}(\cdot)$ and $\mathbf{IFFT}(\cdot)$ are direct and inverse Fast Fourier Transforms and $\bullet$ symbolizes element-wise multiplication of arrays. Thanks to the use of Fast Fourier Transform, the computational complexity of the algorithms is $O(\log N)$ operations per signal sample. Digital filter described by Eq. (9. 32) is called the *discrete ramp-filter*.

Likewise, all DFT based discrete sinc interpolation algorithms, DFT based differentiation and integration algorithms, being the most accurate in terms of preservation of signal spectral components within the base-band, suffer from boundary effects. Especially vulnerable in this respect is DFT-based differentiation because of potential discontinuities at signal borders due to their periodical replication in processing sampled signals in DFT domain. As was already mentioned, this drawback can be sufficiently alleviated using signal extension to double-length by mirror reflection at their boundaries before applying the DFT-based algorithms. For such extended signals, DFT based differentiation and integration are reduced to using fast DCT instead of FFT:

$$\{\dot{a}_k\} = -\frac{2\pi}{N\sqrt{2N}}(-1)^k \sum_{r=1}^{N-1}(N-r)\alpha_{N-r}^{(DCT)}\cos\left(\pi\frac{k+1/2}{N}r\right);$$

(9. 34)

$$\{\bar{a}_k\} = \frac{\sqrt{N}}{2\pi\sqrt{2}}(-1)^k \sum_{r=1}^{N-1}\frac{\alpha_{N-r}^{(DCT)}}{N-r}\cos\left(\pi\frac{k+1/2}{N}r\right),$$

$$\text{(9. 35)}$$

where, $\left\{\alpha_r^{(DCT)}\right\}$ are DCT transform coefficients of the signal. These equations can be obtained as special cases of fast digital convolution algorithms described in Sect. 8.1.2 if one substitutes into Eq. (8.15) frequency responses of differentiation and integration filters given by Eqs. (2.29), (9. 30), and (9. 31). Filters defined by Eqs. (9. 34) and (9. 35) will be referred to as *DCT-based differentiation ramp filter* and *DCT-based integration filter,* correspondingly. Naturally, the computational complexity of these algorithms, implemented using fast DCT algorithms, is $O(\log N)$ operations per signal sample.

9.4.2. Conventional Numerical Differentiation and Integration Algorithms *versus* Perfect DFT/DCT Based Ones: Performance Comparison

In numerical mathematics, signal numerical differentiation and integration are commonly implemented through signal discrete convolution in the signal domain:

$$\dot{a}_k = \sum_{n=0}^{N_h-1} h_n^{(diff)} a_{k-n};$$
$$\text{(9. 36)}$$

$$\bar{a}_k = \sum_{n=0}^{N_h-1} h_n^{int} a_{k-n}.$$
$$\text{(9. 37)}$$

The following differentiating kernels of two and five samples are recommended in manuals on numerical methods:

$$h_n^{diff\,(1)} = [-0.5,\ 0,\ 0.5]$$
(9. 38)

and

$$h_n^{diff\,(2)} = [-1/12,\ 8/12, 0, -8/12, 1/12]\,.$$
(9. 39)

Both are based on the assumption that, on inter-sample distances, signals can be approximated by their Taylor series. These two differentiation methods will be referred to as *D1 and D2 differentiation methods*.

The most known numerical integration methods are the *Newton-Cotes quadrature rules*: the trapezoidal, the Simpson, and the 3/8 Simpson ones. In all the methods, the value of the integral at the very first sample is not defined because it affects only the result's constant bias and can be chosen arbitrarily. When it is chosen equal zero, the trapezoidal, Simpson and 3/8-Simpson numerical integration methods are defined, for k as a running sample index of signal $\{a_k\}$, by equations, respectively:

$$\bar{a}_1^{(T)} = 0, \quad \bar{a}_k^{(T)} = \bar{a}_{k-1}^{(T)} + \frac{1}{2}\left(a_{k-1} + a_k\right),$$
(9. 40)

$$\bar{a}_1^{(S)} = 0, \quad \bar{a}_k^{(S)} = \bar{a}_{k-2}^{(S)} + \frac{1}{3}\left(a_{k-2} + 4a_{k-1} + a_k\right)$$
(9. 41)

$$\bar{a}_0^{(3/8S)} = 0, \quad \bar{a}_k^{(3/8S)} = \bar{a}_{k-3}^{(3/8S)} + \frac{3}{8}\left(a_{k-3} + 3a_{k-2} + 3a_{k-1} + a_k\right).$$
(9. 42)

As was mentioned in Sect. 7.2, continuous and overall frequency responses of digital filters are determined, given signal sampling and reconstruction devices, by their discrete frequency responses (DFT of their point spread function). Applying N-point Discrete Fourier transform to Eqs. (9.38), (9.39), (9.40), (9.41) and (9.42), obtain for discrete frequency responses $\eta_r^{diff\,(1)}$, $\eta_r^{diff\,(2)}$, $\eta_r^{int,T}$, $\eta_r^{int\,S}$, $\eta_r^{(int,3/8S)}$ of the above-described numerical differentiation and integration methods, respectively:

$$\eta_r^{diff\,(1)} \propto \sin\left(2\pi r\,/\,N\right); \quad r = 0,1,..., N_\perp - 1;$$
(9. 43)

$$\eta_r^{diff(2)} \propto \frac{8\sin(2\pi r/N) - \sin(4\pi r/N)}{12}; \quad r = 0,1,..., N_{hf} - 1; \tag{9.44}$$

$$\eta_r^{(int,T)} = \frac{\overline{\alpha}_r^{(Tr)}}{\alpha_r} = \begin{cases} 0, & r = 0, \\ -\dfrac{\cos(\pi r/N)}{2i\sin(\pi r/N)}, & r = 1,..., N_{hf} - 1 \end{cases}; \tag{9.45}$$

$$\eta_r^{(int,S)} = \frac{\overline{\alpha}_r^{(S)}}{\alpha_r} = \begin{cases} 0, & r = 0 \\ -\dfrac{\cos(2\pi r/N)+2}{3i\sin(2\pi r/N)}, & r = 1,..., N_{hf} - 1 \end{cases}; \tag{9.46}$$

$$\eta_r^{(int,3/8S)} = \frac{\overline{\alpha}_r^{(3S)}}{\alpha_r} = \begin{cases} 0, & r = 0 \\ -\dfrac{\cos(3\pi r/N)+3\cos(\pi r/N)}{i\sin(3\pi r/N)}, & r = 1,..., N_{hf} - 1 \end{cases}, \tag{9.47}$$

where N_{hf} is the index that corresponds to the highest signal frequency:

$$N_{hf} = \begin{cases} (N-1)/2 & \text{for odd } N \\ N/2 & \text{for even } N \end{cases}. \tag{9.48}$$

These frequency responses of differentiation and integration filters are presented along with frequency responses of the DFT based differentiation and integration methods in Figs. (**9.13** and **9.14**), correspondingly.

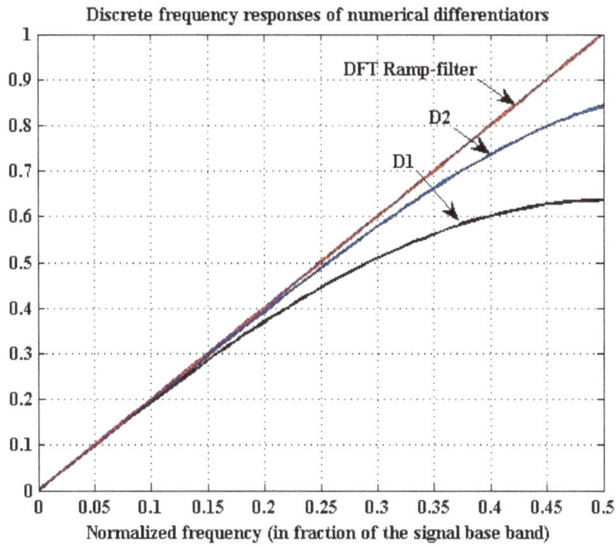

Fig. (9.13). Absolute values of frequency responses of differentiation filters described by Eqs. (9. 43) (curve D1), Eq. (9. 44) (curve D2) and Eqs. (9. 28) and (9. 30) ("Ramp"-filter).

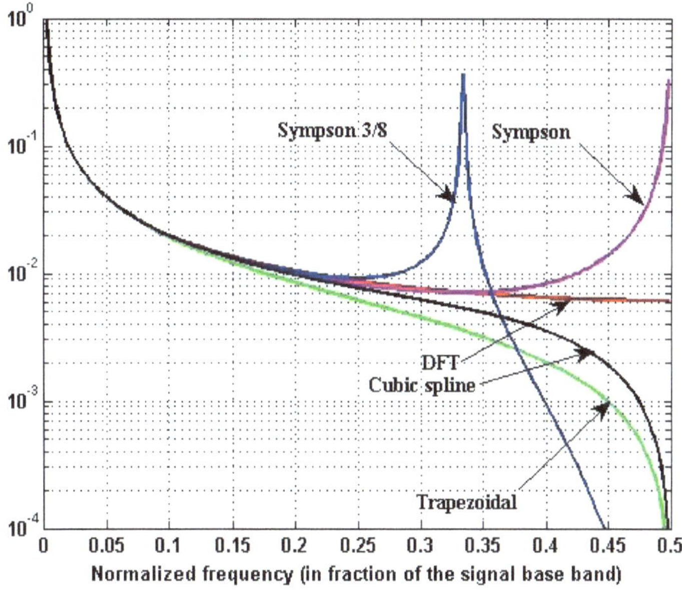

Fig. (9.14). Absolute values of frequency responses of numerical integration filters described by Eqs. (9.45 - 9.47), and that of the DFT-based method (Eqs. 9.29 - 9.31).

One can see from these figures that the standard numerical differentiation and integration methods entail certain and sometimes very substantial distortions of signal spectra at high frequencies. All of them attenuate signal high frequencies, and Simpson and 3/8-Simpson integration methods, being slightly more accurate than the trapezoidal method in the middle of the signal baseband, tend even to generate substantial integration errors if signals contain higher frequencies. Frequency response of the 3/8-Simpson integration method tends to infinity at 2/3 of the signal maximum frequency, and frequency response of the Simpson method has the same tendency at the maximal frequency of the baseband. This means, in particular, that noise that might be present in signal data as well as round off computation errors will be overamplified by the Simpson and 3/8-Simpson methods at these frequencies.

Figs. (**9.15** and **9.16**) present results of an experimental evaluation of the performance of the considered differentiation methods carried out using a simulation program differentiator_comparison_BNTM.m provided in Exercises. The program implements statistical simulation of differentiation by the considered methods of realizations of pseudo-random signals with a uniform spectrum of different bandwidths in the range of 1/6 to 16/16 of the baseband.

In the simulation, 16 runs of statistical experiments with 100 experiments at each run were carried out. In the runs, realizations of pseudo-random signals of 32704 samples with uniform Fourier spectrum were generated to imitate, using 32-fold oversampling, analog signals. At each run, generated pseudo-random signals were low-pass filtered to 1/32 of their baseband using the ideal low pass filter implemented in the DFT domain. The filtered signals are then used as models of analog signals and their derivatives were computed by the DFT domain ramp-filter and used as estimates of the signal ideal derivative. Then the central half part of signal realizations that encompasses 16352 samples taken 8196 samples apart from the signal borders was sub-sampled with the rate 32 to generate 511 signal samples that were used for signal differentiation by D1-method (Eq. (9. 43)), D2-method (Eq. (9. 44)), DFT-based method (Eqs. (9. 30)), and DCT-based method (Eq. (9. 34)). The corresponding central parts of the ideal derivative signals were also sub-sampled with the rate 32 and were used as references for evaluating differentiation error for the tested methods. Differentiation error was computed as a difference between the "ideal" derivative and the results obtained by the tested differentiation methods. It was divided by RMS of the "ideal" derivative over all samples thus producing sample-wise estimates of error mean square value normalized to the energy of the signal derivative. Finally, RMS of the normalized error averaged over 100 realizations were found for each signal sample. In order to evaluate differentiation errors caused by boundary effects of the filtering in DFT and DCT domains, two sets of experiments were conducted: one set for test signals, which before differentiation were multiplied by an *"apodization" window function* that gradually brings signal samples in the vicinity of signal borders to zero, and another set without the apodization.

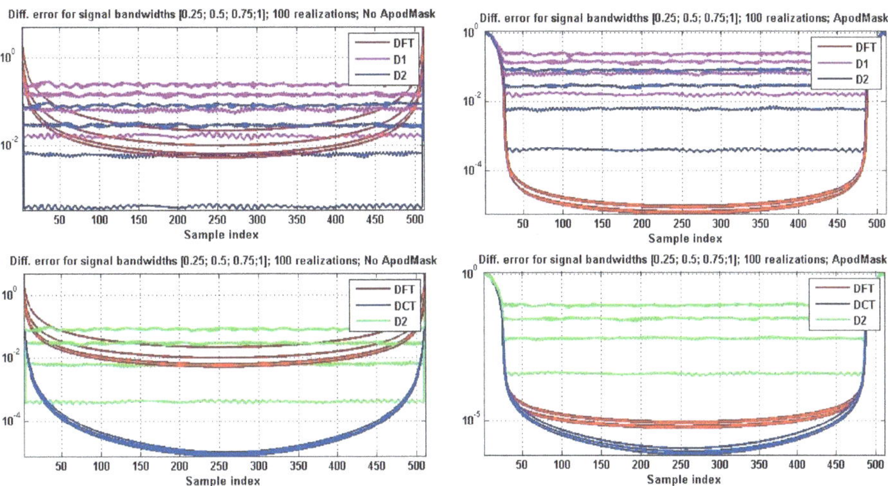

Fig. (9.15). Experimental data on signal sample-wise normalized RMS of the differentiation error. Left column: D1, D2, and DFT-based differentiation methods (upper) and D2, DFT- and DCT-based methods (bottom), without signal apodization. Right column: the same with signal apodization. Numbers at curves indicate the fraction (from one quarter to one) of the test signal bandwidth with respect to the signal baseband.

Fig. (**9.15**) presents plots of signal sample-wise normalized RMS of the differentiation errors for the tested methods *vs.* sample index without (left column) and with (right column) signal apodization. Fig. (**9.16**) presents RMS of the differentiation errors averaged over 100 samples in the middle of the test signal (to decrease the influence of the boundary effects) for D1, D2, DFT and DCT differentiation methods *vs.* signal bandwidth without (upper plot) and with a signal apodization (bottom plot).).

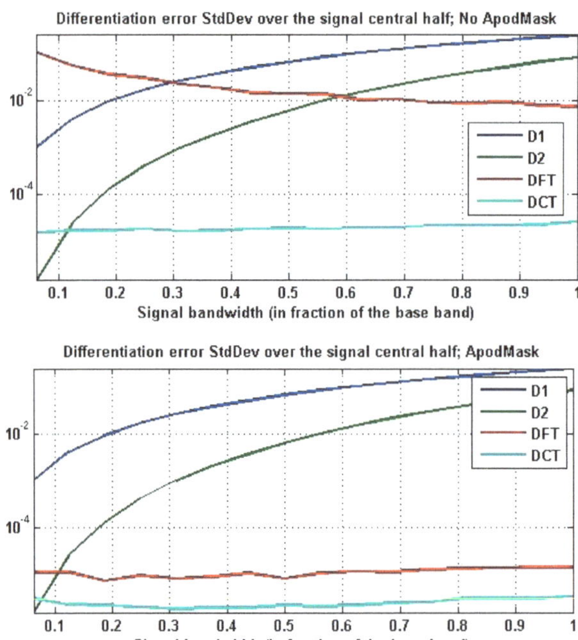

Fig. (9.16). Normalized RMS of the differentiation error averaged over 100 samples in the middle of the test signal (samples from 200-th to 299-th) for D1, D2, DFT and DCT differentiation methods *vs.* test signal bandwidth for the cases without (upper plots) and with a signal apodization (bottom plot).

One can see in the figures that, in terms of the differentiation accuracy,

- The simplest D1 method performs very poorly.
- D2 method outperforms DFT-based method for signals with bandwidths less than 0.6 of the baseband when no signal apodization is used. This can be attributed to the boundary effects of the signal filtering in DFT domain.
- DCT differentiation method very substantially outperforms other compared methods, although it slightly concedes to the D2 method within a couple of tens of signal samples (several percents of signal length) in close vicinity of signal boards and when no signal apodization is used.
- The DFT-based method differentiation accuracy substantially improves with the distance from signal borders and with the use of signal apodization.
- Conventional numerical differentiation D1 and D2 methods maintain relatively good differentiation accuracy if signals are a very narrow band,

i.e., they are very substantially over-sampled, which undermines their only advantage of low computational complexity.

One more way for evaluating the quality of numerical differentiation and integration methods is iterative application to a test signal successive differentiation and integration in tandem and comparison reconstructed signals with the initial signal. Plots in Fig. (**9.17**) obtained using program differentiat_integrat_error_BNTM.m provided in Exercises illustrate results of performed in this way comparison of DCT-based differentiation and integration methods with D2-method of differentiation and trapezoidal method of integration.

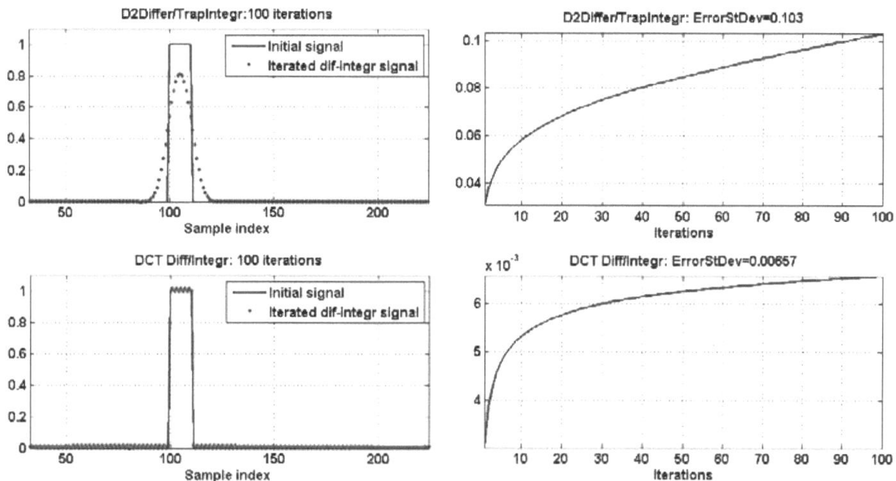

Fig. (9.17). Comparison of signal reconstruction and RMS of the reconstruction error after iterative successive 100 differentiations and integrations applied in tandem to a rectangular test signal for D2 differentiator and trapezoidal integrator (upper plots) and for DCT-based differentiation and integration methods (bottom plots).

Plots in the left column of the figure represent a test rectangular impulse (solid line) and results of its iterative successive differentiation and integration using D2 differentiation method and trapezoidal integration method (upper left, dots) and a result of its iterative successive differentiation and integration by DCT-based methods (bottom left, dots). These plots demonstrate that after 100 iterations of successive differentiation using the D2 method and integration using the trapezoidal method the test rectangular impulse has completely lost its sharp edges, whereas after successive differentiation and integration using the DCT-based methods the test signal has practically not changed. Plots in the right column demonstrate that RMS of the signal reconstruction errors for D2 differentiation and trapezoidal integration methods (upper right plot) is by two orders of magnitude larger than those for DCT-based differentiation and integration methods (bottom right plot).

9.5. LOCAL ("Elastic")   IMAGE RESAMPLING: SLIDING WINDOW DISCRETE SINC INTERPOLATION ALGORITHMS

Above described perfect DFT- and DCT-based fractional shift algorithms are computationally very efficient for performing the same shifts of all pixels. For image resampling in arbitrary irregular sampling lattices, they can be used for generating sufficiently oversampled "quasi-continuous" image models, as was described in Chapter 8. However, this implementation requires additional large memory buffers.

An alternative solution for image resampling in arbitrary sampling lattices is implementation of discrete sinc interpolation in sliding window processing. In signal interpolation in sliding window, the perfect shifting filter is applied only to pixels within the window and interpolated signal samples that correspond to the window central sample have to be computed at each window position from signal samples within the window. Interpolation function in this case is the discrete sinc-function, whose extent equals the window size rather than the whole image size required for the perfect discrete sinc interpolation. Therefore, sliding window discrete sinc interpolation cannot provide the perfect interpolation provided by the whole image size ("global") discrete sinc interpolation. Plots in Fig. (**9.18**) illustrate how well the sliding window discrete sinc interpolation approximates the "global" one. They present 1D frequency responses of sliding window discrete sinc interpolators for window sizes of 15 and 9 pixels, and that of the perfect ("global") discrete sinc interpolations for image $3\times$-sub-sampling.

Sliding window implementation of the discrete sinc interpolation can be regarded as a special case of signal domain convolution. According to the above theory, it has the highest interpolation accuracy among all convolution interpolation methods with the same filter window size. Additionally, being implemented in the DFT or DCT domains, it offers an option of combining image resampling with simultaneous restoration and enhancement by the methods of local adaptive filtering [4].

In local adaptive filtering in sliding window, at each window position, transform coefficients of the window samples are computed and then nonlinearly modified using thresholding low energy transform coefficients to obtain transform coefficients of the output signal samples in the window with a reduced level of noise. Additionally, the modules of transform coefficients, after the thresholding, can be subjected to the **P**-th law transformation (rising to the power **P**<1), which enhances image sharpness, and/or can be multiplied by the exponential shift factor (Eqs. 7.35) to implement window central pixel shift required for the given position of the filter window. Modified, in this way, transform coefficients are then used for generating an estimate of the window central pixel by the inverse transform computed for the window central pixel.

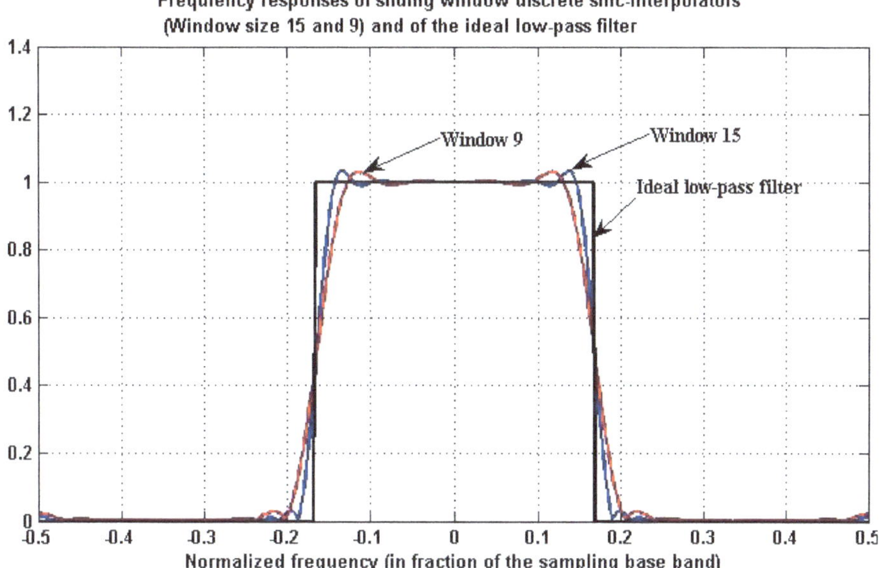

Fig. (9.18). Frequency responses of sliding window discrete sinc interpolators for window size 15 samples (blue) and 9 samples (red) and that of the perfect ("global") discrete sinc interpolations (black) for signal **3×** -sub-sampling.

Fig. (**9.19**) illustrates application of such combined denoising and local shifting for irregular-to regular image resampling. In this example, the left image is distorted by known displacements of pixels concerning the regular equidistant positions and by additive noise. In the right image, these displacements are compensated and noise is substantially reduced by the 9x9 pixels sliding window resampling and denoising algorithm.

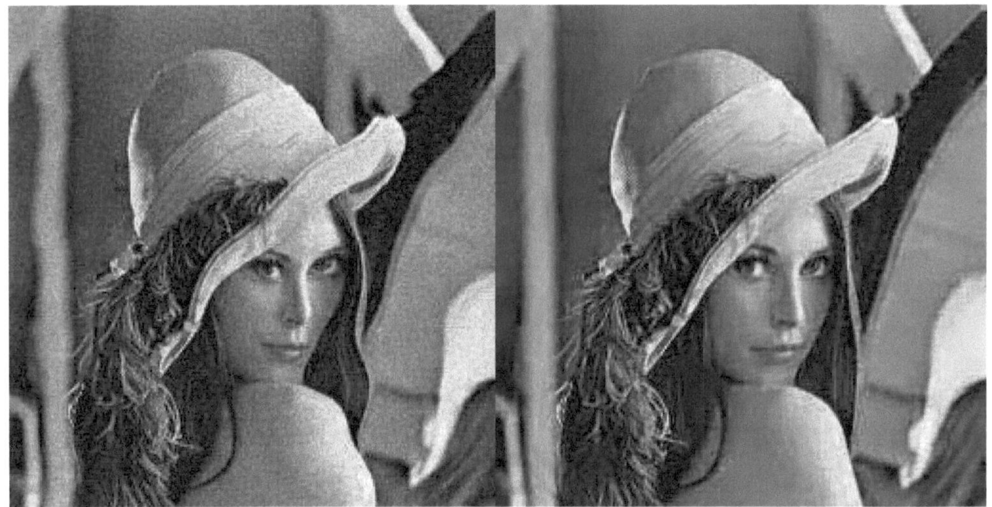

Fig. (9.19). An example of image resampling from irregular to regular sampling lattice and denoising in sliding window: noisy and irregularly sampled image (left) and resampled (rectified) and denoised image (right).

9.6. EXERCISES

- **ContinuousSpectralAnalysis_BNTM.m**

Demonstration of continuous spectrum analysis.

As test signals, sinusoidal signals with non-integer frequencies specified by the user are used.

Displayed are test signal, interpolated signal DFT spectrum, and estimate of the signal frequency.

- **RotateComparis_demo_BNTM.m**

Comparison of three interpolation methods of MATLAB's routine imrotate.m (nearest neighbor, bilinear and bicubic) and the 3-step image rotation algorithm with discrete sinc interpolation implemented in DFT and DCT domains.

Three options are implemented:

 - Single rotation of test image "Text"

- Multiple rotations of test image "Text"
- Multiple rotations of a pseudo-random test image by 10x36 degrees with accumulation of the rotation error spectra over a specified by the user number of test image realizations.

Displayed are:

- images in the process of rotation,
- rotation errors found as a difference between input and multiple 360° rotated images
- rotation error DFT power spectra.
In the titles of rotated images elapsed computation time T is also indicated.

- **radon_invradon_demo_BNTM.m**

Demo of the Direct Radon transform implemented through projecting the rotated image and of image reconstruction using an inverse Radon ramp-filtered back-projection algorithm.

- **differentiator_comparison_BNTM.m**

Comparison of signal differentiation accuracy of two conventional differentiators with point spread functions

- PSFD1 = [0.5 0 –0.5],
- PSFD2 = [–1/12 2/3 0 –2/3 1/12],

and DFT- and DCT-based differentiators using, as test signals, realizations of pseudo-random signals with 16 different bandwidths from 1/16 to 16/16 of the signal baseband width.

User-defined parameters:

- The number N of samples of the signal and its derivative,
- Oversampling rate M,
- The number Ntest of test realizations of pseudo-random signals.

- **differentiat_integrat_error_BNTM.m**

Comparison of DCT-based differentiation and integration and D2&Simpson differentiation and integration using repeated differentiation and integration in tandem of a test rectangular impulse.

User-defined parameter:

- The number of iterations Nit.

REFERENCES

[1] C. F. Gauss, "Nachclass: Theoria interpolation is methodo nova tractata", In: Werke, Band 3, 265-327, Königlishe Gesellshaft der Wissenshaften, Göttingen, 1866 (cited after M.T. Heideman, D.H. Johnson and C.S. Burrus, "Gauss and the history of the fast Fourier transform", IEEE ASSP Magazine, 1 (4), 14-81, 1984)

[2] V. A.Kotel'nikov, "On the transmission capacity of "ether" and wire in electro-communications," *Izd. Red. Upr. Svyazzi RKKA* In Modern Sampling Theory: Mathematics and Applications, J. J. Benedetto and P. J. S. G. Ferreira, Eds. Boston, MA: Birkhauser, 2000)

[3] C. E. Shannon, "Communication in the presence of noise," *Proc.IRE*, vol. 37, pp. 10–21, 1949.

[4] L.P. Yaroslavsky, *Theoretical Foundations of Digital Imaging*, CRC Press, 2013.

[5] L. P. Yaroslavsky, G. Shabat, B. G. Salomon, I. A. Ideses, and B. Fishbain, "Nonuniform sampling, image recovery from sparse data and the discrete sampling theorem", *J. Opt. Soc. Am. A* vol. 26, No. 3, pp. 566-575, March 2009.

[6] D. Donoho, "Compressed sensing," *IEEE Trans. Inform. Theory* 52(4), pp. 1289–1306, 2006.

[7] E. Candès, "Compressed sampling," *Proc. Int. Congress of Math.*, Madrid, Spain, pp. 1433-1452, 2006

[8] D. L. Donoho and J. Tanner, "Exponential bounds implying the construction of compressed sensing matrices, error-correcting codes, and neighborly polytopes by random sampling," *IEEE Trans. Inf. Theory* v. 56, p. 2002-2016, 2010.

[9] L. P. Yaroslavsky, "Can compressed sensing beat the Nyquist sampling rate?" *Opt. Eng.*, v. 54(7), pp. 079701-1-079701-4, July 2015.

[10] L. Yaroslavsky, *Digital Holography, and Digital Image Processing. Principles, Methods, Algorithms*, Kluwer Academic Publishers, Norwell, Ma, 2004.

[11] R. D. Fiete, *"Multiple aperture imaging system"*, US patent US 6,943,946 B2, Sep. 13, 2005 (https://www.google.com/patents/US6943946.

[12] L. Yaroslavsky, B. Fishbain, G. Shabat, I. Ideses, "Super-resolution in turbulent videos: making a profit from damage", *Optics Letters*, vol.32, No. 21, pp. 338-340, Nov. 1, 2007.

SUBJECT INDEX

9 789811 471803